Cyber Security Policy Guidebook

Cyber Security Policy Guidebook

Jennifer L. Bayuk
Independent Cyber Security Governance Consultant
Industry Professor at Stevens Institute of Technology, Hoboken, NJ

Jason Healey
Director of the Cyber Statecraft Initiative
Atlantic Council of the United States, Washington, D.C.

Paul Rohmeyer
Information Systems Program Director
Howe School of Technology Management
Stevens Institute of Technology, Hoboken, NJ

Marcus H. Sachs
Vice President for National Security Policy
Verizon Communications, Washington, D.C.

Jeffrey Schmidt
Chief Executive Officer
JAS Communications LLC, Chicago, IL

Joseph Weiss
Professional Engineer
Applied Control Solutions, LLC, Cupertino, CA

A John Wiley & Sons, Inc., Publication

Library of Congress Cataloging-in-Publication Data:

Cyber security policy guidebook / Jennifer L Bayuk ... [et al.].
    p. cm.
   Summary: "This book is a taxonomy and thesaurus of current cybersecurity policy issues, including a thorough description of each issue and a corresponding list of pros and cons with respect to identified stances on each issue" – Provided by publisher.
   ISBN 978-1-118-02780-6 (hardback)
   1. Information technology–Government policy.   2. Computer security–Government policy.   3. Data protection–Government policy.   I. Bayuk, Jennifer L.
   QA76.9.A25C91917 2012
   005.8–dc23
                                                              2011036017

10 9 8 7 6 5 4 3 2 1

Contents

Foreword

Not long ago, I was the Director of Cybersecurity Policy at the U.S. Department of Homeland Security (DHS). In that role, I routinely met with the department's staff responsible for cyber security operations. In one such meeting, focused on cyber risk management and metrics, we were having a bit of a difficult time seeing one another's perspectives on a related issue. At one point a senior member of the operations staff looked across the table at me and opined, "You actually think policy ought to drive operations?"

Beyond the obvious dysfunction behind his question, it pointed to some of the core themes this book attempts to address: cyber security policy's importance, its relation to both strategy and operations, its relevance to a very diverse set of stakeholders and decision makers, and the inevitable controversy and debate it engenders. These are very much the issues of our time, but they are not issues for the timid.

Perhaps to my DHS colleague's chagrin, in fact, policy does and should drive operations. As the authors clearly point out, policy necessarily drives decisions at many different levels. How many of us have not heard the President of the United States include these words in a speech, "it is the policy of my administration. . . ."? His job is (with Congress) to set national policy, approve appropriate implementation activities to carry out that policy, and then ensure that policy is properly enforced or adjusted as circumstances dictate. Executives at other levels have similar responsibilities.

In the evolution of all things cyber, however, policy has not been a driver. Rather, it has been an afterthought. The authors make this very point in several ways, and in so doing, they raise a vitally important issue: should cyber security policy always be reactive? The obvious answer is "no;" or else the operations and standards it drives will also always be reactive, leading to an inherently untenable situation in which cyber security efforts always lag the attacks they are meant to prevent. If this situation sounds all too familiar, it is because cyber security practitioners have been on this treadmill far too long, with no sign of it ending.

The great problem, of course, is that the setting of proactive cyber security policy is, at least in any democratic environment, an extremely difficult and time-consuming task. Even the simplest perusal of Chapter 6 of this book will be sufficient to inform the reader that the ground on which almost any cyber security policy is contested is muddy ground indeed.

As a general rule, when one is most muddled with the complexity of building a particular system correctly, it is best to take a big step back—and then elevate oneself to see the larger picture. Only then can one ask the all-important question framed in this book, "Am I building the right system?" In my own experience, the too frequent answer to this question is "no." It is incredibly painful for those who are building the wrong system, but building it correctly, and therefore deeply invested in it, to hear that answer.

All of which points, I believe, to the raison d'etre for a *Cyber Security Policy Guidebook* such as this. If read with an unjaundiced eye, it will help the reader to see the bigger cyber security picture and its vitally important policy setting, no matter the vantage point. This cannot help but be an aide.

It is a very happy circumstance that the authors of this book are highly regarded professionals, experts in their respective niches, and that they bring many years of experience to the topic. As they point out, the topic is incredibly expansive—a natural result of the ubiquity of "cyber" anything in today's networked world. Indeed, if the topic were not so incredibly important and relevant, it might be silly even to attempt to get one's arms around it.

But to anyone for whom national security, business operations, or anything related to the Internet is important, and that covers most of us, understanding some measure of the topic is critical. To that end, this book is most useful.

Andy Cutts
Former Director of Cybersecurity Policy
at the U.S. Department of Homeland Security

Preface

The idea for this book coincided with a conference on Cyber Security Policy (SIT 2010). The conference had sessions ranging from security technology investment decisions by venture capitalists to the implications of cyber security policy on personal privacy. Though all speakers were experts in their field and were asked to address cyber security policy topics, many instead focused on strategy or technology issues. Even where it was clear that policy was being discussed, policies were often not articulated clearly enough for panelists and audience members to participate in informed debate. This observation itself became the buzz at the conference and made it a truly memorable experience for many who attended.

The experience made it clear that cyber security policy means different things to different people, even those who work in cyber security. This conclusion led us to the format of this book. That is, the book is designed to lead the reader through concepts that are individually easy to assimilate, and collectively provide a solid understanding of the field of cyber security and the place of policy within it.

We also knew that there is no one person experienced enough in cyber security to have been able to single-handedly write this book. The team was chosen to ensure that all the major fields of experience in cyber security were covered. Each contributed to chapters and sections that were specific to their experience. However, all chapters were scrutinized by all authors to ensure a cohesive presentation for the expected variety of readers. Policy is the domain of authoritative executives. Executive authority may stem from the social contracts by which governments are established or the domain of a private enterprise. This book was written with those executives in mind, but it is not intended solely for their consumption. In order that cyber security policy analysis receive the critical scrutiny essential to sound legislation on both public and private fronts, the audience for this book must extend to executive advisors, educators, researchers, legislative staff, and practitioners in the field. Though each member of the audience brings his or her own background and experience to the material presented herein, we expect that current concepts on cyber security policy will be enriched by sharing this common presentation framework and nomenclature with colleagues in the same field, whose professional experience has exposed them to cyber security issues of varying scope. Most literature about cyber security falls into two categories: technology and advice. This book will refrain from technical jargon and also from recommendations with respect to decisions in any given case of cyber security policy. Although the book endeavors to explain technology issues in cyber security, it does so in layman's terms. At the same time, the book emphasizes the importance of critical and analytical thinking about decisions with respect to cyber security and will equip the reader with descriptions of the impact of specific policy choices, letting the reader decide whether to view that impact as positive or negative.

This guidebook integrates explanations of cyber security policy alternatives across potential executive, legislative, judiciary, commercial, military, and diplomatic action. Readers across these disciplines are expected to view its contents through the lens of their own area of expertise and also gain insights from issues encountered by others. It will be an introductory text for the uninitiated, while at the same time providing a holistic reference for experts in the field of cyber security.

Originally, the outline of the book was divided into policy domains as defined in the conference, and from these were created book sections assigned to each author. Once work began, however, there was immediate skepticism and doubt among the authors on the approach. Some topics at the conference were broad in scope. For example: *Law Enforcement, Privacy, Civil Rights, and Personal Liberties*; *Emergent Technologies, Innovation, and Business Growth*; and *Global Implications of Cyber Security Policies*. Others were focused on a specific type of system, such as *Next Generation Air Transportation System* and *Electric Power Distribution*. No one thought that simply combining policy content from each section would achieve the mission of the volume. The volume could not appear splintered into sets of issues of interest to only one industry while still achieving its goal of educating an outsider on what a cyber security policy issue was. This recognition led to the development of a more holistic, unified view of the guidebook approach.

Chapter 1 introduces the reader to the relationship between cyberspace, cyber security, and cyber security policy. Chapter 2 provides a brief history of cyber security. It provides the background necessary for a lay person to understand the current state of the art as well as the state of the practice in establishing security controls in cyberspace. The chapter is not a chronicle of cyber crime or legislative attempts to establish cyber security controls, but it does highlight significant events that have influenced the evolution of controls.

Chapter 3 describes the state of the practice in measuring cyber security. It revisits the history of Chapter 2 from the perspective of security goals and objectives. It discusses various approaches that have been used to determine whether goals for cyber security have been met. Three case studies of cyber-enabled systems illustrate the approaches. The case studies are of e-commerce, industrial control systems, and personal mobile devices.

Chapter 4 provides guidance for executive decision makers charged with large organizations or constituencies that are cyber security stakeholders. It emphasizes that cyber security management is not unlike other management activities in that successful execution requires clearly articulated goals and corresponding program management. It provides an outline of how to begin to establish a cyber security strategy and associated cyber security policy effort. It suggests a perspective on cyber security issues that is integrated with the mission and purpose of the organization.

Chapter 5 introduces a catalog approach to the examination of cyber security policy issues. It places the history of cyber security and metrics of Chapters 2 and 3 against the context of cyber operations in order to separate the security issues into areas of responsibility. The word "policy" in the domain of cyber security applies to different dimensions of societal issues across multiple organizations and industries. Hence, Chapter 5 describes a demarcation in the scope of issues faced by decision makers in different positions of influence. That is, the policy decisions faced by a telecommunications executive will be very different from the policy decisions faced by a military strategist. However, these divisions are purposely described in chapter sections and not as domains of influence or responsibility because they significantly overlap. The division is made to enhance clarity of explanation and is not meant to introduce nonexistent boundaries.

Chapter 6 builds on the concepts and definitions described in Chapters 1 to 5 to explain the cyber security environment faced by decision makers in each of the five sections of cyber security policy that were introduced in Chapter 5. Each section includes a list of cyber security policy issues faced by different organizations and industries who are stakeholders.

Chapter 7 chronicles the efforts of the U.S. government to align cyber security strategy and policy and observes the impact of historical events on cyber security policy. It closes with references to literature that suggest alternative courses forward.

Chapter 8 presents a summary and shows how the content of each chapter presents different perspectives on the same topic, which is cyber security policy. It emphasizes that approaches to cyber security policy are necessarily different for different cyberspace stakeholders and that the value of security measures must be weighed against their efficacy in achieving individual cyberspace strategy objectives.

We are all five left with a deep appreciation for the depth and breadth of our adopted field. Marcus Sachs' first-hand experience in both the public and private policy arena was invaluable when it came to chronicling history. Jason Healey's wealth of experience in policy analysis in both government service and private research shed light on a rich array of issues in nation-state and global diplomacy. Joe Weiss' in-depth expertise in industrial control systems prevented us from losing focus on critical attributes of our technology infrastructure. Paul Rohmeyer's academic and business experience in technology management consistently made sure that our narratives were not only meaningful to decision makers, but also that the whole carried a strategic purpose that was obvious to our target audience. Jeff Schmidt's career-long immersion in Internet governance and software engineering issues provided a sound sanity check on completeness. Jennifer Bayuk's solid technical background and layman-accessible writing skills framed the presentation of concepts that made sense of it all.

Together, we dedicate this volume to cyber security policymakers, whether vocal or silent. May you achieve success in your respective missions.

Jennifer L. Bayuk
Jason Healey
Paul Rohmeyer
Marcus H. Sachs
Jeffrey Schmidt
Joseph Weiss

Acknowledgments

This book was inspired by the Honorable Mike Wynne, the 21st Secretary of the Air Force, who established considerable capability for cyber security in the Air Force, and was at the time single-handedly responsible for raising the awareness of national security-related cyber security policy issues. Among countless other laudatory and critical advisory appointments, Mr. Wynne serves as the Chair of the Advisory Board for the Systems Engineering Research Center and also as Senior Advisor to the President at Stevens Institute of Technology.

To create awareness within academia of the importance of cyber security policy, Mr. Wynne chaired a conference on that topic sponsored by Stevens Institute of Technology (SIT 2010). Opinions were solicited from experts in a wide variety of fields who are stakeholders in cyberspace. Many of them spoke at the conference or attended the discussions. Some were unable to attend but provided their comments in written form. Our grateful thanks extend to the speakers and other participants who lent their expertise to that conference.

We are most indebted to those who reviewed the first completed drafts of this volume. Their invaluable feedback has considerably enhanced the comprehensibility of the cyber security policy curriculum contained herein. We therefore gratefully acknowledge these individuals for their efforts and expertise: Warren Axelrod, Larry Clinton, Kevin Gronberg, Richard Menta, William Miller, Brian Peretti, Andy Purdy, and Michael zur Muehlen. Others who spoke or sent material to be included in this book are also gratefully acknowledged. They include: Michael Aisenberg, Edward Amoroso, Tom Arthur, Paige Atkins, James Arden Barnett, John Boardman, David M. Bowen, Christopher Calabrese, Ann Campbell, C. R. Collazo, Greg Crabb, William Crowell, Matthew D. Howard, John A. Davis, Christopher Day, James X. Dempsey, Edward C. Eichhorn, Robert Elder, Steve Elefant, Dan Geer, Charles Gephart, Gary Gong, Gail L. Graham, Kevin Harnett, Melissa Hathaway, Husin bin Hj Jazri, Erfan Ibrahim, Robert

R. Jueneman, Jeffrey S. Katz, John Kefaliotis, Alan Kessler, George Korfiatis, Darren Lacey, Pascal Levensohn, Martin Libicki, Chan D. Lieu, Eric Luiijf, Pablo Martinez, Douglas Maughan, Ellen McCarthy, Dale Meyerrose, Gregory T. Nojeim, John Osterholz, James B. Peake, Jim Richberg, Robert D. Rodriguez, Tom Ruff, Brian Sauser, Ted Schlein, Agam Sinha, Ben Stewart, John N. Stewart, Eric Trapp, David Weild, John Weinschenck, and Paul Winstanley. We have incorporated as many opinions as possible from that conference. We are grateful to these experts for sharing their insight. We look forward to continuing the cyber security policy debates in a constructive manner that will secure peace and prosperity in cyberspace going forward.

1

Introduction

1.1 What Is Cyber Security?

Cyber security refers generally to the ability to control access to networked systems and the information they contain. Where cyber security controls are effective, cyberspace is considered a reliable, resilient, and trustworthy digital infrastructure. Where cyber security controls are absent, incomplete, or poorly designed, cyberspace is considered the wild west of the digital age. Even those who work in the security profession will have a different view of cyber security depending on the aspects of cyberspace with which they personally interact. Whether a system is a physical facility or a collection of cyberspace components, the role of a security professional assigned to that system is to plan for potential attack and prepare for its consequences.

Although the word "cyber" is mainstream vernacular, to what exactly it refers is elusive. Once a term of science fiction based on the then-emerging field of computer control and communication known as cybernetics, it now refers generally to electronic automation (Safire 1994). The corresponding term "cyberspace" has definitions that range from conceptual to technical, and has been claimed by some to be a fourth domain, where land, sea, and air are the first three (Kuehl 2009). There are numerous definitions of cyberspace and cyber security scattered throughout literature. Our intent is not to engage in a debate on semantics, so we do not include these definitions. Moreover, such debates are unnecessary for our purpose, as we generally use the term "cyber" not as a noun, but as an adjective that modifies its subject with the property of supporting a collection of automated electronic systems accessible over networks. As well reflected in

Cyber Security Policy Guidebook, First Edition. Jennifer L. Bayuk, Jason Healey, Paul Rohmeyer, Marcus H. Sachs, Jeffrey Schmidt, Joseph Weiss.
© 2012 John Wiley & Sons, Inc. Published 2012 by John Wiley & Sons, Inc.

language-usage debates in both the field of cognitive linguistics and popular literature on lexicography, the way language is used by a given community becomes the de facto definition (Zimmer 2009), and so we request that our readers set aside the possibility that they will be confused by references to "cyberspace" and "cyber security" and simply refer to their own current concept of these terms when it makes sense to do so, while keeping in mind that we generally the term cyber as an adjective whose detailed attributes will change with the system of interest.

At a high level, cyber security is typically explained in terms of a few triads that describe the objectives of security professionals and their methods, respectively (Bayuk 2010). Three that combine to cover most uses of the term are:

- *prevent, detect, respond*
- *people, process, technology*
- *confidentiality, integrity, and availability.*

These reflect the goals of cyber security, the means to achieve cyber security, and the mechanisms by which cyber security goals are achieved, respectively.

Prevent, detect, respond addresses goals common to both physical and cyber security. Traditionally, the primary goal of security planning has been to prevent a successful adversary attack. However, all security professionals are aware that it is simply not possible to prevent all attacks, and so planning and preparation must also include methods to detect attacks in progress, preferably before they cause damage. However, whether or not detection processes are effective, once it becomes obvious that a system is threatened, security includes the ability to respond to such incidents. In physical security, the term "first responders" refers to the heroic individuals in policy, fire, and emergency medical professions. Response typically includes repelling the attack, treating human survivors, and safeguarding damaged assets. In cyber security, the third element of the triad is often stated in slightly more optimistic form. Rather than "respond" it is "recover" or "correct." This more positive expectation on the outcome of the third triad activity, to recover rather than simply respond, reflects the literature of information security planning, wherein security management is recommended to include complete reconstitution and recovery of any business-critical system. Because information technology allows diversity, redundancy, and reconstitution for the data and programs required to operate systems, information security professionals expect that damage can be completely allayed. In either case, the lessons learned in response are expected to inform prevention planning, creating a loop of continuous security improvement.

People, process, technology addresses methods common to both technology management in general and to cyber security management as a specialized field. This triad observes that systems require operators, and operators must follow established routines in order for systems to accomplish their missions. When applied to security, this triad highlights the fact that security is not achieved by security professionals alone, and also that cyber security cannot be accomplished with technology alone. The system or organization to be secured is acknowledged to include other human elements whose decisions and actions play a vital role in the success of security programs. Even if all these people had motivation and interest to behave securely, they would individually not know how to collectively act to prevent, detect, and recover from harm without preplanned process. So security professionals are expected to weave security programs into existing organizational processes and make strategic use of technology in support of cyber security goals.

Confidentiality, integrity, and availability addresses the security objectives that are specific to information. Confidentiality refers to a system's capability to limit dissemination of information to authorized use. Integrity refers to ability to maintain the authenticity, accuracy, and provenance of recorded and reported information. Availability refers to the timely delivery of functional capability. These information security goals applied to information even before they were on computers, but the advent of cyberspace has changed the methods by which the goals are achieved, as well as the relative difficulty of goal achievement. Technologies to support confidentiality, integrity, and availability are often at odds with each other. For example, efforts to achieve a high level of availability for information in cyberspace often make it harder to maintain information confidentiality. Sorting out just what confidentiality, integrity, and availability means for each type of information in a given system is the specialty of the cyber security professional. Cyber security refers in general to methods of using people, process, and technology to prevent, detect, and recover from damage to confidentiality, integrity, and availability of information in cyberspace.

1.2 What Is Cyber Security Policy?

Cyber has created productivity enhancements throughout society, effectively distributing information on a just-in-time basis. No matter what industry or application in which cyber is introduced, increased productivity has been in the focus. The rapid delivery of information to cyberspace often reduces overall system security. To technologists engaged in productivity enhancements, security measures often seem in direct opposition to progress due to prevention measures that reduce, inhibit, or delay user access, detection measures that consume vital system resources, and response requirements that divert management attention from system features that provide more immediately satisfying system capabilities. The tension between demand for cyber functionality and requirements for security is addressed through cyber security policy.

The word "policy" is applied to a variety of situations that concern cyber security. It has been used to refer to laws and regulations concerning information distribution, private enterprise objectives for information protection, computer operations methods for controlling technology, and configuration variables in electronic devices (Gallaher, Link et al. 2008). But there is a myriad of other ways in which literature uses the phrase *cyber security policy*. As with the term "cyberspace," there is not one definition, but there is a common theme when the term *cyber security* is applied to a policy statement as an adjective. The objective of this guidebook is to provide the reader with enough background to understand and appreciate the theme and its derivatives. Those who read it should be able to confidently decipher the numerous varieties of cyber security policy.

Generally, the term "cyber security policy" refers to directives designed to maintain cyber security. Cyber security policy is illustrated in Figure 1.1 using a modeling tool that is used to make sense of complex topics called a systemigram (Boardman and Sauser 2008). A systemigram creates an illustrative definition succinctly by way of introducing components of the thing to be defined (all nouns) and associating them with the activity they generate (all verbs). The tool requires that all major components be connected via a "mainstay" that links the concept to be defined (top left) to its

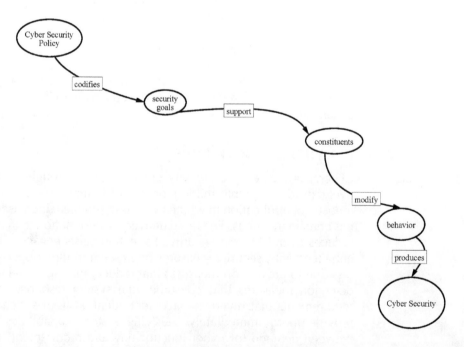

Figure 1.1 Cyber security policy definition.

purpose or mission (bottom right). The mainstay is expected to capture the layman's view of the concept. Other perspectives on the concept to be defined may be represented as supplementary perspectives on the complex concept.

In Figure 1.1, cyber security policy is presented as something that codifies security goals in support of constituents who are expected to modify their behavior in compliance with the policy to produce cyber security. Figure 1.2 fleshes out the concept, adding the color of different perspectives on cyber security policy. Although not all the additional nodes and links are strictly within the scope of a definition of cyber security policy, they provide insight into the scope as defined in the mainstay of the systemigram of Figure 1.1.

In Figure 1.2, the links to and from the "governance bodies" node illustrate that cyber security policy is adopted by governing bodies as a method of achieving security goals. The figure is purposely generic as governing bodies often exist outside of the organizations that they govern. For example,

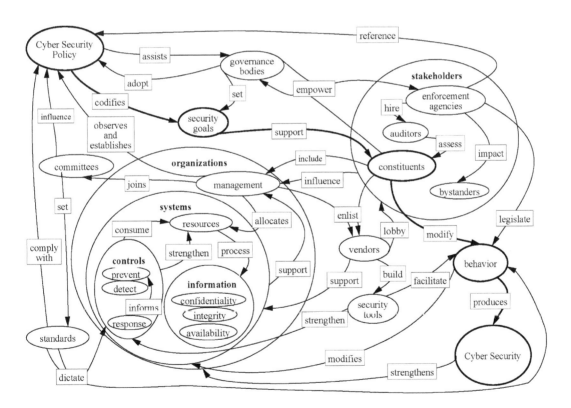

Figure 1.2 Cyber security policy perspectives.

a nation-state may be a governing body, but one may also consider a centralized corporate security office a governing body over multiple independent business units. The links emanating from the "enforcement agencies" node illustrate the role of policy enforcement agencies, who establish laws, rules, and/or regulations that are meant not only to affect constituent behavior, but also affect others, who thereby become stakeholders in the policy process. The links on the far left acknowledge the role of standards that are set by management of organizations who are bound by the governing bodies to comply with policy. The links emanating from the node labeled "vendors" depicts the vendor relationships of constituents and management, who both influence and are influenced by vendors who provide tools for security policy compliance and support systems security with products and services.

The clusters of nodes and links within and adjoining the "organizations" node refer to an organization that is subject to policy. It shows that such organizations observe cyber security policies issued by governing bodies as well as establish their own internal cyber security policies. It also illustrates that organizational management is both supporting and is being supported by systems that are impacted by security policy. The "systems" node refers to the systems used to operate cyberspace, highlighting the interdependent relationship between security controls and system resources. It shows that there is a trade-off between systems resources devoted to security controls and those required to process information; that is, the more security control processes can be integrated into systems operation, the less of a resource drain security will be. A typical goal in an internal organizational cyber security strategy is to optimize this trade-off, using documented policy as a communications tool to create awareness that such decisions have been made.

Note that, as illustrated in Figure 1.2, the role of policy is to provide a foundation upon which to prescribe rules for behavior that are expected to achieve cyber security. There is a wide variety of cyber domains that will have vastly different policy statements and associated rules. These domains are further described in Chapter 6. Goals for cyber security do not directly translate into behavior, but a cyber security strategy based upon cyber security goals is expected to culminate in better cyber security policy. Organizations create standards for implementing technology controls and related operational processes and constituents use these standards to comply with policy. Standards are not themselves policies. Rather, they are translations from policy objectives onto a set of technologies and operational processes. Where a standard is directed at policy compliance, it specifies a combination of process and technology configuration that will achieve policy compliance. However, standards may be issued that are not directed at any specific policy objective, and policies may lack corresponding standards.

1.3   Domains of Cyber Security Policy

As depicted in Figure 1.2, cyber security policy is adopted by a governing body and formally applies only to the corresponding domain of governance. The constituents of a security policy, who may also be considered stakeholders, will vary with the scope of the policy. For example, a nation-state cyber security policy will encompass all citizens and perhaps foreign businesses operating within its domain, whereas a corporate cyber security policy will apply only to staff with which the corporation has employment or other legal agreements which may reasonably be expected to motivate behavioral modification. Even suppliers who are wholly dependent on a single customer cannot be expected to conform to that customer security policy unless under a contractual obligation to do so. The content of security policy will change with the goals of the corresponding governing body. The goals of nation-state security are very different from the goals of corporate security, and so policy statements and corresponding expected activities in support of policy will appear very different.

The way policy is compiled, documented by enforcement agencies, and ratified will also differ with its corresponding governing body and constituency. In government, the process by which goals are codified into policy and the process by which policies are codified into legislation are separate and distinct processes. However, in corporations, it is common to have one central security department responsible for both the cyber security policy and the associated standards and procedures which are the corporate equivalent of regulatory guidance.

Where security is a priority for an organization, it is common to see cyber security policies issued by multiple internal departments with overlapping constituencies, who then sometimes detect policy incompatibility issues in trying to follow them all simultaneously.

1.3.1   Laws and Regulations

Nation-state cyber security policy is currently considered to be a subset of national security policy. Even if nation-state cyber security policy was considered to be on the same plane as foreign policy or economic policy, these policies do not have the same force as law. Rather, policies are established and articulated through reports and speeches, through talking points and negotiations. Policy is used to guide judgment on what laws and regulations to consider. It does not refer to the laws and regulations themselves. Of course, in the best of all possible worlds, treaties, laws, and regulations would reflect a wise and thoughtfully conceived policy. Nevertheless, it is possible to have cyber security executive directives, laws, and regulations without having articulated a cyber security policy at all.

For example, China has clearly established a policy that cyberspace activities critical to nation-state operations shall be controlled (Bishop 2010). This policy states clearly that the Internet shall serve the interests of the economy and the state. The policy has led to laws and regulations that allow the Chinese government to segregate, monitor, and control telecommunications facilities as well as block access to Internet sites they identify as contrary to their interests.

In the United States, by contrast, most laws and regulations that impact cyber security were not developed specifically to address issues of cyberspace, but have emerged as relevant to cyber security in the context of policy enforcement. The policy is often economic in nature. For example, any financial institution that is regulated by the Office of the Comptroller of the Currency has been subject to security audits and assessments of their Internet-facing infrastructure. A 2009 U.S. Cyber Security Policy Review actually redefined the word policy: "Cybersecurity policy includes strategy, policy, and standards regarding the security of and operations in cyberspace, and encompasses the full range of threat reduction, vulnerability reduction, deterrence, international engagement, incident response, resiliency, and recovery policies and activities, including computer network operations, information assurance, law enforcement, diplomacy, military, and intelligence missions as they relate to the security and stability of the global information and communications infrastructure" (Hathaway et al. 2009). This is the full range of issues to be considered when developing security policy. Moreover, the result of this review was not a policy recommendation. It simply outlined a strategy for ongoing communications and cooperation between the public and private sector with the goal of increasing national resilience to cyber attack. The U.S. approach to cyber security policy will be further discussed in Chapter 7.

Whether or not a government cyber security policy is articulated, its cyber security rules will be limited to the scope of its governance domain. That is, a branch or agency of a government will be within the scope of, and thus subject to, any government-wide regulation, so its own policy and rules must be consistent with that broader scope. A branch or agency will only be able to create new legislation for its own constituency and within its own charter. For example, cyber security policy issued by an industry regulator will apply only to those industries in its regulatory domain. An energy regulator will be able to require an energy facility to have redundant communications, but it will not be able to require that telecommunications providers lay redundant cables to each energy facility. Only a telecommunications industry regulator may set rules for the telecommunications industry, and the charter is not likely to include services provided to another regulator's domain. Such gaps in a holistic system-level approach to critical infrastructure regulation leave loopholes in the form of constraints that become excuses for partial and inadequate security coverage. To be effective, cyber security policy would have to span multiple regulatory domains for a single purpose, such as the U.S. Federal Trade Commission.

1.3.2 Enterprise Policy

Private sector organizations are generally not as constrained as governments in turning senior management policies into actionable rules. In a corporate environment, it is typical that policies are expected to be followed upon threat of sanction, up to and including employment termination. For example, human resources, legal, or accounting policies have been codified to the point where any instance of noncompliance may amount to reason for termination. Where mid-level managers support processes such as staff hiring or expense filing, they may be expected to bring department activities into compliance with those policies, and often will have to establish department-level metrics for compliance. As in the case of government, any such suborganization will be subject to constraints of authority in scope. Though there are exceptions in places that take information classification very seriously, a corporation security policy issued by a Chief Executive Officer will generally apply to an entire corporation, but one issued by a Chief Information Officer will typically only apply to the technology staff. A recent change in the organizational landscape is the appointment of a chief information security officer (CISO) or chief privacy officer (CPO) whose is responsible for selected aspects of the organization's security posture. However, the responsibilities in these roles are not as well accepted as those of a Chief Financial Officer (CFO), and sometimes such duties are more about public relations than security management.

An unfortunate difference between most corporate cyber security policies and those issued by a legal or human resource department is that cyber security policies often leave the assessment of cyber security risks to mid-level managers who may not be familiar with cyber security or risk management concepts. By analogy with a CFO policy, this is like leaving the definition of appropriate travel expenses up to the traveler. For example, a cyber security policy may state, "where risk of information confidentiality compromise is high, the information should not be allowed to be shared with a vendor without a duly diligent review of vendor capability to secure information." This type of policy leaves the information risk assessment to a manager who may be motivated to cut costs by outsourcing part of the department information flow. To further reduce those costs, that same manager may decide a due diligence review is not warranted. Such a situation may be caused by the misallocation of security responsibilities to someone who is not qualified, or it may be that the culture of the organization is risk-tolerant, but either way, it presents a segregation of duties issue. These situations are exacerbated by the fact that measures of cyber security are not as mature as metrics in the domains of accounting or human resources. Cyber security metrics are more fully discussed in Chapter 3.

1.3.3 Technology Operations

In an effort to assist clients in complying with legal and regulatory information security requirements, the legal, accounting, and consulting professions have adopted standards for due diligence with respect to information security, and recommended that clients model processes around them. These were sometimes proprietary to the consulting firm, but were often based on published standards such as the National Institute of Standards and Technology (NIST)'s *Recommended Security Controls for Federal Information Systems* (Ross, Katzke et al. 2007) and their private sector counterparts (ISO/IEC 2005a,b; ISF 2007). Where a standard becomes the preferred mode of operation for securing a technology environment, it will often be referred to as a cyber security policy for technology operations and management.

Whether these technology operations policies dictate simply that the standard should be followed, or they customize the standard with specific roles and responsibilities for process execution within the computer operations organization, the scope of the policy will be limited to the management and operations of a well-defined technology platform. It is sometimes even the case that the same organization will run multiple technology platforms, but their cyber security policy will apply only to a subset. This may be the case at a technology services provider who charges extra for security services, so not all of their customers' platforms will be covered by the security policy.

By the strict definition of policy as a high-level management directive, these types of documents may not be considered by all security professionals to be policy at all, but rather processes or standards. However, as the current literature includes this nomenclature, we observe this usage is prevalent. Nevertheless, in this book, we will typically use the term policy to refer to higher level management directives that articulate and codify strategy for overall cyber security goal achievement as opposed to policy for the correct operation of a technology-only process.

1.3.4 Technology Configuration

Because many technology operations standards are implemented using specialized security software and devices, technology operators often colloquially refer to the standard-specified technical configuration of these devices as "security policy." These specifications have over the years been implemented by vendors and service providers, who devised technical configurations of computing devices that would allow system administrators to claim compliance with various standards. This has led vendors to label alternative technical configurations for their products as "security policies." Vendor marketing literature presents these technical configurations as "policy" in an effort to align their solutions with the overall enterprise strategy. For example, "our product allows you to automate your enterprise security policy."

Similar to the use of the word policy to refer to operational processes and standards, this use of the word policy does not correspond to management directives for security. But again, as the current literature includes this nomenclature, we observe this usage is prevalent. Usually, this usage of the term policy will appear with an adjective for the device or technology that is configured. For example, the words "firewall policies" or "UNIX security policy" indicate that the object is a set of technical configuration variables rather than a directive by high-level management. These technologies and devices are further discussed in Chapter 2.

1.4   Strategy versus Policy

Cyber security policy articulates the strategy for cyber security goal achievement and provides its constituents with direction for the appropriate use of cyber security measures. The direction may be societal consensus or dictated by a governance body. We also recognize that independent enterprises need to establish management directives in support of cyber security strategy, and we use the modified term, "enterprise policy" to refer to policies that apply only within a given enterprise community. Though such enterprise policy is often guided by standards for cyber security such as those established by the International Organization for Standardization (ISO) (ISO/IEC 2005a,b) and NIST (Ross, Katzke et al. 2007), those standards by themselves are not policies. Such standards typically contain a combination of process guidance with technology control recommendations. The process guidance recommends that policy be established, but cannot by itself properly be called policy.

In the sense that all policies differ from the implementation standards with which they are enforced, policy can be guesswork, because the simple adoption of policy does not guarantee that the right corresponding rules will be established to achieve security goals. Without a clear conceptual view of cyber security influences, it would be difficult to devise cyber security strategy and corresponding policy. Even if there is widespread consensus on the policy enforcement mechanisms, and these can be directly traced to policy directives, the collective judgment could be misguided, and those mechanisms may fail to achieve security policy goals. Chapter 6 provides many examples of policy statements that may have unintended consequences. Key to cyber security policy formulation is (1) to recognize that security control decisions are made regardless of whether there is a formal policy in place, (2) to understand that policy is the appropriate tool to guide multiple independently made security decisions, and (3) to absorb as much information as possible about how security decisions are influenced in the course of devising security strategy.

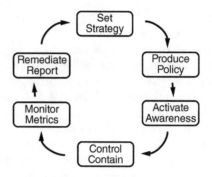

Figure 1.3 Cyber security management cycle (Bayuk 2007).

Given such perspective, cyber security policy is an important security management tool in any organization, government or private. Figure 1.3 demonstrates the place of cyber security policy within an overall cyber security quality management loop. The policy is a "what" compared to a strategy, which is a high-level "how." The establishment of standards in support of policy does not directly translate into behavior that effects cyber security. Policy is one part of an overall organizational security program that includes rules and enforcement mechanisms for the rules rather than the policy itself (Amoroso 2010). Any governing body that establishes policy should also establish monitoring mechanisms to determine whether security goals are met by policy enforcement strategies. To be effective, this monitoring is necessarily outside of the enforcement process, not part of it.

The diagram of Figure 1.3 illustrates that policy flows from an organization's overall cyber security strategy. Individual policy statements are usually debated in the course of cyber security strategy development, and they are an outcome of it. When fully articulated, policy statements are used to facilitate awareness of cyber security strategy to individuals responsible for its execution. The awareness is meant to instill accountability for policy compliance and to motivate the implementation of policy-compliant systems. In mature cyber security programs, policy compliance is monitored. Monitoring may be continuous via automated sensors, periodic checks and balances, and/or it may be intermittent, as in a lifecycle review process. Where such monitoring identifies issues with policy compliance, or cyber security incidents that are not anticipated by policy, remediation plans are considered. Where no remediation plan is considered feasible, this feedback is consumed by cyber security strategists, who use it to refine policy. Different organizations may label the six phases of the security management cycle differently, but they are fairly standard across cyber-security-aware organizations.

For example, a cyber security strategy may include a cyber security policy documentation effort and associated awareness campaign that is supplemented with an oversight capability and associated consequences for deviations from policy compliance. Standards, operating procedures, and guidelines are also often issued by the same organization in conjunction with policy in order to demonstrate how compliance with a given policy may be achieved at a tactical level. These how-to documents also fall into the awareness step of the cyber security management cycle and may be owned by executive management. However, executive management strategy rarely extends into implementation tools and techniques. As both technology and the corresponding threat environment are constantly changing, any executive strategy that dictates technology measures will have a very limited life span within which those measures can be expected to be effective.

Cyber security policy should be flexible and revisited with material changes in situations, but nevertheless should be robust enough to withstand the ever-increasing frequency of changes in technology, and strategy should allow for alternative implementation measures to evolve in conjunction with technology. However, it is important to note that this very evolution may sometimes cause drift between technology implementation and policy. Measures that achieved policy compliance in the past may be inadequate to cover the changes in the current cyberspace environment. Hence, constant monitoring is required to ensure that policy continues to be effected by implementation measures, and exceptions may require remediation in the form of changes in strategy and policy in addition to technology. This is why the management feedback loop in Figure 1.3 directs reports and remediation back to the strategy process. This security management cycle will be further discussed in Chapter 4.

In summary, there is a growing desire among executive decision makers to make informed decisions that reflect their own organizational policy objectives, yet there is little guidance for them on which cyber security-related decisions are likely to help them achieve their objectives. This introduction has served to put the field of cyber security policy in context. The remainder of this guidebook explains cyber security policy alternatives for the sake of clarity with respect to policy alone. It is informed by recent summaries and contains references to them. The guidebook does not propose a cyber security strategy. Rather, it will help the reader to identify the policy components reflected in cyber security strategies recommended by others. The guidebook does not offer a model for cyber security policy. It is intended to assist the reader charged with the creation of cyber security strategy. The overall goal is to facilitate proactive, strategic, and holistic approaches to cyber risk management.

2

Cyber Security Evolution

To understand cyber security policy, it is helpful to appreciate how cyber security has evolved. When computers enabled the first automated processes, the main goal in all such projects was the increase in *productivity* that came with replacing human calculators with automated programs that produced more accurate results. As more software became available, the productivity benefits of computers increased. The introduction of the *Internet* further enabled productivity by allowing quick and accurate communication of information. This led directly to the ability to process business transactions online. This capability was dubbed *electronic commerce (e-commerce)*. By 2000, the economy had become so dependent on e-commerce that it was a frequent target of cyber criminals, and security technology evolved to protect data that could be used to commit fraudulent transactions. Such technology is generally referred to as *countermeasures* because they are security measures designed to counter a specific threat. The chapter chronicles the progression of cyber security technology, and concludes with observations on the *challenges* presented by the ongoing cyber arms race wherein countermeasures are falling behind.

2.1 Productivity

The history of cyber security starts in the 1960s with the mainframe. This was the first type of computer that was affordable enough for businesses to see a return on investment from electronic data processing systems. Prior to this time, the word "computer" referred to a person who performed computations, and the word "cyber" was the realm of science fiction.

Cyber Security Policy Guidebook, First Edition. Jennifer L. Bayuk, Jason Healey, Paul Rohmeyer, Marcus H. Sachs, Jeffrey Schmidt, Joseph Weiss.
© 2012 John Wiley & Sons, Inc. Published 2012 by John Wiley & Sons, Inc.

In those days, computers were secured with guards and gates. Physical security procedures were devised to ensure that only people authorized to work on computers had physical access to them. Computers were so large that hundreds of square feet of space would be customized for their operation, with dedicated security staff. A guard function was sometimes combined with the role of computer operator, called a job control technician. People who needed to use the computer would queue up in front of the guard holding their data and programs in stacks of punched cards. The guard would check the user's authorization to use the computer, receive their stack of cards, and place it into a card reader that would automatically translate the punched holes in the cards into bits and bytes (Schacht 1975). By the late 1960s, remote job entry allowed punched cards to be received from multiple office locations connected via cables to the main computer. Computer security staff then had the added responsibility of tracing these cables under raised floors, and through wall spaces and ceiling ducts to ensure that the authorized person was sitting at the other end.

Managers of these early automated computer systems were acutely aware of security risk, but the confidentiality, integrity, and availability triad was not yet industry standard. Aside from a few installations in the military and intelligence, confidentiality was not the major security requirement. Though businesses did want to keep customer lists confidential, immature software was constantly failing, so their major concern was not confidentiality, but integrity. Potential for human error to cause catastrophic data integrity errors has always been evident in computer software development and operations. Software engineering organizations were the first to raise the security alarm because computers were starting to control systems where faulty operation could put lives at risk (Ceruzzi 2003). In addition, computer crime in the form of financial fraud was common by the early 1970s, and made it to mainstream fictional literature and television (McNeil 1978). Even supposing that the human factor was eliminated from the sphere of security threats, system malfunctions were known to occur without blame, starting with the first actual *bug* discovered among the vacuum tubes in a computer system (Slater 1987, p. 223).

In the 1970s, punched cards were replaced by electronic input and output via keyboards and terminals. Cables and terminals further extended the range within which authorized users could sit while processing data. Systems security expanded to include following the cables through wall partitions and ceiling ducts to ensure that the cables terminated in offices occupied by authorized computer users. This allowed people in offices far removed from the actual computer to be hooked up to an input–output (IO) port and use it from their desks. The guard in front of the computer room door remained, but mostly to sign in visitors who would tour the computer room, or vendors who performed maintenance. Security of the information was moved to the realm of customized business logic. Users were assigned login names, which were associated with menus that provided the screens they needed to perform their job function. Screens literally screened, or filtered, both data fields and menus. The effect was that most users saw the same basic screen, but different data fields and menu selections were available to different users. The screens were limited by *business logic* coded into the software. For example, if clerks had a customer service screen, they may be able to view customer records but not change their balance. However, business logic screens often contained overrides. For example, a supervisor observing the customer service clerk could enter a special code to allow a one-time balance change operation through the otherwise limited screen functionality.

Widespread use of computers enabled by keyboard technology drew attention to the issue of confidentiality controls. Military and intelligence computer use had increased. Government-funded research in cryptography had produced a few algorithms that transformed data into unreadable formats using long sequences of bits called "keys" that would both lock and unlock the data. Such cryptographic algorithms are based on *diffusion*, to disseminate a message into a statistically longer and more obscure formats, and *confusion*, to make the relationship between an encrypted message and the corresponding key too long and involved to be guessed (Shannon 1949). However, advances in computer power had significantly increased the ability of a determined adversary to identify the relationship between messages and keys. It was easy to envision a day when existing automated cryptography methods were not complex enough to frustrate automated statistical analysis (Grampp and McIlroy 1989). In addition, automation of records by government agencies, such as the U.S. Social Security Administration and the Internal Revenue Service, fostered recognition that stakeholders in cyberspace included those whose physical lives were closely aligned to the bits and bytes representing them. In recognition of the growing confidentiality requirements, but without any good way to meet them, the U.S. National Bureau of Standards (now the National Institute of Standards and Technology [NIST]) launched an effort to achieve consensus on a national encryption standard. In 1974, the U.S. Computer Security Act (Privacy Act) was the first stake in the ground designed to establish control over information propagation. The act covered only government use of computers and only information that today would be called personally identifiable information (PII). But it firmly established confidentiality and corresponding efforts to improve encryption technology as mainstream goals for cyber security.

As technology advanced through the 1970s, minicomputers such as the DEC PDP-11 frequently supplemented mainframes in large companies and were rapidly expanding into smaller companies that could now afford them to automate office tasks such as word processing. For those who could not yet afford a computer of any size, technology-savvy entrepreneurs had started services that allowed people to rent time on computers. These were called "timesharing services" because companies in this business would charge their clients based on the amount of computer time they consumed. Once terminal and keyboard technology made it possible to extend IO devices through cables, they used ordinary telephone lines to extend the reach of computer terminal beyond the walls of the building using analog modulation-demodulation technology (modems and multiplexors). These companies began to specialize by industry, developing complicated software such as payroll tax calculations and commerical lease calculations. Such software development was unlikely to fare well in a cost-benefit analysis to a company that was not in the software business, but it was a time-consuming manual processes run by many businesses. Time-sharing services allowed departments that were not the mainstream part of the business to benefit from automation, though they had to access someone else's computer to do it. Today, these services are available over the Internet, though their charging models have changed and they are no longer called "time-sharing" but "cloud computing."

These timesharing services charged for computing resources based on user activity, so they had to have a way to identify users in order to bill them. Often, this user identification was simply a company name, though passwords were sometimes issued where timesharing services were known to have customers who were competitors. However, from the point of view of the customer user, the user name connected them to their information in the computer and the modem connection did not seem like a security risk. Any company large enough to own a computer at the time was obviously a firm of some wealth and substance, so the timesharing service companies were assumed to have physical security around their computer, and passwords were further evidence of their security due diligence. It was considered the risk of the timesharing service vendor to allow customer logical access, and given their wealth and substance, they could be expected to protect their assets accordingly.

Throughout the 1970s into the 1980s, minicomputers became more affordable and eventually allowed people to have an entire computer for their own use. Apple introduced home computers in the late 1970s. These soon made it into the data processing environment and were followed by the IBM personal computer (PC) in 1981. Physical security still was the norm for these small computers, and locked office doors were the primary protection mechanism. Network technologies then allowed desktop computers in the same building to share data with each other, and the names of the computers became important so that people could share information with other computers on the network. The local area network (LAN) cables were protected much like the computer terminals' connection to the mainframe, except that a new type of network equipment called a "hub" allowed the communication, and hubs had to be kept in a secure area. The hubs that allowed a person to hook his or her computer to the LAN were protected via locked closets.

Until the introduction of LANs, access controls were the exception rather than the norm in computing environments. If login IDs were distributed, they were rarely disabled. They functioned more as a convenient method of labeling data so one knew to whom it belonged than to restrict access to it. However, the LAN-connected computing environments and corresponding plethora of PCs made it very difficult to trace network computer activity to individuals, because they generally logged in only to the machine on their desktop. As LANs grew larger, centralized administration schemes from government research labs were developed for corporate mainframes (Schweitzer 1982, 1983). Mandatory access controls (MAC) allowed management to label computer objects (programs and files) and specify the subjects (users) who could access them. These were supplemented with discretionary schemes (DAC) that allowed each user to specify who else could access their files.

As many of the LAN computer users already had a mainframe terminal on their desks, it was not long before these computers replaced the terminal functionality, and the LAN was connected to the mainframe. It was this development that made cyber security become a hot topic with technology management. Though some of the timesharing-type password technology was employed on the LAN, LAN user names were primarily supported to facilitate directory services rather than to prevent determined attacks. That is, it was helpful to know the name of the person who had written a particular file, or posted a memo on a customer record. Assigning login names to computer users allowed programs to use that name as part of its business logic to provide the correct menus and screens. Prior to this point in cyberspace evolution, transactions on a mainframe could still be traced to an individual terminal, in a given physical location, and subsequent investigation using both physical and digital forensics had a fighting chance to identify a suspect. But the LANs and modems blurred distinctions between users, and it was easy for a criminal to deny or—to use a rapidly proliferating computer security version of the word—*to repudiate* activity performed from a LAN desktop. Even where passwords were required, they were weak enough to be guessed. There was no concept of network encryption, so anyone with access to the hubs could see passwords travelling on the network. Moreover, many network programs allowed anonymous access, so user names were not available for every connection.

It only took a few cases of insider fraud for management to understand that the status quo carried too much risk to be sustainable. Hence, security technology that had until that point been the topic of military research was hastily implemented by major computer vendors, and applied to mainframe data sets and LAN file resources. These included user identity, authentication in the form of increasingly more difficult passwords, and management authorization for computer access. A complete set of the system features required to secure operation was soon readily available in a U.S. Department of Defense publication called, "The Orange Book" for the color of its cover (DoD 1985). The complete set of features included both technical implementation standards and terminology for sophisticated processes to ensure that users could be identified and properly authenticated and audited. These features were collectively referred to as *access control lists* (ACLs, pronounced "ak-els"), as they allowed an administrator to specify with some confidence which user could do what on which computers. Encryption was also heralded as an obvious solution to a variety of computer security problems (NRC 1996). But it was a luxury that few outside of the military had enough spare computer processing to afford, so the smaller the computer, the weaker the vendor's encryption algorithms were likely to be, and encryption was parsimoniously applied to specific data such as passwords in storage.

Although accountability for transaction processing was fast becoming a hot topic at fraud conferences, law enforcement activity in the domain of computer operation was limited. Nevertheless, the early 1980s was also the dawn of the age of digital evidence. Cyberspace presented a new avenue of inquiry for law enforcement investigating traditional crimes. Criminals were caught boasting of their crimes on the social networking sites of the day, which were electronic bulletin board services reached by modems over phone lines. Drug dealers, murderers, and child pornographers were prosecuted using the plans, accounting data, and photographs they had stored on their own computers. Law enforcement partnered with technology vendors to produce software that would recover files that criminals had attempted to delete from computers (Schmidt 2006).

Figure 2.1 illustrates cyberspace architecture as it was typically configured at the dawn of the 1980s. Mainframe, micro, and minicomputers

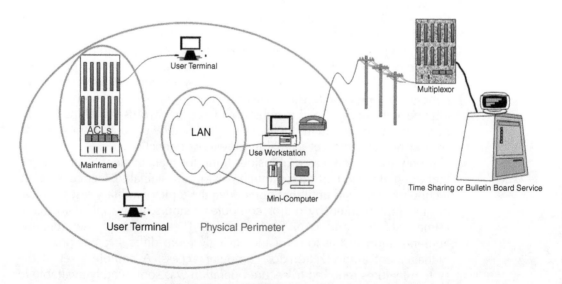

Figure 2.1 Cyberspace in the 1980s.

existed side by side, and were not necessarily connected via networks. However, minicomputers were often used to connect to remote computers via the same types of telephone lines that carried voice calls. However, as the pace of technology innovation was rapid, this situation was constantly evolving, and change was inevitable.

2.2 Internet

By the late 1980s, communication across city boundaries had achieved the same level of maturity as LANs. Directory services were available that allowed businesses to connect, and be connected to, the research and military restricted advanced research projects agency (ARPA) network, or *ARPANET*, whose use case and name were relaxed as it evolved into the public *Internet*. From the point of view of technology management, these Internet connections looked like another modem-like technology service. It was a connection to a large company in the business of connecting the computers of other large companies. The only noticeable by-product of this connection from a management perspective was the ability to send electronic mail. Technology-savvy companies quickly registered their domain names so that they could own their own corner of cyberspace. Only a few researchers were concerned with the potential for system abuse due to the exponential expansion of the numbers of connected computers.

One of these researchers was Robert Morris at AT&T Bell Laboratories. He was an early computer pioneer, to the extent that he actually had computers at his home long before they were marketed to consumers. His son, Robert Tappan Morris, grew up around these computers and was very familiar with the ways in which they could be used without the permission of their owners (Littman 1990). In 1988, Robert Tappan Morris devised the first Internet worm. The "Morris Worm" accessed computers used as email servers, exploited vulnerabilities to identify all the computers that were known to each email server, and then contacted all of those computers and attempted the same exploits. Within a few hours, most of the Internet had been affected and the damage was severe. Internet communication virtually stopped, computing resources were so overwhelmed by the worm's activities that they had no processing cycles or network bandwidth left for transaction processing, leaving business processes disrupted.

The only organization on the ARPANET that was safe from the Morris worm was AT&T Bell Laboratories. The reason for the safety had nothing to do with Morris but instead was due to an experiment being conducted by some other computer network researchers. They had developed a method of inspecting each individual information packet within a stream of network traffic that they called a *firewall* (Cheswick and Bellovin 1994). The firewall was designed to allow network access to only those packets whose *source* and *destination* matched those on a previously authorized list. The sources and destinations in the network access rules were formulated using the *network addresses* of communicating computers, as well as a *port number* that serves as the access address for software running on each computer that is expected to be accessed via the network. The Bell Labs firewall was hastily employed to safeguard AT&T's email servers, and the impact to AT&T from the Morris worm was minimal. Since then, cyber security policy has included management directive to safeguard the network periphery. The primary cyber security implementation strategy of choice since then has been to deploy firewalls.

The Morris Worm had a profound effect on the Internet community. As ARPA still officially managed the network, it responded by establishing the Computer Emergency Response Team (CERT) to provide technical assistance to those who suffered from cyber security problems (US-CERT ongoing). Detection and recovery had officially joined prevention as standard cyber security controls.

Introspective postmortems following the Morris worm revealed that the same types of vulnerabilities in Internet-facing email servers existed in systems that presented modem interfaces to the public. Hackers would dial every number in the phone book and listen for the tell-tale hum of a computer modem. Once identified, they would call these modems with their own computer and often find little security. Hackers shared the numbers on bulletin boards and met on vulnerable computers to play games or other activities unbeknownst to the systems owners. Those that stole computer time only to play games were called joyriders. There had been a few public examples of hackers mining such systems with profit motives, but these had largely been directed at theft of phone service, and phone companies would occasionally partner with law enforcement to make a sting (Sterling 1992).

However, it was not just the phone companies that were targeted, they were just the most visible. One month in 1986, Cliff Stoll, an astrophysics graduate student with a university job as a timesharing services administrator, noticed a billing error in the range of 75 cents of computer time that was not associated with any of his users. Though neither his management at Lawrence Berkeley National Laboratory nor law enforcement was concerned, he was curious how the error could have occurred on such a deterministic platform as a computer. Stoll ended up tracking the missing cents of computing time to an Eastern European espionage ring. He published an account of his investigation in 1989 in a detective-like tale called *The Cuckoo's Egg* (Stoll 1989). *The Cuckoo's Egg* set off a large-scale effort among technology managers to identify and lock down access to computers via modems.

No firewall-like technology had been developed for modems, but various combinations of phone-system technology met the requirements. One such combination is caller ID and dial-back. Caller ID is a method of identifying the phone number attempting to connect, and this allows comparison of the caller to a database of home phone numbers of people allowed to connect. However, anyone with customer premise phone equipment can present any number to a receiving phone via the caller-ID protocol, basically impersonating an authorized home phone number, or *spoofing* an authorized origination. So it is not secure simply to accept the call based on the fact that caller ID presents a known phone number. After verifying that the number is valid, the dialed computer hangs up and *dials-back* the authorized number to make sure it was not spoofed.

Seemingly safe behind firewalls and slightly more complex dial-back modems, organizations allowed their users to dial in and use their networks from home and also to surf the fast-growing Internet, which still mostly consisted of universities and research libraries. The first easy-to-use browser made it simple even for nontechnical people to use the Internet, and it was fast becoming the phonebook of choice for those familiar with it. Small, single purpose servers were becoming more affordable, and many companies had an area of the network dedicated for shared server connectivity, called a server farm. Growing familiarity with both server operation and the Internet led most companies who had their own domain names and email servers to establish web servers as well. These were mostly brochure-ware sites that allowed an Internet user to download a company's catalog and find its sales phone number.

Figure 2.2 illustrates how these networks were typically connected in the early 1990s. The circles show where physical security is heightened to protect network equipment. The devices represent the logical location of the firewalls and telecommunication line connections to other firms. The telecommunication lines are portrayed as logically segmented spaces where lines to business partners terminate on the internal network. These were, and still are, referred to as "private lines" because there is no other network communication on the lines except that which is transmitted between two physical locations.

Unfortunately, all these network periphery controls did not prevent the hackers and joyriders from disrupting computer operations with viruses. Viruses were distributed on floppy disks (i.e., removable media, the 1990s equivalent of universal serial bus [USB] sticks), and they were planted on websites that were advertised to corporate and government Internet users. Virus specimens were analyzed by cyber forensics specialists, who had earned their security credentials helping law enforcement identify digital evidence. They were able to create a "digital signature" for each virus by identifying each file it altered and the types of logs it left behind. They created "antivirus" software, which they sold to industry and government. Antivirus vendors committed to their clients that they would keep their list of signatures up to date with every new virus introduced on the Internet. As there were already thousands of viruses circulating, companies quickly devised the means to install antivirus software on all of the PCs of all of their users.

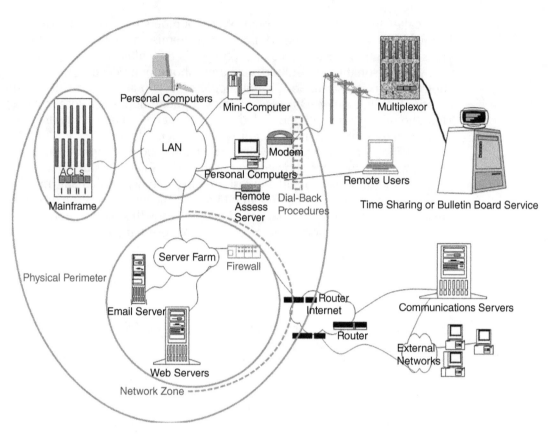

Figure 2.2 Cyberspace in the early 1990s.

The antivirus software vendors' cyber forensics specialists were also usually able to identify the software security bugs or flaws in operating systems or other software that had been exploited by the viruses. As the signature that identified one virus was not tied to the software flaw but to the files deposited by the virus itself, a virus writer could slightly modify his or her code to take advantage of the same software vulnerability and evade detection by antivirus software. It thus became important not only to update antivirus signatures, but also to demand that software vendors correct the security bugs and flaws in the software that allowed viruses to cause damage in the first place. Software companies were under pressure to fill the demand for Internet applications, and a common software business model was to build skeletal applications that were of minimal utility while their graphical user interfaces (GUIs) communicated a vision for more advanced features (Rice 2008). Customer feedback on the initial software release determined which new features would be added and which bugs and flaws would be repaired.

These fixes were known as "patches" to software. The word "patch" is derived from the physical term meaning a localized repair. Its origin in the context of computers referred to a cable plugged into a wall of vacuum tubes that altered the course of electronic processing in an analog computer by physically changing the path of code execution. Now the term patch refers to a few lines of code that repair some bug or flaw in software. Patches are small files that must frequently be installed on complex software in order to prevent an adversary from exploiting vulnerable code and thereby causing damage to systems or information.

The software rush to the Internet marketplace in the mid-1990s heralded a new era of e-commerce, a generic term for the exchange of goods and services using the Internet as a medium. Software replaced the online catalogs and allowed Internet users to purchase goods and execute financial transactions over the network. Vulnerabilities in software became the source of what was then called "the port 80 problem." Port 80 is the port on a firewall that has to be open in order for external users to access web services. Web application developers recognized this and knew how web server technology could be exploited to gain access to an internal network. Starting from port 80 on a server facing the Internet, a web server program was designed to accept user commands instructing it to display content, but it would also allow commands instructing it to accept and execute programs provided by a user. What every web developer knew, every hacker knew, and hackers were using port 80 to attack the web server and use it as a launch point to access the internal network. The immediate result of the port 80 problem analysis was that firewalls were installed not just at the network periphery but in a virtual circle around any machine that faced the Internet.

A Demilitarized Zone (DMZ) network architecture became the new security standard. Coined by the Bell Labs researchers who had created the first firewall, a DMZ was an area of the network that allowed Internet access to a well-defined set of specific services. In a DMZ, all computer operating software accessible from the Internet was "hardened" to ensure that no other services could be accessed from those explicitly allowed, or that were considered "sacrificial" systems that were purposely not well secured, but closely monitored to see if attackers were targeting the enterprise (Ramachandran 2002). These sacrificial systems were modeled on a fake national security system that Cliff Stoll had used to lure espionage agents. They were also called "honeypots" in analogy of the practice of trapping flies with honey rather than actively swatting at them.

Like its military counterparts, a cyber DMZ is surrounded by checkpoints on all sides. In the cyber case, the checkpoint includes firewall technology. The design of a DMZ requires that Internet traffic be filtered so packets can only access the servers that have been purposely deployed for public use, and are fortified against expected attacks. It further requires that traffic filters be deployed between those servers and the internal network. It became standard procedure that the path to the internal network was opened only with the express approval of a security architect, who was responsible for testing the security controls on all DMZ and internally accessible software. This practice of security review prior to deployment matured into methods of integrating security review within the systems development life cycle and was christened "systems security engineering." The process has since become internationally standard (ISO/IEC 2002, 2009c).

This isolation of the path from the consumer to an e-commerce site soon became a liability. As competitors became aware that rivals were growing their businesses by allowing easy online access to catalogs, competing sites attempted to stop the flow of e-commerce to competitors by intentionally consuming all the available bandwidth allowed through the competitor firewall to the competitor websites. Because these attacks prevented other Internet users from using the web services of the stricken competitor, they were designated "denial of service" attacks. To evade detection, attackers used multiple, geographically dispersed machines to execute such attacks, and this practice was dubbed "distributed denial of service" or "DDOS." At this time, there was no way to mitigate such attacks other than to increase the bandwidth allocated to Internet services.

As companies realized how hard the Internet boundary was to police, it became apparent that the timesharing systems to which they were directly connected had also established markets in online services. This means that the Internet was not only outside their firewall, but was also on the other side of telecommunications lines facing service providers. These were connections that had previously been considered secure. In addition, the introduction of easy-to-carry laptop computers had vastly increased the number of people who wanted to dial in from home and also while traveling, so dial-back databases were becoming hard to securely maintain. Caller ID and dial-back were gradually replaced by a new handheld technology that used cryptography to generate one-time passwords, called *tokens*. Multiple vendors competed to produce the most convenient handheld device that would be able to compute unguessable strings that provided user authentication in addition to passwords.

Security researchers had long envisioned that passwords would not be considered secure enough for user authentication. Handheld devices were referred to as a second factor, which if required during authentication, would make it harder to impersonate a computer user. A third factor, biometric identification, would be even stronger, but then was still in proof of concept stages. So credit card-sized handheld devices capable of generating tokens were issued to remote users. These contained encryption keys that were synchronized with keys on internal servers. Token administration servers supplemented passwords for authenticating user network connectivity.

Increases in the numbers of remote users exacerbated the virus problem. In addition to installing antivirus software and patches on workstations, companies also enlisted security software vendors to track the spread of viruses on websites so they could block their users from accessing websites that hosted viruses, and thereby reduce the propagation of viruses on their internal networks. The term "blacklist" became to be known in computer security literature as the list of websites that were known to propagate malicious software ("malware"). *Web proxy* servers work by intercepting all user traffic headed for the Internet, comparing the content of the communication to a set of communication rules established by an organization, and not letting the intercepted traffic proceed if there is a conflict between the traffic and the rules. The first use of this technology made use of a list of the universal resource locations (URLs) corresponding to Internet sites called a "blacklist." A web proxy server blocks a user from accessing sites on the blacklist. The proxy is enforced because browser traffic is not allowed outbound through the network periphery by the firewalls unless it comes from the *proxy server*, so users have to traverse the proxy service in order to browse. Vendors quickly established businesses to hunt down and sell lists of malicious software sites.

As the lists of viruses, patches, and malware sites changed continuously, enterprise security management needed a way to know that all of their computers had in fact been updated with antivirus signatures, patches, and proxy configurations. All too often, a user who had been on vacation during a patch or antivirus update became the source of network disruption by bringing a previously eradicated virus back onto the internal network. Headlines in the mid-1990s repeatedly described the travails of many reputable companies whose computing centers were devastated by the latest Internet viruses and worms. Given the amount of effort that they were expending internally to keep up with the latest security technology, it occurred to technology management that they could estimate the cost burden this would place on their service providers and often doubted that those to whom they connected for software services were not keeping up. This type of service provider review was often motivated by increasing regulatory scrutiny on handling of personally identifiable data. When an online transaction occurs between a customer and a company, these two entities are considered the first and second party to the transaction, respectively. If the company outsources some of the data handling for the customer to a service provider, this entity is referred to by regulators as a "third party" to the transaction. It did not take much skepticism to guess that technology services vendors were not keeping up with ever-increasing security requirements. This recognition led to a new standard for protecting the network periphery, not just from publicly accessible network connections, but even from trusted business partners. All network connections were now sources of potential threat of intrusion. Firewalls were placed on the Internal side of the telecommunications lines that privately

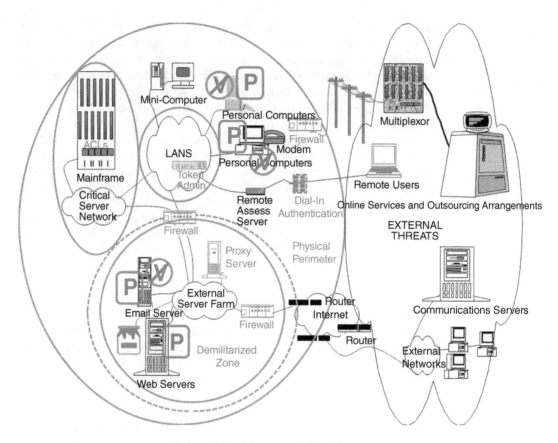

Figure 2.3 Cyberspace in the mid-1990s.

connected firms from their third party service providers. Only expected services were allowed through, and only to the internal users or servers that required the connectivity to operate.

Figure 2.3 depicts a typical network topology in the mid 1990s. The Vs with the lines through them indicate that antivirus software was installed on the types of machines identified underneath them. The Ps stand for patches that were, and still are, frequently required on the associated computers. The shade of gray used to identify security technology is the same throughout the diagram. The dashed line encircles the equipment that is typically found in a DMZ.

2.3 e-Commerce

Despite its complicated appearance, the illustration in Figure 2.3 is dramatically simplified. At the time, LANs were propagating across remote locations; even relatively small companies might have hundreds of PCs and dozens of servers. All of the security software is very difficult to manage, and antivirus vendors came up with *antivirus management* servers that track each PC in a company inventory to make sure it had the most up-to-date signatures. The situation was not comfortable, but seemed controllable, and e-commerce opportunities beckoned. Customers now expected to not just find a catalog or phone number on company websites, but actually place orders and receive reports. The first such sites were fraught with risk of fraud and threats to confidentiality because of the number of telecommunications devices that suddenly gained unfettered access to customer information, including credit card numbers.

To enable businesses to cloak customer communications in secrecy, a web software company introduced a new encrypted communications protocol called Secure Socket Layer (SSL). This was 1995, and in 1999, the protocol was enhanced by committee and codified under the name Transport Layer Security (TLS) (Rescorla and Dierks 1999). Despite an occasional vulnerability report (Gorman 2012), TLS has been the standard communications encryption mechanism ever since.

The TLS protocol requires web servers to have long identification strings, called certificates. These were technically difficult to generate, so security staff purchased and operated certificate authority software. The software allowed them to create a *root* certificate for their company, and the root certification was used to generate server certificates for each company web server. The way the technology worked, a customer visiting the web server would be able to tell it was stamped with the identity of the issuing company by comparing it to the company's root certificate. For critical applications that facilitated high asset value transactions, certificates could also be generated for each customer, which the SSL protocol referred to as a *client*. The SSL protocol thus made use of certificates to identify client to server and server to client. Once mutually identified, both sides would use data from the certificates to generate a single new key they both would use for encrypted communication. This allows each web session to look different from the point of view of an observer on the network, even if the same information, such as the same credentials, are transmitted. When a user visited an SSL-enabled site for the first time, the site owner would typically redirect them to a link where they could download the root certificate. Thereafter, these browsers automatically checked the corresponding web server certificates. If client certificates were required, the user would be asked a series of questions that installed the client certificate on their desktop.

But this SSL security configuration was difficult for e-commerce customers to manage, and users were confused by the root certificate downloading process and the questions about certificates. So browser software vendors started to preload their browsers with the root certificates from security software vendors, who for a price, would sell a company web server certificates that corresponded to a root certificate delivered with the browser.

The default behavior of this new version of browser when encountering a web server with a certificate that did not come from one of these preselected certificate vendors was to declare a security alert. This meant that the clients of any company who had invested in a certificate authority rather than buying certificates from a company like Verisign would receive a warning that the certificate was "untrusted." The alert caused Internet users so much angst that the result was that most companies abandoned their own certificate authorities and instead purchased certificates from one of the vendors already installed in browsers, creating a new market in encryption keys. To add insult to injury, the certificate vendors periodically expired the certificates. So those who previously made their own keys and switched to avoid the "untrusted" warning had to keep track of the date on which the key was purchased, and repurchase before that day to avoid system failure. The client-side certificates could also be purchased, but due to major variances in customer desktops, these proved so difficult to use they were abandoned by all but high risk e-commerce financial companies like payroll service vendors.

Even without certificates, dealing with customers over the Internet was hard to manage. Due to the dispersed nature of many sales organizations, customer relationship records had always been difficult to manage centrally, and now login credentials and email addresses had to be associated with customer records. Other than timesharing vendors, companies had rarely issued login credentials to anyone who was not in their own phone directory. Managing external users required specialized software. *Identity management systems* were developed to ease the administration and integrate customer login information and online activity with existing customer relationship management processes.

This new development of widespread customer access to internally developed software made the software development and deployment process very visible to customers, and thus to management. Software programming errors were routine and hastily assembled patches often caused as much damage as they were intended to fix. The insider threat to computers had previously been focused almost solely on accounting fraud now turned to the software developer. Security strategies were devised to control and monitor code development, testing, and production environments. Source code control and change detection systems became standard cyber security equipment.

By the late 1990s, most e-commerce companies were highly dependent on their technology workforce for software support and had long been paying for dedicated dial-up lines to workers' homes, and now so many of the users relied on the Internet to perform their job functions, they started to subsidize Internet access. Rather than pay for both, they allowed users to access servers remotely from the Internet. Although it was recognized that the plethora of telecommunications devices that could see this user traffic on the Internet presented the same eavesdropping threat that had been recently solved for customer data by using SSL, most of the people who used this technology were not using customer data, but rather doing technical support jobs. Moreover, remote access still required two-factor authentication, and this was judged an adequate way to maintain access control, particularly when combined with other safeguards, such as a control that prevents a user from being able to have two simultaneous sessions. However, once the speed of Internet connectivity became superior to that provided by modems, even business users handling customer data wanted to connect over the Internet. To maintain confidentiality of customer information, the entire remote access session would have to be encrypted. *Virtual private network* (VPN) technology answered this requirement, and also, if so warranted, would allow restrictions on network communication on a home network while a PC was VPNed into the corporate network. The network periphery was also extended to Blackberrys and other smartphones so that remote users could have instant access to their email without connecting via VPN, and this required specialized *inbound proxy servers* that encrypted all traffic between the handheld devices and the internal network.

While many of these security technologies ran on their own devices, they nevertheless required computer processing cycles on user workstations and servers. Firewalls were constantly challenged by increasing needs for network bandwidth. Innovative security companies sought to relieve workstations from their virus-checking duties by providing network-level *intrusion detection systems* (IDSs). The idea behind IDS was the same as that behind signature-based antivirus technology, but rather than compare the virus signatures to files that were deposited in a network, they were compared to what viruses would look like as they traveled across the network. This level of virus-checking was also appealing because it provided more information about where on the Internet a virus had originated. Network IDSs could also identify attacker activity prior to its resulting in the installation of destructive software by looking for patterns of search activity commonly used by hackers scanning a potential target. An IDS could also spot network-borne attacks such as DDOS.

Although the set of viruses to be checked by network IDS was the same as that compiled over the years by antivirus vendors, the way the antivirus software checked for the signatures on the desktop required different technology than the way it was checked on the network. Security managers began to notice that the end result was that some viruses were identified by some technologies and not others. Even vendors of the same technology widely differed in their ability to identify viruses, and had different levels of false positives, which is where software that was not actually a virus was mistakenly identified as such (McHugh 2000). Many companies created new departments called security operations centers (SOCs) to weed through the output of these systems to try to determine the extent to which they may or may not be under attack.

In the early 2000s, network security challenges were exacerbated by wireless. Like the demand for connectivity by traveling users in the mid 1990s, demand for wireless connectivity became irrepressible in the early 2000s. VPNs and handheld tokens were commonly among the technologies enlisted to maintain confidentiality of those communications, though they were not widely used for wireless access control until researchers demonstrated how easily native wireless security features were broken (Chatzinotas, Karlsson et al. 2008).

Note that, whether these security technologies were newly adopted or redeployed for a new purpose into a company network, their use required installation of a server and specialized software which had to be configured and customized for that use. As described in Chapter 1, Section 1.3.4, these technical configurations such as firewall rule sets, security patch specifications, wireless encryption settings, and password complexity rules were colloquially referred to as "security policy." As more and more security devices such as firewalls, proxy servers, and token servers had to be replicated to keep up with the escalating scale of technology services, security departments established management servers from which to deploy technology configurations. They did this not only for virus signatures, but also for all of the security technologies. *Security policy servers* were established to keep track of which configuration variables were supposed to be on which device. If a device failed or was misconfigured, it would take too much work to recreate the policies. Security policy servers economically and effectively allowed the technology configurations to be centrally monitored and managed.

Despite the best intentioned management-level security policy supported by technical security policies, cyber security incidents continued to occur anyway. In the course of an incident investigation, security devices were often found to be out of compliance with technology configuration policy. Security managers would have to investigate the root cause of such incidents and often had to track down logs of user activity on multiple machines. These efforts were streamlined by the introduction of *security information management* (SIM) servers, which were designed to store and query massive numbers of activity logs. Queries were designed in advance for events that were captured by logs that might indicate that systems were under attack. A SIM server can also verify that logs were in fact retrieved from inventory, so may serve a dual role for security managers: incident identification and policy compliance.

Figure 2.4 demonstrates the state of security technology in the early 2000s. e-Commerce security requirements had motivated the start-up of a plethora of security software companies that produced the additional gray security boxes that appear in the figure. The patch management processes had been enhanced to add *tripwires* to detect and report software changes. Though originally the subject of a Master's thesis on security, and then the name of a security software company, the generic use of the word tripwire

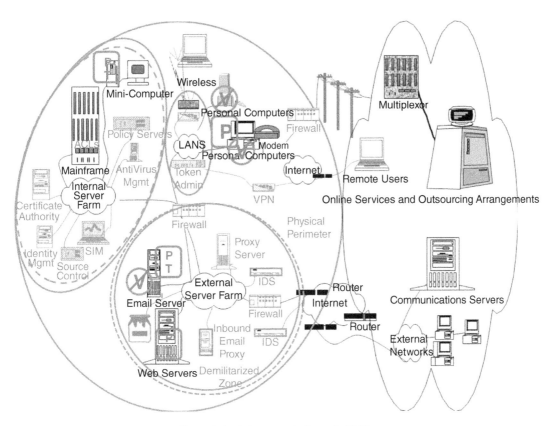

Figure 2.4 Cyberspace in the early 2000s.

now has the same connotation in software as its original use in physical security: a triggering mechanism (e.g., in physical security, a wire) that detects change in the environment (Kim and Spafford 1994). These internal software change detection mechanisms were also called host intrusion detection systems (HIDSs) to differentiate them from the network intrusion detection (IDS) that was deployed at the network periphery (Amoroso 1999). The feature also reflects the recognition that segregation of technology services and system change controls are safeguards against insider threats and accidental changes as well as external threats. For this reason, the term "zone" has taken on more of the connotation of local ordinance designating an area for a specified use. Network zones are now designated for isolating critical processes such as payroll from large sets of enterprise users who have no need to see those systems. Hence, many companies have created multiple network zones with different operational security policies of the type described in Section 1.3.3, even where machines do not face the Internet.

2.4   Countermeasures

Notwithstanding these security technology innovations, cyber attacks continued to be successful. Emails that look like normal communication from financial institutions contained links to malicious look-alike sites that either trick users into typing their passwords into the malicious sites, or into downloading malicious software ("malware") from malicious sites (Skoudis and Zeltser 2004). Cyber criminals attacked the methods used to direct users to Internet addresses and change the addresses to those of look-alike sites. These attacks were called *phishing* and *pharming* in analogies with casting a hook into the ocean to see who would bite, or planting seeds for later attacks, respectively. One type of malware logs user keystrokes and send user names and passwords to criminal data collection websites ("spyware"). Antivirus and intrusion detection vendors still create signatures for the latest spyware and malware, and SOC staff develop routine procedures to eradicate the software once it is identified. The network intrusion detection technology vendors offer the SOC staff a feature that would sever the network connection of any user who was downloading malware, but to accomplish it, they had to replace all of their IDSs with *intrusion prevention systems*.

The mid-2000s also saw a dramatic increase in organized crime on the Internet, and identity theft was rampant (Acohido and Swartz 2008). There were also many highly publicized incidents of lost laptops and backup tapes that contained large quantities of the type of PII used to commit identity theft. This raised awareness of the habits of remote users, who frequently kept such data on the laptops that they took with them on travel and also used removable media such as USB devices to carry data with them between home and work. While some of the technologies had been configured with the threat of device theft or loss in mind (e.g., smartphones containing software and data programmed to destroy all data if a user enters too many inaccurate passwords), many had never even been the subject of security review. Vendors hastily provided methods to encrypt laptop disks and USB devices. Companies adopted standards and procedures for the authorized use of digital media, and restricted access to the devices. It is hard to purchase laptops without these USB ports and DVD writers. Security software to control them can be very intrusive, expensive, and hard to monitor. So it is not uncommon to see security staff adopt tactical measures such as applying crazy glue to USB ports and removing DVD writers from laptops before they are delivered to users.

Theft of storage devices extended even into the data center. So many devices were being encrypted, it became difficult for administrators to keep up with procedures to safeguard encryption keys. Simple key management systems such as password-protected key databases had been around since the 1990s, but the rate at which the keys needed to be produced to perform technology operations tasks such as recovering a deleted file was rapidly increasing. Security vendors stepped in with automated key storage and retrieval systems. Often keys are stored on special hardware chips physically protected in isolated locations and accessible only by the equipment used to control access to the devices. This way, if the device is stolen without the hardware chip, the storage media itself cannot be decrypted. Unfortunately, it became so hard for users to get the data they needed to work at home on their home PCs that they would email it to themselves in order to bypass the security controls on removable media.

There has been no evolution in email security since the Morris Worm, only patches for known vulnerabilities. Even today, the protocols by which servers communicate and share information are not encrypted without very specialized agreements on both sides of the communication. Email is easy to observe with network equipment and is routinely routed via multiple Internet service providers before landing at its destination. Although there have been some attempts to identify authorized email servers via certificate-like keys, they are often ignored for fear of blocking legitimate email users by accident. Email security vendors created software to assist in the analysis of email content, and many companies who suspected that confidential data such as PII was being sent via email for work-at-home purposes thereby found that many of their business processes routinely emailed such data to customer or service providers. Even those with policies against sending PII in email sometimes had customers who demanded that their reports be delivered via email and were willing to accept the risk of identity theft for the convenience of receiving reports via email. Internal users would bow to customer wishes and ignore security policy. Although this risk acceptance was acceptable in some industries, in others, regulatory requirements prevented its continuation. The security technology response to this issue was content filtering. Patterns were created for identifying sensitive information. These included generalized social security numbers and tax identification numbers from other countries. They also included snippets common in internally developed company software, and "internal use only" stamps hidden in proprietary documents. All information sent by users to the Internet, or other publicly accessible networks, is routed through a device that either blocks the information from leaving or silently alerts security staff, who investigate the internal user. Frequent or blatant offenders are often subject to employment or contract termination.

Still, hackers are finding holes in the network periphery to exploit, and many are still in vulnerable web servers. The network control of the DMZ does not prevent a web software developer from deploying code that can be used to imitate any network activity that is allowed by the web server itself. This can, of course, include access to sensitive customer data because that is how a customer gets it. Developers innovate by sharing the software source code via both public ("open source") and proprietary development projects. In starting a new project, they typically will try to reuse as much existing code as possible in order to minimize the amount of effort required to build new functionality. They may also use free software ("freeware") for which no source code is available. Much of this code has known security bugs and flaws. These have been dubbed software security "mistakes" by security software consultants and vendors. Like the lists of viruses and software vulnerabilities, software security mistakes have been cataloged as part of the National Vulnerability Database project (MITRE 2009; MITRE ongoing). Cyber security vendors have created security source code analysis software to be incorporated into source code control systems so these bugs can be found before software is deployed. These work using static software analysis, which reads code as written, or dynamic software analysis, which reads code as it is being executed. Other cyber security vendors have created systems that observe network traffic destined for web server software, as well as the web server response. These devices, called *web access firewalls* (WAFWs), are programmed to detect unsecure software as it is used, and block attempts to exploit it in real time.

Figure 2.5 depicts the state of the practice of cyber security. Encryption mechanisms are deployed on both critical servers and remote devices.

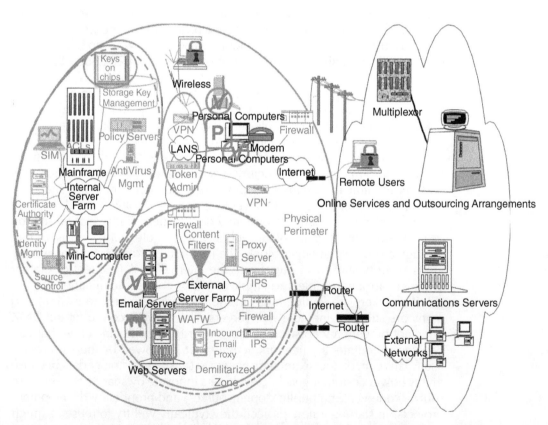

Figure 2.5 Cyberspace and cyber security countermeasures.

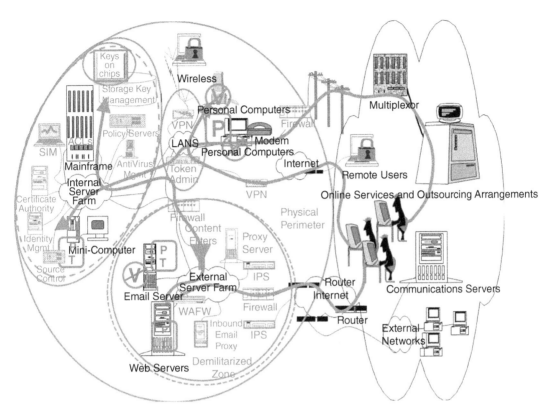

Figure 2.6 Cyber crime attack paths.

Content filters prevent users from sending sensitive information to the Internet. Intrusion prevention devices have replaced intrusion detection devices. Web access firewalls accompany Internet-facing applications. Moreover, though Figure 2.5 includes most of the security technologies so far mentioned in this chapter, not all existing security technologies are represented in this figure. Only the major security technologies are included.

2.5 Challenges

Note that we now use the adjective "cyber security" to refer to all of these countermeasures, while the history includes terms like computer security and information security. Though the terminology has morphed over the last half century from computer security to information security to cyber security, the basic concept has remained unchanged. Cyber security policy is concerned with stakeholders in cyberspace. However, the number and type of cyberspace stakeholders far exceeds the scope envisioned with the first Computer Security Act. In a world where computers control financial stability, health-care systems, power grids, and weapons systems, the importance of informed cyber security policy has never before been more significant, and is only likely to increase in significance over the next several decades, if not longer.

Threat, countermeasure. Threat, countermeasure. Threat, countermeasure. None of the threats has disappeared; hence all of the countermeasures are still considered best practice. Nevertheless, cyber security breaches continue. Figure 2.6 depicts the paths taken by today's hackers. It is the same path that cyberspace engineers have created to allow authorized users into systems. Done correctly, cyber security can keep out the joyriders. In many domains, joyriders are not even perceived as an issue anymore, as the more dangerous threats come from hardened criminals and espionage agents. Note that our description of the evolution of cyber security in no way implies that the way it has evolved is in fact effective, or even appropriate.

New paradigms of thinking about cyber security protection are needed to face these challenges. Nevertheless, every one of the security devices in Figure 2.6 (and we have skipped or glossed over dozens of others it would be possible to include) is recommended by current cyber security standards. These standards have been proposed as the subject of legislation, and this is just one of numerous reasons why the history of cyber security presents policy issues. To paraphrase Hubbard, "Ineffective risk management methods that somehow manage to become standard spread vulnerability to everything they touch" (Hubbard 2009).

3

Cyber Security Objectives

Given the complex nature of cyber security technology, and the fact that cyber security threats only escalate, it might be expected that policymakers are constantly confronted with decisions on how to react to the latest threat. However, because it is often the case that decisions concerning cyber security measures are delegated to technologists, a policymaker may not actually see these decisions being made, and thus not have a chance to weigh in on the organizational impact of various alternative approaches. In fact, the cyber security arms race often seems to offer very few alternative options. Almost immediately after cyber security technology is introduced, its usage is declared industry standard by some regulatory body, and this locks organizations into the identified countermeasure approach. For example, if a regulated organization decided to use a cyber security approach that did not make use of firewalls, they would face detailed scrutiny by their regulatory auditors. It seems easier to continue keeping up with the latest security tools and technologies than rethinking an organizational approach to cyber security.

Nevertheless, if there is any lesson in Chapter 2, it is that new paradigms for cyber security are sorely needed. In this chapter, we critically examine the policy objectives that evolved with the history of cyber security as described in Chapter 2. Note that these cyber security policy objectives did not then and do not necessarily now correspond to organizational goals for cyber security. Nevertheless, in this chapter, we also review methods used to determine that cyber security policy goals have been met. We observe that those who set security objectives often mistake achievement

Cyber Security Policy Guidebook, First Edition. Jennifer L. Bayuk, Jason Healey, Paul Rohmeyer, Marcus H. Sachs, Jeffrey Schmidt, Joseph Weiss.
© 2012 John Wiley & Sons, Inc. Published 2012 by John Wiley & Sons, Inc.

of objectives for accomplishing security goals. We conclude that current cyber security metrics do not measure security at all. The chapter ends with three case studies that illustrate how cyber security goals may be established and how cyber security goal achievement may be measured.

3.1   Cyber Security Metrics

Measurement is the process of mapping from the empirical world to the formal, relational world. The measure that results characterizes an attribute of some object under scrutiny. Combinations of measures corresponding to an elusive attribute are considered derived measures and are subject to interpretation in the context of an abstract model of the thing to be measured (ISO/IEC 2007). *Metrics* is a generic term that refers to the set of measures that characterize a given field. Cyber security is not the direct object of measurement, nor a well-enough-understood attribute of a system to easily define derived measures or metrics. So those engaged in cyber security metrics are measuring other things and drawing conclusions about security goal achievement from them. This challenge has spawned a field of study called security metrics (Jaquith and Geer 2005).

Metrics in physical security traditionally have concentrated on the ability of a system to meet the goal of withstanding a design basis threat (DBT) (Garcia 2008). A DBT describes characteristics of the most powerful and innovative adversary that it is realistic to expect to protect against. In New York City, it may be a terrorist cell equipped with sophisticated communications and explosive devices. In Idaho, it may be a 20-person-strong posse of vigilantes carrying automatic assault weapons on motorcycles. Adopting a DBT approach to security implies that the strength of security protection required by a system should be calculated with respect to a technical specification of how it is likely to be attacked. In physical security, this process is straightforward. If the DBT is a force of 20 people with access to explosives of a given type, then the strength of the physical barriers to unauthorized entry must withstand the ton of force that these 20 people could physically bring into system contact. Barrier protection materials are specified, threat delay and response systems are designed, and validation tests are conducted accordingly.

In cyber security, the terms perpetrator, threat, exploit, and vulnerability are terms of the trade, their meaning is distinct and interrelated. As depicted in the systemigram of Figure 3.1, a perpetrator is an individual or entity. A threat is a potential action that may or may not be committed by a perpetrator. An exploit refers to the technical details that comprise an attack. A vulnerability is a system characteristic that allows an exploit to succeed. Thus, the mainstay of the systemigram of Figure 3.1 is read as, "Security thwarts perpetrators who enact threats that exploit system vulnerabilities to cause damage that adversely impacts value" (Bayuk, Barnabe et al. 2010).

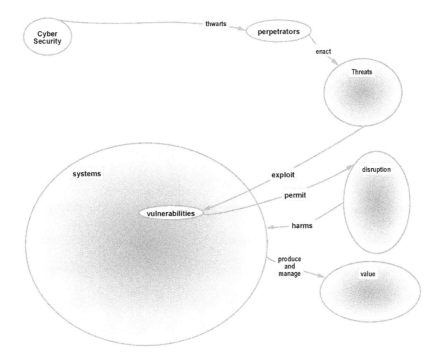

Figure 3.1   Security systemigram mainstay.

Since the advent of computer systems, DBTs for computer security have considered potential perpetrators such as hackers in the form of joyriders, malicious agents of cyber destruction, and espionage agents. However, unlike a physical security analysis of DBT, the countermeasures designed in response to the threat did not concentrate on the threat actors themselves, and what their latest tactics might be, but on the technology vulnerabilities that were exploited to enact the most recent threat. As each type of system vulnerability reached the stage of security community awareness, a corresponding set of security countermeasure technologies came to the market, and became part of an ever-increasing number of best practice recommendations. Countermeasures were applied to vulnerable system components, and threats to systems were assumed to be covered by the aggregated result of implementing all of them. Figure 3.2 illustrates this approach by adding these concepts and the relationships between them to the systemigram of Figure 3.1. Figure 3.2 shows that cyber security metrics, management approaches, audits, and investigation techniques are based on security tools and techniques. Unfortunately, as described in Chapter 2, they have been derived from the tools and techniques in use rather than specified as system requirements.

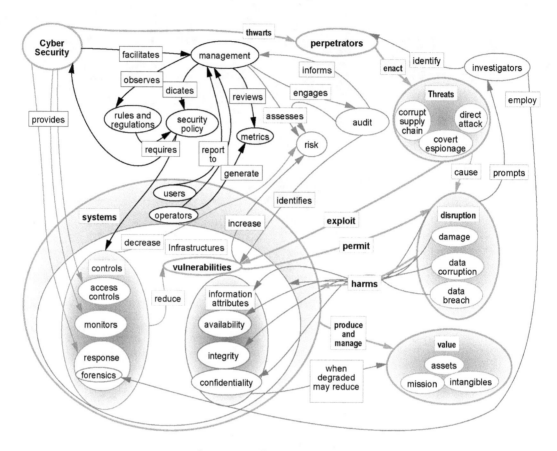

Figure 3.2 Full security systemigram.

The consensus that security goals are met by countermeasure technology has come at the expense of addressing DBTs as part of the system design itself. Figure 3.3 illustrates the difference between this traditional approach to security architecture and a more holistic, system-level approach. It depicts vulnerable attributes of a system as a subset of system attributes, and perpetrator targets as a subset of the system's vulnerable attributes. Traditionally, security engineering has attacked this problem with security-specific components, derogatorily referred to as "bolt-ons." These are often labeled "compensating controls," which is a technical term in the audit that refers to management controls that are devised because the system itself has no controls that would minimize damage were the vulnerability to be exploited. Bolt-ons are by definition work-arounds that are not part of the system itself, such as the firewalls described in Chapter 2. The lower part of Figure 3.3 illustrates the contrast between a bolt-on approach to

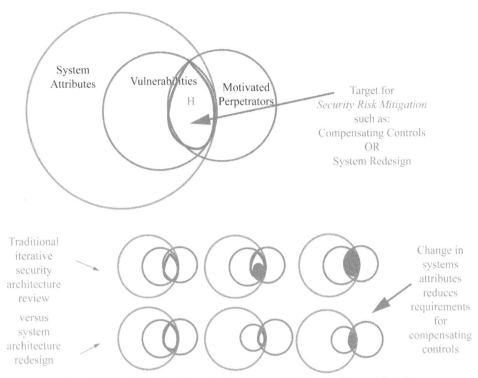

System Attributes

Vulnerabilities
H

Motivated Perpetrators

Target for
Security Risk Mitigation
such as:
Compensating Controls
OR
System Redesign

Traditional iterative security architecture review

versus system architecture redesign

Change in systems attributes reduces requirements for compensating controls

Area of vulnerability is either reduced, or covered with security-specific bolt-ons.

Figure 3.3 Bolt-on versus design.

solving security problems and a security design approach that instead is expected to alter system-level attributes to eliminate or reduce vulnerability. If this approach is tried first, the number of security-specific compensating controls should be minimal.

Nevertheless, there instead seems to be an almost unconscious adoption of the list of security technologies as described in Chapter 2. The effect is that a typical security goal presentation shows the progress of implementation of those security technologies listed by business area and computer operating system. Figure 3.4 is a typical example. In the analysis that would typically accompany the figure, the fact that the marketing business area does not have as much security as the finance area might be explained with reference to a higher risk tolerance on the part of marketing versus finance. As may be evident from the cycle of threat, countermeasure, threat, countermeasure reviewed in Chapter 2, cyber security professionals have their hands full just getting the business areas that want to reduce risk up to the full measure of security technologies available. It is a reactive approach that leaves little time to evaluate what the threats really are, and

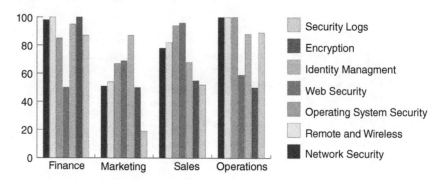

Figure 3.4   Example of cyber security metrics.

thus what overall enterprise goals of security should be (Jaquith 2007). Also, although some surveys indicate this situation may be improving (Loveland and Lobel 2011), cyber security practitioners historically have had relatively little input from the business stakeholders they are protecting. A few good examples are the situations described in Section 2.4 wherein business users used email to send sensitive material to customers as well as to their own home PCs even though these actions were prohibited by security policy. In fact, it would appear that the security staff were at odds with the goals of the business. Cyber security activity to date has been characterized by a heads-down approach, concentrating on applying controls and countermeasures. It is a method of problem solving by reacting to external threats with constraints on operations. A focus on enterprise-level goals for security has been missing.

Compare this phenomenon to management issues in other complex areas. If a manufacturing line is having trouble keeping the equipment running, do they continue despite its obvious negative effect on the product? In a well-run manufacturer, strategic thinkers prevail, and the manufacturing line is redesigned, perhaps pruned, before returning to operation. If components of a transportation system are chronically under repair and causing service delays, are they patched while they are running? At least in efficiently run organizations, they are pulled out, and perhaps replaced or reconfigured. By contrast, in cyber security, it has often been the case that an examination of the underlying business process is not presented as part of the engineering tradespace. This is particularly true in organizations where technology operations are managed independently from business operations. The business runs in parallel to security measures, not in conjunction. Security practitioners are exhorted not to interfere with systems operation, and security itself is not considered a critical component of system functionality. Hence, its failures often take management by surprise, often with devastating effects.

In nonsecurity areas, where specific goals are included in system requirements, there is always a recognition that the goals may not be achieved, and corresponding contingency plans are made for business operations. If revenues do not meet projections, business expansion plans may be revisited. If a new marketing plan does not increase customer traffic, alternative ad campaigns are made ready. If a new customer service strategy alienates customers, it is immediately revised. If security goals are seen in the same light, then security strategy planning would receive similar scrutiny. For example, the goal of "protect intellectual property" would have a corresponding definition of intellectual property that would allow its protection to be monitored to ensure goal achievement. Such monitoring would include both verification that the plan was properly executed, and validation that the plan achieved its security objectives. Failure in either such verification or validation would trigger remediation measures.

3.2   Security Management Goals

Many executives have no articulated goal for security other than "I want to be secure." In such cases, there is also an element of the goal that goes without saying, as the full articulation would typically be, "I want to be secure with little or no impact to my organization." They provide this directive to security professionals the same way they delegate balance sheet management to the accounting staff, saying, "I want the numbers to be accurate." Putting aside the parallels in the two professions concerning the need to be legal and regulatory compliance the delegation amounts to trust that the professional to whom the executive delegates understands the issues involved in the assignment and is capable of working closely with all those in the business who are stakeholders in the delegated functions to achieve the executive's goal.

However, the accounting profession has a well-established, several-thousand-year history supporting its ability to define trust in terms of relationships that involved a combination of circumstances and sanctions (Guinnane 2005). By contrast, the cyber security profession has just a half century or since the first industry or national security standards, and far less than that since the advent of international security standards (a small sample includes DoD 1985; ISO/IEC 2005a,b; FFIEC 2006; Ross, Katzke et al. 2007; PCI 2008). Moreover, rather than any agreed-upon industry standard, such as accounting's generally agreed upon accounting principles (GAAP), there are so many multiple competing standards in cyber security that a business has been established to catalog and compare them (UCF ongoing). The product is delivered in a spreadsheet or other structured data format. It is meant to be imported into a security information management (SIM) system, and it allows a security manager to demonstrate compliance with multiple standards without having to read them all.

Security programs that are motivated by regulatory compliance are not specifically designed to achieve organizational goals for security, but instead are designed to demonstrate compliance with security management standards. Hence, the standards themselves have become de facto security metrics taxonomies that cross organizational borders. Practitioners are often advised to organize their metrics around the requirements in security management standards against which they may expect to be audited (Herrmann 2007; Jaquith 2007). There is even an international standard for using the security management standards to create security metrics (ISO/IEC 2009b).

The disadvantage to this type of approach to security management is that details of standards compliance are seen as isolated technology configurations to be mapped to a pre-established scorecard, as opposed to the scorecard being designed to reflect enterprise goals for security. None of these standards comprise a generally accepted method of directly measuring security in terms of achievement in thwarting threats (King 2010). They are typically used to ensure that management has exercised due diligence in establishing activities that should result in security, not to measure whether those activities have been effective.

Contrast this with the layman's view of security. For example, individuals who have changed jobs sometimes measure the security at the old and new firms in terms based on the degree of difficulty for them to access important data and information, both locally and remotely. For example, they may identify the number of passwords they have to use from their desktops at home to access customer data in the office, and decide that the firm that makes them use more authentication factors is more secure. Figure 3.5 shows this type of layered-defense depiction of system security. Such layering is often called *defense in depth*. The term refers to an architecture where security controls are layered and are redundant, and vulnerability in one part of the system will be compensated for by another. That is, no one control should present a single point of failure, because at least two controls would have to break for an intruder to get in.

Figure 3.5 provides a layered perspective on a typical network of the type in Figure 2.6. It has multiple security "layers," as described in the central lower part of the diagram. At the top of the diagram, the "Remote Access" user is illustrated as being required to authenticate a workstation, which may or may not be controlled by the enterprise. The user then authenticates via the Internet to the enterprise network. From the network access point, the remote user can directly authenticate to any of the other layers in the internal network. This is why remote access typically requires a higher level of security, because once on the internal network, there are a variety of choices for platform access.

This remote access path is contrasted with the access path for the Web application in Figure 3.5. In the case of the web application, the existence of the layers does not actually constitute defense in depth. This is because

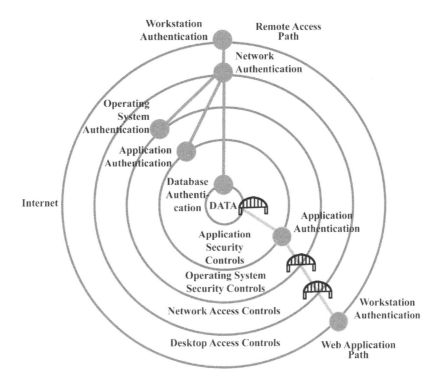

Figure 3.5 A layered defense.

such Internet accessible applications are usually accessible with just one log-in. The web application path shows that Internet users typically authenticate to their own workstations, which are not controlled by the enterprise. A user then can access the application without authenticating to the network because the firewall allows anyone on the Internet to have direct access to the login screen of the application on the web server. There is also no need to authenticate to the operating system of the server itself. Once within the application, the data authentication layer is not presented to the user; the application automatically connects to it on behalf of the user. These conveniences are depicted in the figure as bridges through the layers that the remote user would have to authenticate to pass, but the application user does not. Hence, to apply the term defense in depth to this case would be a misnomer.

Recalling the technology required to fortify these layers as presented in Chapter 2, it is obvious that multiple devices must be configured in coordination to ensure that each lock on each layer is actually closed to those who do not have a key. Hence, in much of the literature on security metrics, the goal is assumed to be correct configuration of all of these layers (Hayden 2010). However, despite this assumption, there is not a standard

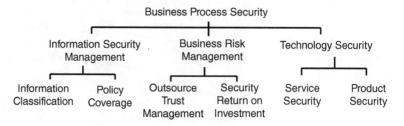

Figure 3.6 Security management metrics.

taxonomy for security metrics. Principles to be used in such classification have been explored by different researchers, and these explorations have produced different results. A survey of security metrics taxonomy efforts was compiled a few years ago and still accurately described the field from the practitioners' viewpoint (Savola 2007). It reported that common a theme in security metrics literature was that taxonomies of security metrics tended to address technical configuration and operational process from the point of view of security management rather than to directly described business goals for security. Even taxonomies that include *governance* in addition to management tend to focus on the security management tasks that are evidence of governance, and those metrics could easily be considered part of the management category (CISWG 2005). As illustrated in Figure 3.6, it is recommended that security metrics be raised to consider business-level requirements for security.

However, there is an issue with this approach. It is that there is currently no convergence around a *single* organizational management structure for security, so there can be no corresponding authoritative business-level security metrics taxonomy. Instead, there has been a great deal of consensus around standards for security process (ISO/IEC 2005; ISO/IEC 2005; ISACA 2007; ISF 2007; Ross, Katzke et al. 2007).

Yet even within the standards community, there is a debate on what makes a good measure of security. For example, the National Institute of Standards and Technology (NIST) sets standards for creating security metrics (Chew, Swanson et al. 2008), but is also on the record with a report that observes that current systems security measures are inadequate, and has called for research in security metrics (Jansen 2009). This report acknowledges a difference between managing security consistent with some standard and providing effective security. This *correctness* and *effectiveness* distinction is analogous to an engineering distinction between verification and validation, which highlights a distinction between the statements, "the system was built right" and "the right system was built" (INCOSE 2011). The former refers to the conformance to design specifications and the latter refers to the ability of the design to achieve desired functionality. The NIST report also suggested a classification of security metrics into leading, concurrent, and lagging indicators of security effectiveness. An example of a leading indicator is a positive assessment of the security of a system that is about to be deployed. Concurrent indicators are technical target metrics that show whether security was currently configured correctly or not. Lagging indicators would be discovery of past security incidents due to inadequate security requirements definition, or failures in maintaining specified configurations. If the goal is to know the current state of system security, concurrent indicators would make better metrics. However, as there is no systems attribute currently recognized to be security, there is no agreement on what a concurrent security metric looks like. That is, any one organization can judge whether its systems were built "right," that is, to their specifications. But no organization has reached the holy grail in cyber security, which is to know that the "right" security was built.

Recommendations for security metrics often suggest a hierarchical metrics structure where business process security metrics are at the top, and the next level includes support process metrics like information security management, business risk management, and technology products and services (Savola 2007). As illustrated in Figure 3.6, the supporting processes are expected to achieve the security via goal decomposition into more granular measures, perhaps through several decomposed layers until there are only leaf-level measures, that is, considering the hierarchy as a tree, and reading the lowest level at the end of a branch. Each leaf-level measure is combined with its peers to provide an aggregation measure that determines the metric above them in the hierarchy. For example, the leaf in Figure 3.6 labeled "Product Security" would be filled in with the accumulated totals of security products from the graph in Figure 3.4 that corresponded to security products. This number would be combined with the Security Service metric to provide an overall Security Technology metric. Assume that Security Logs, Web Security, Operating System Security, and Network Security are considered products and Encryption, Identity Management, and Remote and Wireless are considered services. The average percentage target goals achieved in each subset for the four business areas would be called the "Product Security" and "Service Security" metrics, respectively. The average of those two would be the "Technology Security" metric. This method of measurement is still verification that the design for security was implemented (or not) as planned, rather than validation that the top-level security goals are met via the process of decomposition and measures of leaf performance.

3.3 Counting Vulnerabilities

A notable exception to the technology management approach to security metrics, though still one that does not directly measure security, is vulnerability and threat focused. This is the enumeration of system vulnerability and misuse techniques. NIST and MITRE encouraged a consortium of security product vendors and practitioners to contribute to an endlessly growing repository of structured data describing known software vulnerabilities in a project known as the National Vulnerability Database (NVD) (MITRE ongoing). The first *Common Vulnerability Enumeration* (CVE) was published in 1997 (MITRE ongoing). This provided some standard by which security protection efforts would be judged to be effective by providing a "to-fix" list. Starting with the second antivirus vendor, it has been hard for security practitioners to know whether the security software they use protects them from any specific piece of malware. This is because antivirus vendors give names to malware that are different from competitor names for the same malware if they feel they should get credit for being the first to discover it (a product manager from a large antivirus company actually admitted this in a conference panel; Gilliland and Gula 2009). Just listing the vulnerabilities that allowed malware to work did not address the concern that malware had to be identified in order for it to be eradicated, so in 2004, the CVE was followed with a *Common Malware Enumeration* (CME) that catalogs malware that exploits vulnerabilities. This facilitates the development of automated methods to detect and eradicate malware. The MITRE NVD data was extended in 2006 to include the *Common Weakness Enumeration* (CWE), which is a list of software development mistakes that are made frequently and commonly result in vulnerabilities. An example of a specific issue would be the identification of a software security flaw that appears on the "Never-Events" list. The list is a metaphorical reference to the National Quality Forum's (NQF) medical Never-Events list (Charette 2009). That list includes medical mistakes that are serious, largely preventable, and of concern to both the public and healthcare providers for the purpose of public accountability such as leaving a surgical instrument in a patient. The software integrity version of the Never-Events list is the list of the top 25 mistakes software developers make that introduce security flaws (previously identified as CWEs). *SQL Injection* in the metric example for this category refers to one of those never-events. An SQL-injection mistake allows database commands to be entered by web page users in such a way that the users have the ability to execute arbitrary database queries that provide them with information that the application is not designed to allow them to access (Thompson and Chase 2005, ch. 21). The metric is the number of applications that allow SQL injection to occur. Measurement would rely on an application inventory to provide the 100% target of SQL-injection-free applications, as well as systematic source code scanning processes run by someone familiar with how system authentication is designed to work. To cover the possibility that some system access feature may have been intended, but nevertheless introduces a security vulnerability, in 2009, NIST introduced a *Common Misuse Scoring System*, which provides a method to measure the severity of software "trust" flaws by correlating them with estimates of negative impact (Ruitenbeek and Scarfone 2009).

Figure 3.7 Security badness-ometer. *Source*: McGraw (2006).

All types of vulnerabilities in the NVD are used to create security metrics by using them as a checklist and checking a technology environment to see if they exist. This database is also used by security software vendors used to create a set of test cases for vulnerabilities against which security software should be effective. These are not only anti-malware vendors, but vendors of software vulnerability testing software. Penetration tests of the type used by malicious hackers (also known as "black hats" in reference to old Western movies where the heroes always wore white hats) are designed by cyber security analysts ("white hats") to exploit any and all of the vulnerabilities in the NVD. They are automated so they can be run from a console. The security metric is usually the inverse of the percentage of machines in inventory that test positive for any of the vulnerabilities in the database.

If a stated security goal is to have no known vulnerabilities, this type of test may seem to provide a good cyber security metric. However, in practice, this type of measurement process is fraught with both false positives and negatives due to the difficulty of designing and executing tests in multiple environments (Thompson 2003; Fernandez and Delessy 2006). Moreover, while such vulnerability metrics may be useful to a security practitioner whose goal is to protect only against commonly known attacks, this is a flawed approach to security goal-setting in general. These metrics will necessarily miss the zero-day attack, and so, if a complete technology inventory test for all the known NVD vulnerabilities was passed with flying colors, then this would not mean that the system was secure. It could simply mean that *if* the system had security bugs and flaws, those bugs and flaws were not yet identified. As one software security expert puts it, they are a *badness-ometer* (McGraw 2006). As illustrated in Figure 3.7, these types of measures can provide evidence that security is bad, but there is no number on the scale that would show security is good.

3.4 Security Frameworks

So far, the usage of cyberspace in this book has generally corresponded to Internet-related technologies and how they have been used by various e-commerce and government constituents. However, this is only one way to view cyberspace. Where cyberspace is connected to something other than a database of sensitive information, the understanding of the impact of any given metrics on a goal will change considerably. Cyberspace occupies automobiles, trains, boats, planes, buildings, amusement parks, and industrial control systems (ICSs). At a smaller end of the spectrum, it occupies radio antennas, refrigerators, microwaves, audiovisual systems, and mobile phones. Goals for cyber security, and methods to achieve those goals, will vary considerably with the framework within which cyber components operate.

In this chapter, we describe e-commerce systems generically as a framework in order to contrast it with other types of frameworks. There are as many systems frameworks as there are ways to use electronics, so we first chose e-commerce systems and then follow with two at opposite ends of the spectrum for illustration purposes: ICSs and personal mobile devices.

3.4.1   e-Commerce Systems

e-Commerce systems are Internet-facing systems that allow facilitative transactions. The word itself is short for of the now obvious adjective, "electronic," as in "electronic commerce." e-Commerce has matured to the point where many retailers only exist online, and many brands are only available via online stores and businesses. In addition to traditional customer-to-business relationships (C2B), e-Commerce also includes business-to-business (B2B) transactions conducted between manufacturers, suppliers, distributors, and retail stores.

e-Commerce systems are called "Internet facing" because they are designed to be directly reached by any other system on the Internet. In order to be Internet facing, a system must be connected to an Internet service provider (ISP). ISP is a generic term for different types of companies that provide Internet connectivity services. They may be a local cable company, a large telecommunications carrier, a municipal network operator, or a web hosting service provider. The common element of the service is that network traffic between the customer and the Internet traverses the ISP. Figure 3.8 illustrates a few alternate ISP connections in the context of the Internet as a whole. Because of the large numbers of systems that must be represented in any diagram of the Internet, the Internet itself is depicted in Network diagrams as a cloud. The cloud symbol has been in use since the 1970s and in no way is meant to refer to the subset of Internet services that today utilize the word "cloud" as a marketing term.

Note that in Figure 3.8, the connection from the customer to the hosting service provider is not itself a direct Internet connection. Rather, it is facilitated by a telephone line, cable, or wireless link that becomes a conduit to the Internet through the hosting provider network. This line is typically leased from a large telecommunications carrier, but that carrier

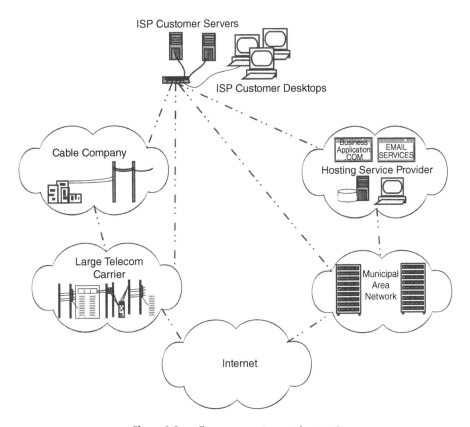

Figure 3.8 e-Commerce system environment.

is not the ISP for the customer; the hosting service provider connects the customer to the Internet via their own relationship with a telecommunications carrier. Where a hosting service provider and a client have offices in the same building, they may just arrange for a wire to connect their equipment through a wall or ceiling duct. The diagram is meant to illustrate that there is no single type of company that provides Internet service. Different companies will offer different types of services, including cyber security services, to its customers. Some types of cyber security services, such as denial of service attack mitigation, may only be possible to perform as an add-on to a carrier service. Others, such as mail spam filtering, may only be possible to perform as an add-on to a hosting service. Hence, the way a system connects to the Internet may constrain its options for cyber security.

Once Internet is connectivity established, a typical e-commerce system will follow the general architecture of Figure 3.9. There will be firewalls between the enterprise border and any external network. All computers

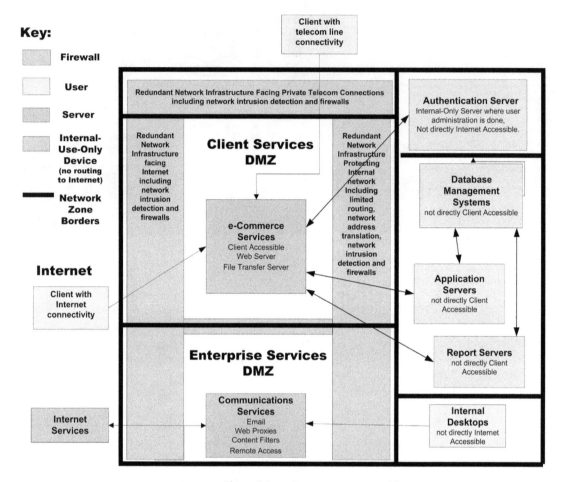

Figure 3.9 e-Commerce system architecture.

that face the Internet will be enclosed within an isolated network zone. Any security-critical system will be connected to an internal network zone with no direct routing to external networks. User desktops will also typically be segregated into their own network zone. Various security technologies will be placed at network zone interfaces to facilitate tasks such as remote access to the internal network, intrusion detection, and communications monitoring.

In addition to the in-house architecture, many e-commerce systems will be dependent on fellow e-commerce business partners to complete the user experience for their application. For example, their website may contain a link for directions to their retail stores, or a link to their stock performance, and that link will take the user to a site that specializes in maps and equity analysis, respectively. The map may look like it is part of the original vendor's site, but the actual image will be delivered by another company with whom it has a business relationship that includes an agreement to provide subsets of the features on the original vendor's website. Hence, the complete availability of the original site will necessarily be dependent on services that are outside their control. These techniques are used to deliver advertising as well.

It is also the case that providers of frequently used website features, such as store locators or news releases, will allow their software to be used for free in return for being able to advertise to the customers of the original vendor's site. Scenarios where the user experiences a composite of e-commerce websites are sometimes referred to as mashups. A mashup is a website wherein multiple companies' e-commerce services are combined into a single web page under the heading of a single e-commerce vendor.

The purpose of an e-commerce system is usually to provide continuous transactions for customers on Internet-facing servers, while simultaneously facilitating the business transactions received from the Internet with robust and reliable transaction execution. Security features that facilitate this purpose include, but are not limited to:

- System redundancy—if one system goes down, another takes its place.
- System diversity—if one system is vulnerable to an attack in progress, transactions it supports can be supported with alternative technology.
- System integrity—systems are not changed unless there is a well-defined and tested plan to maintain service continuity while the system undergoes change.
- Transaction accountability—counterparties are identified in a manner that does not allow them to repudiate their activity on the e-commerce site.

Note that these four security features, if accomplished, would be sufficient to support an overall goal of transaction security. Each feature may require the integration of multiple technology components. Each feature will have its own set of goals that indicate whether security features have been implemented as designed, that the system was built right. However, security measurements that determine whether security goals are met are validation rather than verification metrics, and answer the question of whether the right system was built. Validation of security goals requires measurements of the system in the context of its operation rather than measures of the system conformance to security specification. It requires evidence that the purpose of the system will not be adversely impacted by security threats.

It has been our observation that everyone's first instinct in proposing security validation metrics is to measure successful attacks or intrusions. For example, in the book, *How to Measure Anything*, the author suggests that security goals be measured by the absence of successful virus attacks (Hubbard 2007). The process described in the book is to start with what you know, structure that knowledge, identify what you would like to know, and use the structured data you have to reduce uncertainty concerning your object of measure. Applied to security, this approach makes sense; however, the suggested metric of "absence of successful virus attacks" suffers the fatal flaw that it measures progress toward a goal by the absence of an event rather than by any positive indicator that the goal is met. Using this approach, a system that is rarely attacked will be judged to be more secure than another simply because its security has not often been tested.

It is therefore common to attempt to bolster the "absence of virus metric by planning and executing attacks on one's own system." This combines the absence of viruses with the absence of the vulnerabilities known to be exploited by the set of all currently identified malicious software. This practice is called "penetration testing" and makes use of *badness-ometers* as described in Section 3.2. As these attacks are fully understood at the time security features to thwart them are designed, this practice demonstrates that a design specification was verified, not that a design goal was validated.

Validation of security goals for an e-commerce system can only be achieved with reference to its purpose in the context of its operation. It requires not just evidence that the latest set of known attacks will fail, but evidence that it is not possible (or at least extremely difficult) to enact security threats that impact system performance. Such a demonstration requires that the system in operation be subject to the types of failures that would be caused by a determined attacker rather than some simulation of any one or more known methods of attack. Hence e-commerce business continuity measures typically include failure mode testing that demonstrates that the failovers among redundant and diverse components are routine and are capable of being conducted without impact on system integrity and transaction accountability and without warning to system operators. However, this does not require a fully automated environment as accidents and false alarms may inadvertently trigger security responses. In these cases, to automate a response would cause unnecessary failover activity. As noted in Chapter 1, systems security includes people, process, and technology working in concert. Note also that validating all security goals requires that system integrity and transaction accountability features are also included in redundant and diverse alternative system configurations. Though no system will ever be 100% secure, there are known technology architecture patterns for design of e-commerce systems that facilitate these capabilities. Validation metrics should show that the system both properly works as designed and that the design thwarts attacks that are known examples of e-commerce crime.

One way to create such metrics is to model criminal activity using attack path analysis techniques. In this approach, attack goals are decomposed into subgoals, and activity required to achieve each subgoal is measured in terms of time, cost, or other quantifiable effort on the part of the attacker. Each path leading to system compromise is then measured in terms of overall capability required to complete all subgoals leading to system compromise. This technique allows for strategic placement of security measures to deter and delay attackers, as well as corresponding incident management processes designed to respond to attacker activity while it is in progress, and before it causes harm. Ideally, the metrics would be used to show that successful system compromise is beyond the capability of any known adversary.

3.4.2 Industrial Control Systems

ICSs operate the industrial infrastructures worldwide including electric power, water, oil/gas, pipelines, chemicals, mining, pharmaceuticals, transportation, and manufacturing. ICSs measure, control, and provide a view of the physical process ICSs monitor sensors and automatically move physical machinery such as levers, valves, and conveyor belts. When most people think of cyberspace, they think of Internet-enabled applications and corresponding information technology (IT). ICSs also utilize advanced communication capabilities and are networked to improve process efficiency, productivity, regulatory compliance, and safety. This networking can be within a facility or even between facilities continents apart. When an ICS does not operate properly, it can result in impacts ranging from minor to catastrophic. Consequently, there is a critical need to ensure that electronic impacts do not cause, or enable, misoperation of ICSs.

Figure 3.10 is an example of ICS architecture. A typical ICS is composed of a control center that will house the human–machine interface (HMI), that is, the operator displays. These are generally Windows-based workstations. Other typical components of an ICS control center include Supervisory Control and Data Acquisition (SCADA) and Distributed Control Systems (DCSs). The control center communicates to the remote field

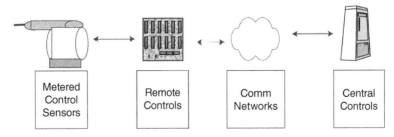

Figure 3.10 Industrial control system framework.

devices over communication networks using proprietary communication protocols. These protocols may be transmitted in Internet format, but the data still include fields that are unique to control system packets. The packets generally are sent via wired or wireless local area networks (LANs). The control center generally communicates to a remote control device such as a remote terminal unit (RTU) or directly to a controller such as programmable logic controller (PLC) or an intelligent electronic device (IED, e.g., a smart relay or smart breaker). A PLC or IED is preprogrammed to perform control actions automatically and send information back to the control center. The PLC or IED communicates via serial, Ethernet, microwave, spread spectrum radio, and a variety of other communication protocols. The communication is received by sensors, gathering measurements of pressure, temperature, flow, current, voltage, motor speed, chemical composition, or other physical phenomena, to determine when and if final elements such as valves, motors, and switches need to be actuated if the system requirements change or if the system is out specification. Generally, these changes are made automatically with the changes sent back to the operator of the control center. However, it is possible for an ICS to merely report status to an operator, who may make manual changes.

There are major differences between the type of information technology that runs e-commerce (IT) and that which is used to run an ICS. In the IT world, major issues concern information content. In the ICS world, major issues are reliability and safety. In the IT world, unintentional attacks are not seen as a major issue; in the ICS world, unintentional is just as bad. Security events do not have to have a malicious origin to be of major significance.

Both types of systems include networks and workstations for the HMI. The HMIs of ICSs are generally IT-like systems and may be susceptible to standard IT vulnerabilities and threats. Consequently, they can utilize IT security technologies, and traditional IT education and training can apply (see, e.g., Byres, Karsch et al. 2005). However, ICS field instrumentation and controllers generally do not utilize commercial-off-the-shelf operating systems and are designed to consume the least possible amount of both silicone and energy (Stouffer, Falco et al. 2009). They often use proprietary real-time operating systems (RTOSs) or embedded processors. Due to their unique position in a physical workflow, field instrumentation and controllers often have operating requirements and constraints that IT systems never face. For example, harsh weather conditions and extremely short mean time to repair (MTTR) specification. These systems can be impacted by cyber threats typical of IT systems and also cyber threats unique to ICSs.

It has long been recognized that a cyber attack against ICS system, such as those that control an electric grid, could be more than just a single attack against a single target, and it could also be blended with a physical attack (Schewe 2007). The North American Electric Reliability Corporation (NERC) held a High-Impact, Low-Frequency (HILF) Conference to address those attacks beyond the design basis (NERC 2010).

There are only a limited number of ICS suppliers, and they supply most industrial processes worldwide. Nevertheless, there is significant ambiguity in the industry's literature on key terms that are used to describe ICS technology and security capabilities. Key terms such as *SCADA* and *field instrumentation* carry different meanings to different organizations. For example, the term SCADA can refer to the master station or the entire control loop from the master station to the final field devices. Thus, when these terms are used in security standards, utilities often adopt their own interpretation.

Even within a single industry, security carries many definitions. Though a cyber security definition of security in the energy industry will invariably refer to ICSs, other perceptions of energy industry security range from references to dependence on foreign oil to interties allowing energy to flow from one area to another. Recent NERC regulatory guidance required energy utilities to apply technology security standards to their critical infrastructure. Several of the regulated utilities reported that none of their infrastructure was critical, and hence they did not have to comply with proscribed security standards (Assante 2009). Until we have agreed-upon nomenclature on components of national infrastructure and some common understanding of what it means to be secure, we will continue to have these roadblocks to policy implementation.

The root of the ICS security problem is that ICSs are very different from each other, and there is not one characterization of all possible control configurations that would correspond to any set of definitions that would be valid for all industries (Igure, Laughter et al. 2006). In physical security, cyber security terms have different meanings and implications for security control implementation. For example, the term intrusion detection systems (IDSs) with respect to physical security implies monitoring algorithms using images from cameras and personnel badge or physical access card readers, while in cyber security, the term IDS refers to host or network monitoring for known malicious software and/or damaging impact to cyberspace resources. Moreover, in security and in control systems environment, there are also many overlapping acronyms that are used much more fluently than the actual words they represent, and so initial conversations among these communities start out disadvantaged. For example, among physical security professionals, the term IED refers to improvised explosive devices. To control systems professionals, it means intelligent electronic devices. (Unfortunately, these may be used in combination to facilitate automated destruction.)

Nevertheless, the limited number of suppliers has the consequence that the ICS cyber security-related differences between industrial facilities are not large and this should allow common ICS cyber security policies and

Industry	Cyber security incident	Actual impact
Electric	2008 Florida Outage, power plant equipment failures	Loss of power to almost 3 million people
Oil/gas	Pacific Gas & Electric nature gas pipeline failure	9 killed, impacts of more than $400 million to date
Pipelines	Olympic Pipeline Company gasoline pipeline rupture	3 killed, $45 million in 99 dollars and bankruptcy of the Olympic Pipeline Company
Agriculture/food	Food processing plant PLC failure	Plant shutdown
Water	Contamination from Superfund site	Drinking water contamination
Transportation	DC Metro train	9 killed

Figure 3.11   Impacts from ICS cyber incidents (NTSB 2010; Weiss 2010).

standards. What is different is the domain of industrial operation and corresponding control equipment, sensors, and physical material flowing through the system. Examples of impacts from different industries are shown in Figure 3.11. These differences highlight the different impacts on society of cyber security failure. Cyber security failure impact for a nuclear power plant would obviously be different than cyber security failure impact for a water treatment plant. (Unfortunately, these may be used together to facilitate destruction.)

Note that the worst case impact of a cyber security event in an ICS may not be shutting the system down, but rather corrupting the process which it controls. Consequently, denial of service, though it has dire consequences for an e-commerce system, is not the worst case for an ICS; rather, *denial of control* or *denial of view* can be much worse. This can be done either by attacking the process directly or compromising the operator displays with misleading information; this may lead the operator execute commands intended to resolve an issue that is not present. Note also that the Internet is not necessarily the biggest threats to ICSs, as they generally can operate for long period of time without direct Internet connectivity. Rather, its biggest threat is the exploit of any access necessary to maintain the operation of the field devices, including physical access.

The goal of an ICS is typically to operate some type of physical process. Environmental sensors provide status information which is processed by the system using rulesets that may or may not trigger valves or levers to achieve stability in operational process. Sometimes these triggers are operated by humans, the "wetware" component of the system. At other times, they are triggered automatically. Even with a human in the loop, cyber components of these systems receive and send electronic signals that operate equipment in response to operator commands. Security features that facilitate these goals include, though are not limited to:

- ICS device (could include sensor, relay, controller) reliability—if one sensor goes down, another takes its place.
- Sensor diversity—if one sensor is vulnerable to an attack in progress, environment conditions that it monitors can be achieved with alternative technology.
- Software containment—the extent to which incorrect commands may be automatically entered by software is limited by compensating factors such as range limits or input validation routines.
- System resiliency—system should continue to operate despite component failures, even if at reduced capacity.

Note that these four security features, if accomplished, would be sufficient to support the overall goal of controlling an ICS, which includes preventing its falling under the control of outsiders. Of course, many other manual and business processes are required to support the actual industrial process that the ICS supports. As in the e-commerce example, each security feature may require the integration of multiple technology components. Each feature will have its own set of verification procedures and validation will require evidence that it is not possible (or at least extremely difficult) to enact security threats that impact system performance.

Validation of security goals for an ICS system can only be achieved when the system in operation is subject to the types of failures that could be caused by inappropriate actions or by malicious attacks. Failure mode testing should demonstrate that the failure of any one software component cannot adversely impact the operation of the process controlled by the ICS. Unlike the case of e-commerce, there are not well-established architecture patterns for testing such processes, and the risk of deliberately failing an ICS is considerably higher. Hence, validation tests must resort to modeling the impact of the failure of any single component and the cyber interconnections between components. Physical flows through the industrial system should be modeled to the most detailed extent possible in order to ensure that each physical control point is represented and that each cyber component is correctly associated with the physical sensors, electronic switches, or mechanical levers that may be affected by its operation. Models should extend to system interfaces so that potential cascading impact of any one component failure is made transparent.

Research is needed to develop ICS cyber forensics, resource-constrained device authentication, and security models for simulation. Yet the cyber security problems of ICS do not require advances in science to be solved, simply determined security engineering. Research into technology architecture patterns for design of secure ICS systems should be able to facilitate these capabilities. Agreement on the goals of failure mode avoidance should allow an associated security policy to be established in support of goals to maintain control over mechanisms. This type of exercise is common in the Nuclear Regulatory environment (Preckshot 1994) but is not prevalent in other industries that support ICS infrastructure.

3.4.3 Personal Mobile Devices

Many people think of mobile personal devices simply as small computers. To some extent this is true, because they are produced using computing technology. But from a security perspective, mobile personal devices are missing many elements that have typically been taken for granted in computer operation. Security features for computer operating systems that have been standard specifications since the early 1980s. As described in Chapter 2's discussion on the *Orange Book*, these were designed to facilitate administrator control of a machine as well as user operation for data processing in an uninterrupted and confidential control flow. A standard computer had been designed to be operated in isolation and has utility for many users whether or not it is connected to the Internet. Yet the design of a mobile operating system does not incorporate most standard operating system security features. Rather, mobile devices are designed to allow the mobile carrier service providers to control the device. Mobile operating systems are in some sense tethered to the mobile carrier and unable to fulfill their purpose without it. This is why the mobile carrier has more interest in ensuring that the configuration of the device can be accessed remotely than in providing the user control over its content.

Some mobile carriers share these device control features with enterprise administrators. For example, some device operating systems may have configurable security settings that allow an administrator to disallow installation of applications, but allow installation of applications from the corporate server. In effect, the corporation plays the role of the mobile phone administrator. Even though phone users may pay the mobile carrier directly for the service, once the device is registered under the corporation's service contract, the primary customer for the device in the eyes of the mobile carrier becomes the corporation, not the mobile phone user.

Figure 3.12 illustrates mobile phone connectivity. Phones signal cell towers, which relay the signals to equipment that identifies the transmitting device and allocates land-based telecommunications bandwidth to the mobile device based on the tower operator's agreements with the mobile carrier who administers the phone (of course, the tower operator and mobile carrier may be one and the same company). Where device configuration is administered via the cell service, administration occurs from computers in the mobile carrier's data centers. They identify the device that is connected and send it data and commands that update the software on the device. Note that this administration process uses part of the same bandwidth that is reserved for cell service itself, and mobile carriers do not charge the customer for the service time spent updating software. This

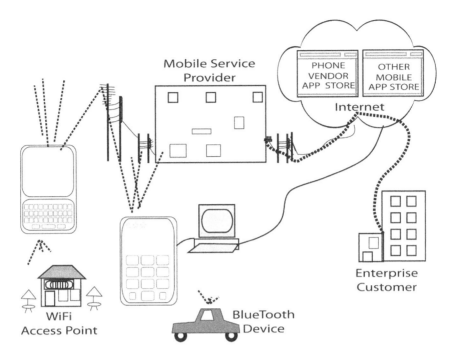

Figure 3.12 Mobile device system framework.

keeps mobile carrier updates to a minimum and thus may actually delay
the implementation of security patches if they become available during
times of peak mobile service requirements. This is one reason why some
mobile carriers require that a device be connected to a computer with an
Internet connection in order to download its configuration updates and
patches. The device administration process may be run out of a company,
the device vendor's company, or directly from the cellular carrier.

Mobile devices have a wide range of capabilities. Although the devices
may also facilitate game play and office utilities like calendars and
calculators, these services are not core to the system mission, but rather
conveniences that create competitive advantage between devices and
associated mobile telecommunications carriers. The commonality, or core,
function in mobile devices is to provide personalized voice and messaging
connectivity services via data transmission. Hence, the purpose of a personal mobile device is to facilitate that communication. But a mobile
device cannot communicate on its own. As illustrated in Figure 3.12, it
must be part of a larger communications system in order to achieve its
mission. Currently, this means that it must be a node on a telecommunications network that includes other nodes with which to communicate. A
phone by itself has some functionality, but to be used for communication,

it requires access to a multiple independently operating systems that interface using well-defined protocols. It is one system in a *system of systems* (SoS). An SoS is characterized by a situation in which full functionality in operation of an individual system is not achievable without the larger SoS in which it participates, and that the larger SoS has functionality that cannot be ascribed to any of its individual component parts, nor is simply an aggregate of them. Interaction between individual working systems creates emergent properties that are the functionality of the SoS. All social networking systems share this characteristic. Individual systems may come and go as the SoS continues to function without interruption.

Security features that facilitate these goals include, though are not limited to:

- Possession—the phone number associated with the device is not transferable without permission of the owner.
- Reliability—transmissions sent by one user are received by the specified recipients.
- Connectivity—the system is available to transmit and receive.
- Confidentiality—mobile users expect that data transmissions will not be intercepted by parties other than those with whom they specifically choose to communicate.

Note that these four security features, if accomplished, would be sufficient to support the overall goal of mobile transmission security. Each feature may require the integration of multiple technology components. Some, most notably confidentiality, have no current technology implementation but may be accomplished in part by features at telecommunications carriers like encrypted wireless transmissions.

Verification that mobile devices security features work as designed is complicated by the fact that the owner of the device has limited control over its operation. Security features are constructed by mobile carriers and phone vendors working in concert to serve their own priorities for service provision rather than expectation of customer security requirements (Barrera and Van Oorschot 2011). All phone vendors have implemented some form of process isolation to separate their own software on the device from applications provided by others. This software may generally be used by the mobile carrier to uninstall software, suspend service, and even erase all the data on the device if it is known to be stolen or maliciously corrupted.

To accommodate user preferences for device use, many vendors have included a permissions file that lists the user-controllable device settings and lets users change them. However, some phones also allow applications acting as users to change the settings, in which case the user would be unaware that the settings had changed. At the other end of the spectrum, some vendors restrict all permission settings to the phone administrator, who may be an enterprise customer. Settable permissions may include the ability to read and write to files such as the user's contacts and calendar, the ability to access hardware on the device like microphones and cameras, and the ability to run applications from a given source.

The application-level permissions on a mobile device are typically implemented via some form of application code digital signature via certificates that work much like the web server certificates that were discussed in Chapter 2. Each application vendor has their own root certificate that is used to stamp the applications they produce. The root may be checked at any time by mobile devices programmed to check the provenance of software before installing it.

Though not all mobile devices require authentication to operate, many have a feature for password protection. The password unlocks the keyboard and screen of the device, allowing operation. However, the device will not operate unless the device itself can authenticate to the cellular service. This authentication may be built into a chip or entered by a device distributer when provisioning the device for the user. Another pin or password for authentication may be used to secure other network connections supported by the device, such as the close range protocol Bluetooth. A typical mobile device user is confused by these options, much less by the options for basing decisions about file system access on the question of whether the requesting application is digitally signed (Botha, Furnell et al. 2009).

Verification that all security features are configured as per user requirements at this stage can only be done with extensive user education and forensic analysis of mobile device software configuration. Such verification will reveal whether or not all device permissions are set as expected, but as design goals are not shared between mobile carriers and their customers, it may still not be possible to verify that the system was built correctly.

Validation of security goals for mobile personal devices is even less straightforward both because different users will have different security goals and because carrier and vendor security goals are very different from those of the end user. Carrier goals are focuses on service integrity and billing accountability, while end user security requirements for mobile devices need to take into account the cell phone use cases of the owner. Some people may keep valuable client contact lists in mobile devices and thus have confidentiality requirements, while others never store more than nicknames and so do not have confidentiality requirements. Others may use a key stored on their mobile phone as a second factor of authentication for online banking transactions, and so have data confidentiality requirements, while others use it for nothing but voice communication, and thus may only have voice but no data confidentiality requirements.

In order to identify security validation metrics, a specific purpose for the system must be well articulated, and it is simply not possible to clearly articulate security goals for the SoS that is mobile communications as a whole. Nevertheless, while within the larger SoS a subset of the communicating systems may have a joint goal that may be well articulated, it may be impossible to identify a specific purpose that applies to the entire SoS. Only when both the users and network operators are the same, such as in an enterprise-controlled mobile network, might all stakeholder goals be consistent enough to identify validation measures.

We therefore must reduce the scope for this example to identify security validation metrics. Let us say that it is an enterprise mobile communications systems, the cell phone issues by a company, a communications gateway server supported by the company, and the specific cellular operator service that the company had contracted may comprise a system. The purpose of that system may be to provide confidential communications between internal users while allowing them access to messages from external sources. In this more narrow case, it is possible to identify measures by which the security goal of confidentiality may be validated.

Confidentiality is a hard thing to validate because when information is leaked or stolen, the original owner still has it and may not be aware that it has fallen into unauthorized hands. Hence, the only way to validate confidentiality is to identify all the places where the data are authorized to be, and monitor whether the data stay there. In engineering terms, this is to create a model of the information flow, and devise methods to sample whether it has been subverted. In the mobile network case, data communications between mobile user and enterprise should have only preauthorized end points, and no data should be able to travel to external parties without being filtered at a gateway. If all data in the authorized communications flow could be marked with some "internal use only" identifier, it would be easy to see if any such data made its way out of the authorized path. Presumably, the gateway would not let it through without a reference monitor that would determine whether the data are confidential. This type of validation test, however, would be difficult to implement in today's mobile networks because typically the only data that are marked confidential are those that have already been deemed sensitive. Moreover, not all communications channels between the user and external parties traverse the enterprise gateways. The mobile carrier still has a direct link to the device. This approach also acknowledges that it is well understood among security professionals that security fails in the same way an underground economy fails (Nelson, Dinolt et al. 2011). Those who are constrained by it develop work-arounds that meet their needs. Mechanisms to mark all data confidential allow for identification of leaks via monitoring outside the network for the confidential mark.

Major additions to mobile technology features would be required to create mechanisms to mark all data confidential and then unmark them if they were allowed out. Nevertheless, the fact that security validation goals are not easy to achieve should not prevent them from being set. Unfortunately, these scenarios often are addressed not by changing the way technology works, but by bolting on layers of security overhead around it (e.g., the intrusion detection mechanisms described in Chapter 2).Goals that are presently untestable due to technology limitations should be viewed as requirements for security features that should be incorporated into products to enable such testing.

3.5 Security Policy Objectives

It is typically taken for granted that *you can't manage what you can't measure*. Unfortunately, this observation calls attention to the fact that there are significant obstacles to managing cyber security. Security policy-makers must be aware that selecting a policy that supports a strategy is a simple task compared to validating that the policy actually is effective. The state of the practice in the cyber security profession is to design for security and verify that designs are correctly implemented, and it seems enough of a technical challenge to verify that an implementation is correct, much less effective. This is probably why security standards are so often used as a substitute for customized security objectives. Of course, substituting security standards for objectives introduces another oft-quoted phrase, "metrics drive behavior." It must be acknowledged that there is no one-size-fits-all strategy that will satisfy every security framework. Although security standards have some utility in ensuring that verification techniques for design decisions are sound, all cyber security systems should have, in advance, set some customized design goals that form the basis for cyber security validation metrics. That is, if you measure compliance with standards, you will get compliance with standards, but you will not get security goal achievement because you are not measuring security goal achievement.

Security policy statements should always be phrased as goals that are capable being validated. Even within security frameworks, it is evident that the nuances of a business model will affect the operation of technology, and thus impact the implementation of security standards. Chapter 4 provides some security policy guidance for decision makers who are accountable for security strategy.

4

Guidance for Decision Makers

4.1   Tone at the Top

Chapter 3 made a brief comparison between the accounting profession and the cyber security profession. One reason why this comparison is informative is because many of today's information security controls were first established as standards by the Electronic Data Processing Auditor's Association (EDPAA, now the Information Systems Audit and Control Association, ISACA) (Bayuk 2005). A key take away from that comparison is that the accounting profession's mantra concerning the integrity of financial management applies across the board to cyber security management. That is: *"the tone is set at the top"* (COSO 2009). Management tone in any endeavor exists whether policy is formally established or not, and management tone is not the same as formal policy establishment. In the domain of cyber security, policy is a documented enterprise agreement on cyber security goals and objectives, and tone is the level of commitment that management has toward that documented policy and corresponding enforcement measures.

There is no single right way for a decision maker to make sure people are really understanding and following cyber security policy. But consciously or unconsciously, every good leader has a method of getting important messages across (Bayuk 2010). For example, one manager will make it a practice to always be at the same level of calm in order to get maximum value out of showing emotion with respect to an important issue. Another will work at a brisk pace, but slow down when explaining something they think is really important. The way a manager behaves toward

Cyber Security Policy Guidebook, First Edition. Jennifer L. Bayuk, Jason Healey, Paul Rohmeyer, Marcus H. Sachs, Jeffrey Schmidt, Joseph Weiss.

issues of importance to cyber security policy will set the tone for the enterprise.

The day-to-day decisions made by middle and lower-level managers to facilitate their own business occasionally have unintended consequences on an organization's overall cyber security posture and require a timely response. Singular policies that seem necessary to adopt in the context of a security crisis may also be inconsistent with an enterprise-level cyber security strategy. Adjustments in both strategy and policy must be customized to the evolving requirements of the organization, which means cumulatively they point to where formal policy should evolve.

For example, it is often the case that responsibility for cyber security policy is set within a low-level information technology department. In many organizations, cyber security planning is seen as a technology risk management function. Although cyber security strategy should be designed to minimize risk, it is not only technology risks that may be minimized with adequate cyber security, but business risks as well. In order to be effective, cyber security strategy must be a mainstream part of business, system, or mission planning, not a subcomponent of a technology-only function. For example, it is not uncommon for a technology department that has no set security strategy to set unreasonably hard standards for user-selected passwords, while sharing administrative passwords among themselves via email. Cyber security in this case would be disruptive to business and at the same time provide poor protection against a determined hacker.

It takes time to craft policy to make sure it is not disruptive to business and interim steps to reduce risk do not always qualify as long-term solutions. A decision maker will often count on an information security professional to shepherd cyber security policy (e.g., a Chief Information Security Officer, or "CISO"), ensuring it remains effective and relevant. If it is not relevant, the void will doubtless be filled with what some security professionals call *"security theater."*

Security theater is created when security concerns within the business prompt action, but the action is more visible than effective. This is because people think something needs to be done about security, so they create activity that looks like security where they think people want security to be in place (Schneier 2003). Security theater does not actually prevent anything bad from happening. It just creates the illusion that security is in place. For example, in a building that has experienced a recent rash of thefts, a guard is installed behind a desk in the lobby of a building, and told to ask for identification, but anyone with any kind of laminated card with a name and photo on it can get in. Though it seems like a good return on investment, because it "solves" the security problem, the value here is questionable. Compare it to a true security control designed for the same situation. For example, those authorized to access the building are prescreened for criminal records, have photos taken, and are issued a badge that initiates activation of a floor-to-ceiling turnstile that permits entry into the building. The card has electronic identification on it that is used to check a database for a picture of the person to whom the card had been issued. The guard checks the picture against the person using the card. The turnstile activation is completed by the guard's active acknowledgement that the photo matches the person attempting entry. A similar procedure is used for internal building doors and building exits. True security controls, such as this one, provide measurable value. In this case, the value is the knowledge of exactly who is in what area of the building at what time.

A common approach to ad hoc security theater is to make it apparent that cyber security policy affects technology usability. Make it harder for people to get into the network, to get to their data, to use applications, and so on. Security is somehow perceived as equivalent to cumbersome levels of approval, and authorization workflows present obstacles to gaining cyber access. Often, it is thought that more security control means less cyberspace usability. But it is also true that usability of technology may be strengthened by security policy that supports productive use cases. Once cyber security policy is well understood, it can be appreciated as a shining light with which to illuminate strategy, and to evaluate alternative courses of action to achieve cyber security goals, the majority of which should not require red tape. Policies that constrain rather than guide result in work-arounds rather than work-withins.

True security and security theater may have the same requirements, for example, to hire guards and subject people to authorization processes. The difference between security and security theater is that in the first case, the process behind the authorization is designed for an outcome wherein unauthorized individuals are kept out, and in the second case, the process behind the authorization is more for show and the outcome is random. Of course, any specific decision on how important it is to authorize access as well as to know what people are where should differ depending on the risk to the enterprise. While it is advisable to make risk-based judgments, these should be consistent with a defined policy. It is not unusual for the same company to have inconsistent security measures in two buildings of similar function, wherein one building sports effective security measures, while the other displays security theater. The same people may sheepishly follow both processes, but this does not mean they are blind to the difference. This makes security policy throughout the entire organization seem like a joke, something that is detrimental to management's credibility. Security theater is a symptom of an ad hoc security strategy. Development of a well-structured, formal security policy exposes the holes in existing strategy and that paves the way to true security.

4.2 Policy as a Project

As described in Chapter 1, cyber security easily lends itself to a Drucker-style management cycle for managing by objectives and self-control, observing and revising plans based on observations (Drucker 2001). The management style also follows military security recommendations for managing battle-action: observe the situation, orient observations based on background knowledge and analysis, decide on a course of action, act, and observe the impact of actions on the situation (Boyd 1987). These activities, in combination, comprise the management cycle of an enterprise security program. Where cyber security is managed as a program, the program structure provides organization, strategy, and operational process to maintain activities in support of cyber security. Where security is viewed as part of, or integrated with, other business or mission goals, it becomes evident that the strategy to achieve security objectives cannot be a stand-alone project, but must be part of a larger program. Within an enterprise management structure, the cyber security program will be a set of inter-related discrete projects and combined with processes managed in a coordinated way to obtain benefits and control not available from managing them individually (PMI 2008).

The process by which cyber security policy is established is a part of that program. As with any important initiative, the establishment of cyber security policy requires task definition, planning, and clear objectives. That is, to create cyber security policy is a project, and should be managed as one. As with any project, cyber security policy creation starts with goals and objectives. It is also helpful to begin with the recognition that policy follows business or enterprise strategy, not the reverse. Figure 4.1 is a more prescriptive and direct version of the security management life cycle presented in Chapter 1. It shows that cyber security management starts with strategy designed to achieve cyber security goals and objectives consistent with enterprise objectives. Policy is an extremely important component of strategy execution because it is used to communicate desired outcomes. Even if an executive issues only one policy statement, that statement will be interpreted in the context of other plans, objectives, and operational environments that complete an organization's cyber security posture. Clear

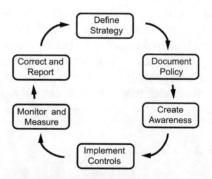

Figure 4.1   Security cycle.

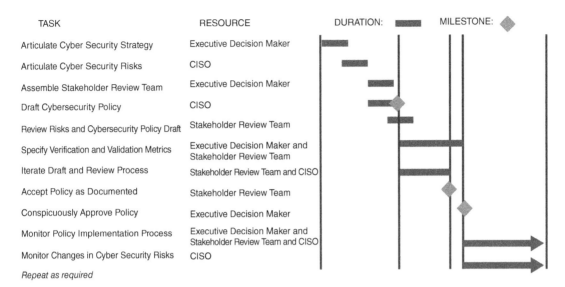

TASK	RESOURCE	DURATION:	MILESTONE:
Articulate Cyber Security Strategy	Executive Decision Maker		
Articulate Cyber Security Risks	CISO		
Assemble Stakeholder Review Team	Executive Decision Maker		
Draft Cybersecurity Policy	CISO		
Review Risks and Cybersecurity Policy Draft	Stakeholder Review Team		
Specify Verification and Validation Metrics	Executive Decision Maker and Stakeholder Review Team		
Iterate Draft and Review Process	Stakeholder Review Team and CISO		
Accept Policy as Documented	Stakeholder Review Team		
Conspicuously Approve Policy	Executive Decision Maker		
Monitor Policy Implementation Process	Executive Decision Maker and Stakeholder Review Team and CISO		
Monitor Changes in Cyber Security Risks	CISO		

Repeat as required

Figure 4.2   Gant chart.

documentation of desired outcomes is a critical element of enterprise communication and is required for awareness activities that motivate members from executives to first-level employees of the organization to achieve security goals. Progress in goal achievement should be monitored, and gaps in policy compliance or difficulties in following strategy should be corrected if possible, and if there is too much difficulty in complying with policy, that fact should be captured in a management feedback loop.

Given that business, system, and/or mission risk management should drive cyber security strategy and corresponding policy, articulating the risks presented by threats to business, system, and/or mission cyberspace is a good way to begin a cyber security policy project. Though the description of these risks may not be included in the final policy document, it is helpful in creating awareness among stakeholders of why the policy has been deemed necessary. The articulated risks also provide a sanity check against the resulting policy. The policy should be focused on reducing cyber security risk rather than on any externally set goals such as compliance with industry best practices. Such a sanity check should be a formal milestone in the policy project. Figure 4.2 is typical gant chart for a cyber security policy project.

4.3   Cyber Security Management

Many companies have established a Chief Security Office or Chief Information Security Office. However, those offices generally do not have line authority over operations that are critical to asset preservation and other security goals. These offices generally are skilled in the tools and techniques necessary to enforce security policy, but often do not have the understanding of business or mission that would be required to establish one. This observation is not meant to belittle the role of security professionals; they simply are not as intimate with the daily workflow of each business unit as are their leaders. Also, many security professionals were trained in industries that were early security adopters such as military or finance. It would be unreasonable to expect someone who spent 20 years in one industry to know what business processes should take priority in a completely different one. This is also true of Chief Financial Officers or Human Resources Officers. Though many skills are transferrable, there is always an industry learning curve.

Hence, the team an executive needs to determine security policy is the same team convened to create other important strategic objectives. It should include the Chief Operations Officer or equivalent. It may include business leaders and/or trusted advisors from any area of the enterprise. Of course, if there is a high-ranking individual whose sole job is security, then that person will undoubtedly be a good sounding board when discussing the potential efficacy of a suggested policy, whether or not they are also well versed in the business.

4.3.1 Arriving at Goals

To begin the process of developing cyber security policy, executives may ask themselves:

- What assets need to be in place to maintain operations? Which are the "crown jewels?" Are these changing and/or evolving with our long-term business plans?
- What cyberspace infrastructure houses or impacts our most critical assets?
- Do we have any information that should be kept from general circulation? If so:
  - What criteria would we use to release it to someone within the organization?
  - What criteria would we use to release it to someone outside the organization?
  - If someone with access to it left the organization, should it still be protected?
- Do we participate in socio-technical networks with communities who are hostile to our interests? Are we subject to cyber threats simply from being a bystander within a larger community?

Once these general environmental aspects of the cyber security environment within the enterprise are understood, more detailed questions can be probed with the help of a cyber security task force composed of operations, financial, and technology staff. Such questions may be found in industry standard literature. For example (ANSI and ISA 2010):

- Have we analyzed our cyber liabilities? What legal rules apply to the information that we maintain or that is kept by vendors, partners, and other third parties? What laws apply in different states and countries in which we conduct business?
- Have we assessed our exposure to suits by our customers and suppliers? Have we protected our company in contracts with vendors?
- What is our biggest single vulnerability from a technology or security point of view? How vulnerable are we to attack on the confidentiality, integrity, and availability of our data and systems? How often are we re-evaluating our technical exposures?
- If our system goes down, how long until we are back up and running, and are there circumstances where we do not want to be back up quickly? How prepared are our business continuity plans? What is our risk exposure of technology or business operation failures at our vendors and service providers?
- Do we fully understand the overall financial impact of mishandling communications with our key stakeholders following a cyber security event? Have we budgeted for a cyber security event?
- Do we have a documented, proactive crisis communications plan? Have we identified and trained all the internal resources required to execute the communications plan? Do we have contacts at specialist crisis communications firms if we need their services? In the case of a cyber security event involving personally identifiable information (PII), do we have a system in place to quickly determine who should be notified, and how?
- Have we evaluated the appropriate communication responses to our key stakeholders? Do we have a template timeline for executing the communications plan? Have we considered that, depending on the situation, we may need to craft different messages for different types or levels of clients or employees?
- How do we attract, acclimate, invest in, and engage critical cyber security technical and leadership talent, including those in functional areas requiring cyber security savvy?

From these types of questions, an information classification system can be developed (e.g., customer info, financial info, and marketing info). The classification should be as granular as the corresponding business processes. It may be possible to merge classifications into a hierarchical taxonomy, but in the initial effort, it is important not to miss any distinctions in the value of information that may be blurred by lumping similar-sounding business records into a single bucket.

The answers to questions such as those above should provide the foundation from which to articulate security goals. Because committees are often motivated by regulatory requirements, the temptation is to use regulation as the foundation for security strategy. We caution against start-ing with that approach. Everyone's business process is different and regula-tions are not always concurrent with change in industry. A strategy to protect a business process should also protect regulatory-specified informa-tion, but the opposite is rarely true. By concentrating on a business process rather than regulatory requirements, it is likely that efficient and economi-cal techniques will cover both. Once a cyber security policy serves the needs of the business, a simple internal audit should confirm that it also meets the needs of the regulators, or identify a gap that can be closed in a way compatible with the agreed-upon business security requirements.

Cyber security business or mission goals should be focused on how security can contribute to enterprise mission or purpose. Sample cyber security goals are:

- Make operations safe from hackers
- Make it extremely hard to steal information stored on physical assets without insider collaboration
- Always detect cyber-space-enabled asset fraud or theft.

Note that it is not reasonable to expect that cyber security goals are 100% achievable. They are simply guideposts and sanity checks meant to ensure that any cyber security strategy and policy established have some tangible value. They lay the foundation on which to specify the scope of system and process level security efforts. However, executives should not mistake progress in technology implementation of cyber security best practices for cyber security goal achievement. As discussed in Chapter 3, verification measures that cyber security technology is deployed provide a completely different information from validation measures that systems are safe from hackers. It is incumbent on the decision maker to understand the validation measures and contribute to an assessment of whether they have been achieved. Any cyber security program that does not make progress toward its goals is not achieving its objective. These security goals, in conjunction with asset and information inventory terminology, should be discussed in the context of business operations. There should be some agreement on a strategy appropriate for validating them.

Armed with tangible goals, a cyber security program can justify both its strategies and corresponding policy. Cyber security policy statements should be phrased in a language native to the same team of executive decision makers that set cyber security goals. For example, if customers are called clients in the business literature, the policy should use that term, or if telecommunications lines are called facilities in the business literature, that term should not be used to describe buildings. Sample cyber security policy statements based on the three sample goals above might be:

- Critical program information includes the software, systems configura-tions, documentation, and test generation methods for all business applications, and these include electronically enabled controls for mechanical equipment. The integrity of all critical program information shall be maintained.

- Physical access to all information assets shall be restricted to those required to operate them via job functions. Any physical device capable of storing information that is small enough to be portable shall be centrally encrypted with keys that do not leave the internal network.
- Where any asset is capable of being disbursed via online mechanisms, the software controlling the disbursement shall require end-to-end non-repudiation using physical, geographical, and logical authentication, authorization, and robust delivery verification.

Note that a policy statement does not dictate how the situation described in its "shall" statements will be accomplished. As part of an overall strategy, the implementation mechanisms may be central or distributed among various stakeholders within the policy scope. The policy should be specific enough for its outcomes to be measureable, but general enough to allow for appropriate information handling procedures to be described at the business process level.

Nevertheless, it is important to compose an information security policy document so that the organizations within scope are unmistakably aware of the existence of well-defined objectives for security and an agreed-upon management approach for securing information. If there is debate over the content of the policy, the debate will continue through attempts to enforce it, with the consequence that the Information Security Program itself will be dysfunctional.

It is also true that cyber security policy statements that reflect a poor security posture do not stand alone. An executive may accept that the negative aspects of a given policy statement are more likely to occur than the positive ones, but may issue such a directive in the context of an overall strategy that provides compensating controls intended to shore an organization's resiliency to the negative impact expected due to lack of security measures.

4.3.2 Cyber Security Documentation

As illustrated in Figure 4.1, policy awareness is a necessary step to complete after policy development and before implementation. If people are not aware of the decisions made in strategy and policy, then they will have no reason to implement in accordance with them. This is why security standards, operating procedures, and guidelines are also often issued in conjunction with policy to demonstrate how compliance with a given policy may be achieved. Though every organization draws the line between what types of directives are mandated policy and which are relegated to standards as they see fit, standards typically document the implementation details for specific technology platforms, while policy statements are reserved for higher-level management control objectives. There may be multiple, equally effective, methods of implementing policy within a technology platform and standards are generally adopted for economy and efficiency. They are often stated in the form of settings for technology configuration variables, that, when configured and combined with control activities such as procedures, will achieve policy compliance.

Procedures are documented step-by-step implementation instructions that a technician may follow in order to be successful in implementing policy and standards. They are used not only to guarantee a policy-compliant technical configuration, but also to train new technicians on the mechanics of configuring the technology. Procedures therefore must be written at a much lower level of detail than policies or standards, and they must fully explain how to operate technology.

Guidelines are the most general type of security document. They are designed to raise awareness among those who must comply with policy. They provide options for policy compliance. They do not dictate exactly how to comply or what must be done, but instead contain education and advice for individuals who must make daily choices about security as part of their job function.

Because security professionals like CISOs are often the people who document cyber security policy, it is important to understand that these are not necessarily the same set of people as the cyber security strategists. Cyber security specialists often act as trusted advisors to executive decision makers, but are not as well-versed on overall organizational mission as the executives who would be expected to create cyber security strategy. Cyber security specialists usually advise on matters of cyber security technology and implementation while leaving the organizational goals that form the basis of the policy to executive decision makers. Once an executive decision maker clearly articulates goals for cyber security, a cyber security specialist may be drafted to translate those goals into cyber security policy directives. As illustrated in the gant chart of Figure 4.2, these directives would then be reviewed, circulated among stakeholders, and refined by executive management. It is, after all, the executive who signs, and thereby owns responsibility for, the resulting cyber security policy, and its overall impact to the organization strategy and operating plan.

The Chief Security Officers today are similar to the Chief Information Officers (CIOs) in the 1990s. The title was new, and the function was not quite like technology advisors before them, cyber security advisors are a recent addition to the executive staffroom. They comprise a new specialist field because there is a significant requirement to address cyber security issues, but as yet no common understanding in the general public, nor even the general research community, as to what is meant generically by a cyber security. Like CIOs in the 1990s, their job is not well understood even by those who hired them. Their responsibilities change frequently, and their tenure is often short due to matters beyond their control. They will seek to establish standard ways in which to configure technology so that it can be easily verified to be policy-compliant. They will seek to supplement those standards with education and training for individuals responsible for configuring equipment. They may mandate that staff perform step-by-step procedures in areas that previously had no need for them (e.g., the guard at the door). They may draft guidelines and expect others to follow their advice. Only an executive who truly understands the end goal of their activities will be able to provide the tone at the top necessary to support such a CISO-led cyber security program.

There is also a technique used by cyber security professionals, both security staff and auditors, where policy and standards are translated into a set of questions about the technology environment. Rather than directly evaluate technology, a cyber security assessor may instead present management with a series of questions about the security of a given technology environment. These questions are typically formulated with a specific cyber security policy or standard in mind, but they do not replace the standard. They are information-gathering conveniences for the assessor. People who participate in this type of process often treat the questions themselves as policy, but they are not. Such sets of security questions lie entirely outside of the cyber security management process. Moreover, although this type of the question and answer routine is typically used in due diligence processes where security must to some extent be evaluated, it should not be mistaken for a professional technology audit (Bayuk 2005).

When an executive fully understands the motivation and origin for enterprise security policy, the process for implementation should be as easy to manage as any other technology endeavor. This is not to say that technology endeavors are ever easy to manage. However, typical managerial techniques such as continuous monitoring in the style of Drucker and Deming go as far in cyber security as they do for any other domain (Drucker 2001; Pande, Neuman et al. 2001). Applied to cyber security, such techniques allow for advancement of the enterprise purpose or strategic mission, and fortify its resiliency against currently unknown threats. Moreover, the application of sound management practices to the domain of security carries the happy unintended consequence of the ability to pass technology audits.

4.4   Using the Catalog

The next two chapters of this book describe a catalog approach to cyber security policy and provide numerous examples of cyber security policy statements that have been adopted by others. A thorough read of these chapters will provide an appreciation for the breadth and depth of issues that come under the general heading of cyber security, most of which will never be faced by any one individual. However, it also makes it easy to see how policy decisions made by some individuals in their own domains will affect others.

As in a physical security environment, each significant social, economic, institutional, and political segment of the community has a number of potential resources that can be brought to bear (NCPI 2001). There is a role for the police, for private security services, for technology vendors, for government, for the insurance industry, for civic groups, for the business community, for industry associations, and for citizen organizations. Each group's role needs clarity in its scope and potential impact on the overall problem. The cyber security policy issues in Chapter 6 have been organized in a role-based manner accordingly.

However, the policy statements in Chapter 6 are not meant as a pick-list from which to choose a cyber security policy befitting one's role. Not only is the chapter not customized to the nomenclature of any given enterprise, there are certainly statements concerning cyber security policy of use to executive management that do not appear in this guidebook. The list is not expected to ever be exhaustive. Even if it were possible to complete such a list before the time this guidebook went to publication, by the time the publication process was finished, there would be some change in cyberspace that necessitated new ways of policy formulation. At best, this book provides executives with the capability to properly analyze new cyber security situations within a well-understood framework of policy issues.

There is also a large class of policy statements that were omitted intentionally. These are technical security configurations for hardware and software components of cyberspace of the sort described in Section 1.3.4. While many organizations publish technical security specifications under the heading of policy, they do not reflect management objectives themselves. Rather, they provide implementation standards for technical professionals charged with executing management policy directives. Where it is imperative that these technical standards are implemented consistently without exception, they may qualify as cyber security policy. However, depending on the enterprise or mission, there are in fact implementation standards that executive management may not be expected to completely understand, much less to dictate.

Cyber attacks require coordinated response. However, in order to coordinate response, one first needs an ability to detect cyber attacks, access to intelligence with which to analyze them, and a method and means of response (Amoroso 2006). An individual organization may lay plans to coordinate its own response, but for response to cross all communities of interest, more coordinated policies are required on common fronts. As you read through Chapter 6, you may find a way to self-categorize issues into those you may be able to control, those you may have influence over, and those concerning which the most you can do is maintain awareness.

Although there are circumstances under which influence should be sought as well as provided, we caution against the active solicitation of customers or other end users to participate in the cyber security policy goals of any given enterprise. Citizen participation should not be solicited until policymakers understand the point and purpose of individual action. Citizen awareness programs that stimulate fear but provide no effective response to attack are not useful in minimizing the potential societal effect of any threat (Siegel 2005). However, where problems are obvious and remedies are easily available, citizen groups may be counted on to recognize issues in their own domains and unite along lines that may preexist in various communities. Bridge clubs and book club discussions may lead to local community participation in crime surveys and then to government meetings and eventual legislation. Where there is an opportunity for self-policing to occur, for example, neighbors on the same cable connection, it should be as supported and encouraged just as much as physical neighborhood crime watches. It may be well within an enterprise policy framework to actively court such interests to contribute to well-defined cyber security strategies.

Policy should not only address goals, but also identify key barriers to goal achievement and anticipate resistance to change. The resistance may come from sources both internal and external to the organization. Those with experience in accountability for security measures well understand that security policy is often used as a shield against change. Where the security policy mandates that are composed for a given business operation seem to work well, the evolution of that business operation may be at risk due to an inflexible security policy. That is, those who oppose a proposal for innovation may use a legacy system's security policy as an excuse to resist change. Where policy has been mistakenly framed as an enterprise-level directive in support of the elusive concept of "security" rather than framed as support of a given operation or mission, this attitude receives considerable support because no one wants to be accountable for introducing vulnerability. However, a true enterprise strategist will see security policy as a flexible tool with which to achieve objectives, not as a barrier or disincentive to innovation.

When things are quiet, it makes sense to plan. As the CISO of AT&T, historically one of the most hacked targets on the planet, has put it, "During a period of seeming quiet, never confuse good luck with improved cyber security"(Amoroso 2006).

5

The Catalog Approach

A recent attempt to catalog all possible ways in which cyber security may be measured resulted in a list of over 900 items (Herrmann 2007). The full spectrum of issues that may one day be laid before cyber security policy decision makers would be similarly long. A listing of all cyber security policy issues is not feasible to attempt because it is the type of list that would be out of date as soon as it was done. Nevertheless, a catalog approach provides structure for classification and examples of cyber security policy issues. Chapter 6 uses a catalog approach to isolate and explain decision criteria on which cyber security policy mandates are frequently based.

The primary reason for listing and explaining a set of issues is to introduce and explain the foundations of concepts that frequently recur in cyber security policy debates. A secondary reason for presenting a catalog is to impress the reader with the variety and breadth of the field of cyber security policy. A third reason is to include enough detail in the explanation of cyber security policy issues for decision makers to recognize how the consequence of a given policy may affect their enterprise, whether or not it is a policy they themselves adopt, or a policy that has been adopted by others. Given that the list is necessarily incomplete, and its purpose is elucidation and awareness, it is first necessary to present the nomenclature used to create the list, which has itself become a taxonomy of cyber security policy issues.

The original taxonomy for this Catalog transformed considerably as this book took shape. The process of listing the issues and the corresponding discussion among authors while contributing to the list altered the taxonomy several times. As more issues were added to the list, more prior

Cyber Security Policy Guidebook, First Edition. Jennifer L. Bayuk, Jason Healey, Paul Rohmeyer, Marcus H. Sachs, Jeffrey Schmidt, Joseph Weiss.
© 2012 John Wiley & Sons, Inc. Published 2012 by John Wiley & Sons, Inc.

explanatory guidance was needed for them to be comprehensible to the reader.

Moreover, debate in cyber security typically centers on the impact of cyber security incidents. Root cause analysis of cyber security incidents, as in any root cause analysis exercise, will produce two types of causes: events and conditions. Events are the proximate causes, and conditions are the situations that allowed the event to occur. For example, a situation in which dry kindling is left next to a gasoline soaked rag is a condition, an event is a discarded cigarette that ignites the rag and causes a fire that burns out of control due to the presence of the kindling. Events are by nature unpredictable and difficult to control. But conditions that allow events in cyberspace to become security issues may be controlled with policy. Concentration on conditions rather than events led to the current taxonomy for the catalog of cyber security policy issues. Although other taxonomies may be equally valid, the current catalog is a viable method to promote education and awareness of cyber security policy issues. It is an alternative to the typical fear, uncertainty, and doubt (also known by security professionals as the *FUD factor*) that surrounds the conventional presentation of security issues in terms of events. Rather than accept the current situation as described in Chapter 2, where the latest threat is typically unanticipated, an overview of cyber security policy alternatives provides a comprehensive look at what might be done to avert the high impact of an unexpected threat. Rather than give up on security validation metrics because they are as difficult as described in Chapter 3, an overview of cyber security policy alternatives presents a comprehensive picture of the significance of metrics data that we are capable of gathering. Cyber policy issues faced by individual agencies and organizations seem hopelessly complicated in isolation, but in the context of the issues faced globally, sense can be made of the individual organization's choices in the context of the cyber-enabled community. For many of the seemingly hopeless situations, a solid understanding of cyber security policy issues suggests potential solutions not only for the organization, but provides a solid foundation for the organization to lobby for choices made by others that affect them.

For example, nearly everyone who uses cyberspace is affected by mechanisms that govern the allocation of Internet domain names and numbers. But only those who have been affected to the extent that policy choices in this domain have facilitated incidents that cause negative impact to their enterprise have likely investigated these issues. Even then, the investigation is typically into how Internet governance works, rather than how it could work if policy was different. From the Catalog's clear presentation of the issues related to Internet Governance, it is apparent that no matter how many lawyers one has, all domains will continue to be subject to threats of impersonation unless several policies are changed globally. If more organizations came to this recognition, we may collectively realize that our combined resources may be better spent in diplomatic efforts and cooperative prevention pacts than in law tribunals. A comprehensive catalog that describes conditions under which cyber events turn into security issues should assist all organizations to better use their own sphere of influence to further their own cyber security strategies.

To that end, we present the Cyber Security Policy Catalog of Chapter 6. Like each chapter before it, this chapter looks at cyber security from a different dimension. The dimensions in this case are suggested by the policy issues themselves. The chapter divides cyber security policy issues into sections based on five aspects of cyber security policy goals:

6.1 Cyber Governance Issues
6.2 Cyber User Issues
6.3 Cyber Conflict Issues
6.4 Cyber Management Issues
6.5 Cyber Infrastructure Issues

This classification scheme was chosen in order to explain the types of issues that build on each other so as to provide a more thorough understanding of the entire set. Figure 5.1 illustrates that these sections build on each other to produce comprehensive insights into how policy is expected

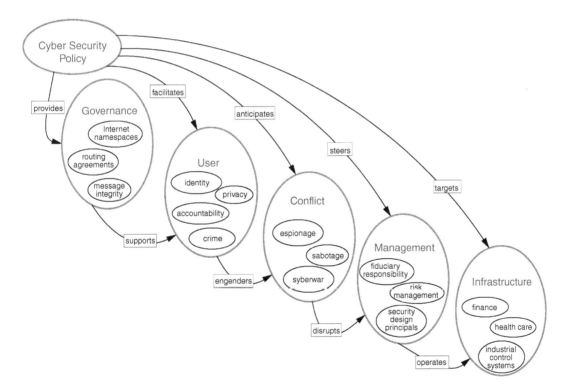

Figure 5.1 Cyber security policy taxonomy.

to contribute to cyber security. *Cyber Governance* is concerned with issues relating to Internet operation and its continued utility and feasibility. Of course, where cyberspace networks are privately operated, these issues will also apply, but their scope will be smaller. The resolution of issues in the governance arena undoubtedly will heavily influence the e-commerce environment, which is how most users are exposed to cyber security policy issues. *Cyber Users* are concerned with the stability of cyberspace as a platform upon which to conduct business, as well as their own personal expectations for Internet communication. Cyber security policy issues decided in that arena may have downstream consequences, both intended and unintended, on *Cyber Conflict* between political factions and nation-states. These conflict issues will drive cyber security requirements and thus present policy issues in the practice of technology operations and management. *Cyber Management* policies in some sense form a baseline of due care with respect to security, although each industry will face issues of unique concern. Hence, we provide examples of *Cyber Infrastructure* issues.

None of the policy domains in Figure 5.1 stands alone. They are presented in an order that allows the conditions presented under one to be used as background explanations for those that follow. However, in practice, the policy discussions in these areas are often intertwined to the point where it is difficult even for experts to dissect the issues to the level included in Chapter 6. The point of this introductory discussion before the actual presentation of cyber security policy issues is to foster an understanding of the various types of policy issues in order to prompt recognition that they are separate and distinct. For example, most cyber governance issues may be resolved independent of user issues, though some may constrain the policy choices made on behalf of users. Also, the resolution of user privacy issues may limit choices or introduce constraints in alternatives for cyber policy concerning cyber conflict issues. The interaction and overlap between the sections of Chapter 6 are often highlighted in the discussions. The chapter also attempts to clarify the difference between major policy issues that often capture headlines, such as cyber crime and cyber war.

It is understood that some executives will find that a few sections of Chapter 6 offer enough education on, and diversity of, cyber security policy examples to allow them to peruse one or two and then skip to Chapter 7. Others may find the high-level description of each section to provide enough understanding and so skip reading the example policy issues in themselves. However, those interested in public policy on cyber security will read all sections and all of the debates with interest, as each brings richer understanding of the differing perspectives on the overall domain of cyber security.

Note also that government and private sector policy decision makers will have different issues to face in the policy debate. However, they may be very interested in the way issues are resolved in other domains. For example, telecommunications sector executives will be most involved in the issues of Internet Governance on a day-to-day basis, but they may also be very interested in the cyber security policy decisions made with respect to cyber conflict, although these are issues more directly faced by government officials in their role as public steward or servant. Also, although government officials do not confront decisions on cyber security issues faced by executives who manage large industrial control systems that are part of the nation's critical infrastructure, they may nevertheless be very interested in the resolution of the issues because they may have consequences for the nation's critical infrastructure. There are also policy issues that are common to large segments of the executive decision-maker population, no matter what their industry. For example, all of the technology practice issues that are faced by a corporate executive managing his or her own enterprise generically are also faced by leaders of government agencies.

5.1   Catalog Format

Each section of the Catalog follows a uniform format. Each section begins with an overview of the issues of interest for that section. The overview is meant to shed light on cyber security policy concerns and introduce a taxonomy for the issues within the general section heading. Each item in the taxonomy will have its own subsection introductory description. These descriptions are followed by a categorization of cyber security policy issues that illustrate the concerns of the subsection and may include examples of events that illustrate major cyberspace developments and corresponding security impact. The opening discussion in each subsection is followed by a table that lists specific examples of cyber security policy issues.

Each policy statement in a tabular list is enhanced with both explanation and opinions that indicate why cyber security policy constituents may be concerned about the issuance of executive mandates with respect to the issue. Rather than take sides on these opinions, they are neutrally presented as "reasons for controversy." Readers should also keep in mind that cyber security policy that makes sense for one organization does not necessarily make sense for any other, and two organizations with inconsistent internal cyber security policies may nevertheless coexist in harmony. Hence, no sides are taken on whether any given proposed policy statement should be issued as policy in any given constituency. Instead, the reasons why a statement may stir controversy are presented in the form of virtual constituent opinions.

There are at least two reasons for controversy cited for each policy statement. However, the reasons for controversy reveal that there are often more than two sides to a cyber security policy debate. Note that many of the policy statements identified in this book are already mandated in the context of existing policy directives or published doctrines within some constituency, but many are not. Even those that have been adopted as policy may not have any corresponding enforcement structure. Nevertheless, all issues and corresponding literature have surfaced in published information security standards, government directives, or academic literature.

Many executives today are faced with responsibility for creating their own organizational cyber strategy and cyber security policy statements. These reasons for controversy are highlighted solely to enhance awareness of debates in progress while encouraging development of new opinions on the issue. In line with the objective of providing a comprehensive guide to cyber security policy issues for executive decision makers, an attempt has been made to phrase the cyber security policy issues in such a manner that an executive in the domain sees the consequences of mandating these statements as policy within their own sphere of organizational control. The members of the list have been grouped by subject of concern to the corresponding domain in order for an executive to quickly get a sense of how cyber security policy issues within a given domain may be related to each other. The adoption of one may entail the adoption of another, or it may conflict with the opportunity to adopt another. These lists are not intended to be a complete enumeration of all policy issues in a given domain that will serve as an executive menu (although such menus do exist; Peltier 2001). Rather, they are intended to provide insights which will allow the reader to build their own comprehensible framework to cover their own goals with respect to cyber security policy.

The catalog approach is intended to ensure that policy issues are captured systematically and without prejudice toward one overarching global strategy to accomplish any given organization's objective for the utilization of cyberspace. Again, note that there are an infinite variety of policy statements that would serve to identify a cyber security policy issue for the purposes of discussion, and no attempt has been made at a complete enumeration.

A key goal of the Catalog is to provide well-articulated constituent opinions with respect to each policy statement. These opinions are clearly demarcated from the explanation of the policy issue itself, as the explanation is intended to be fact-based. Inclusion of a policy statement in this document in no way implies endorsement. A reason for controversy with respect to a policy statement is not highlighted as either a pro or a con. Though they may be grouped by category or similarity of opinion, reasons for controversy are not listed in any purposeful order. Note that all policies are subject to unanticipated, as opposed to unintended, consequences. Unanticipated consequences are inherently unknown and so will not be listed. By contrast, unintended consequences may be anticipated, though they are not certain to occur. Hence, an unintended consequence carries a likelihood value that is subject to opinion. If unintended consequences are included in the catalog in the context of a policy statement, they will be listed as opinions, that is, as reasons for controversy.

It is important for the reader to keep in mind when reading these opinions that many organizations have differing requirements for cyber security. An opinion that seems like it is a pro cyber security policy statement by one organization may be considered a con by another. Also keep in mind that enforcement of any policy relies on accompanying strategy, technically feasible strategy implementation, and enforcement. Therefore, expected benefits stated in opinions are not likely to be gained unless it is certain that the policy can be enforced.

5.2 Cyber Security Policy Taxonomy

As previously mentioned, each of the catalog sections is further broken down into subsections. The resulting taxonomy provides a methodology for examination of cyber security policy issues. The sections and subsections are:

6.1   Cyber Governance Issues
    6.1.1 Net Neutrality
    6.1.2 Internet Names and Numbers
    6.1.3 Copyrights and Trademarks
    6.1.4 E-mail and Messaging
6.2   Cyber User Issues
    6.2.1 Malvertising
    6.2.2 Impersonation
    6.2.3 Appropriate Use
    6.2.4 Cyber Crime
    6.2.5 Geolocation
    6.2.6 Privacy
6.3   Cyber Conflict Issues
    6.3.1 Intellectual Property Theft
    6.3.2 Cyber Espionage
    6.3.3 Cyber Sabotage
    6.3.4 Cyber Warfare
6.4   Cyber Management Issues
    6.4.1 Fiduciary Responsibility
    6.4.2 Risk Management
    6.4.3 Professional Certification
    6.4.4 Supply Chain
    6.4.5 Security Principles
    6.4.6 Research and Development
6.5   Cyber Infrastructure Issues
    6.5.1 Banking and Finance
    6.5.2 Health Care
    6.5.3 Industrial Control Systems

Just as it is always possible to add more policy lists, it is always possible to find specific sectors of the population for whom cyber security policy will contain different and unique sets of issues. The original domain sub-sections for the Catalog were loosely modeled on the U.S. Department of Homeland Security Critical Infrastructure domains. Experts in these areas were invited to speak on cyber security policy at a conference of cyber security experts hosted by Stevens Institute of Technology (SIT 2010). The opinions of these experts, invited reviewers, and the authors, after over a year of discussions, were finally determined to correspond to the taxonomy of this list.

Each subsection is prefaced with a discussion of issues unique to that domain, and combined with background information with which to under-stand the point of some of the policy statements contained within its list. Sections 6.1–6.4 are generally applicable to any industry, but there are cyber security policy issues that do not apply generically to all organiza-tions. Details on such industry-specific issues are not covered in the more general sections, but a few examples appear in subsections under the heading of Cyber Infrastructure Issues. For example, Section 6.5.2 concerns the Health-Care industry, wherein the pressure to digitize record-keeping and associated electronic health-care initiatives has called public attention to a variety of issues in the dominion of cyber security policy. These have motivated both legislation and enterprise cyber policy directives.

Each subsection discussion is followed by a table that contains the list of policy issues to be explained for that subsector. The table has three columns. Each row in the table begins with a clear articulation of a cyber security policy statement. The second column in each row is a fact-based explanation of the policy statement. The third column contains the list of the reasons why the policy statement may be controversial. This format is illustrated in Table 5.1.

The lists of issues in each table are representative. Though some sections will have more than the others, there is no expectation that any list is complete. It is always possible to add issues or include more opinions sur-rounding them, and enough issues have been listed in these tables to com-municate a sense of the challenges in cyber security policy strategy to be

Table 5.1 Format for Policy Lists

Policy statement	Explanation	Reasons for controversy
This cell contains a statement of policy in the form it would be stated if it were a management directive.	This is a brief explanation of why the policy has significance in the domain of cyber security.	This column contains two or more cells. Each cell states a different reason why a policymaker might be motivated to issue the policy statement in the form of a management directive, or defer from association with the policy statement.

accomplished by domain executives. Refreshing these lists with new unique and innovative cyber security policy issues and arguments will occur naturally in experienced readers. This is especially true in conjunction with new societal developments, and thus, after our publication of this initial subset, the development of other current and emerging cyber security policy issues will be left as an exercise for the reader.

6

Cyber Security Policy Catalog

The Cyber Security Policy Catalog is organized according to the taxonomy introduced in Chapter 5. There are five major topics that correspond to sections of the catalog. Each topic has several subtopics. Each topic and subtopic is introduced with some background information, some of which may appear technical, but the level of technical detail required to understand the issues has been purposely kept to a minimum and may be skimmed without loss of continuity. The background information is followed by a table that contains a list of policy issues that are of relevance to the topic. Each table has three columns. Each row in the table begins with an articulation of a cyber security policy statement. The second column in each row is an explanation of the policy statement. The third column contains a representative list of the reasons why the policy statement may be controversial.

The authors recognize that it is easy to confuse *collecting* policy statements with *endorsing* them, other than as statements that, in our judgment, are good examples. This chapter contains the policy statements that we collected. Please do not read the catalog as if it is a policy document. It is not. The catalog exists because participation in policy debate requires recognition of a policy and reasoning about it. As repeated several times in both Chapters 1 and 5, the statements in this catalog are not contrived as endorsements but as *examples*. None of the statements in this chapter should be mistaken for the opinion of the authors. In fact, some of the statements seem extreme to the authors. All will seem extreme to one set of readers or another. For any given individual, some statements may offend and others may seem banal. It is important to recognize that all policies are controversial. To that end, all have been presented with corresponding reasons for controversy. Many readers will easily be able to

Cyber Security Policy Guidebook, First Edition. Jennifer L. Bayuk, Jason Healey, Paul Rohmeyer, Marcus H. Sachs, Jeffrey Schmidt, Joseph Weiss.
© 2012 John Wiley & Sons, Inc. Published 2012 by John Wiley & Sons, Inc.

elaborate on those reasons, and also to add more reasons to the list for each statement. This is an expected response from our readers. No issues have been intentionally left out of the list because they were deemed offensive. To do so would leave the reader unaware that controversy exists.

6.1   Cyber Governance Issues

The Internet began as the Advanced Research Projects Agency Network (ARPANET), a U.S.-military-funded network designed to survive a nuclear attack. It quickly became a tool for sharing information among computer science researchers in the military, its contractors, and its academic collaborators. Those with an idea for a communications protocol would share it via a formal process managed by the Internet Engineering Task Force (IETF). These were published as Requests for Comments, which allowed others to quickly learn the new protocols, as well as extend them (IETF ongoing).

While the vast majority of Internet infrastructure and functions are decentralized (a design goal of the Internet), certain centralized planning and coordination functions are required. The most visible are the allocation of names (i.e., http://www.whitehouse.gov) and numbers (i.e., Internet Protocol, or IP, addresses, the cyberspace equivalent of postal addresses; they are used to find routes to locate computers). These coordination functions were initially performed at Stanford Research Institute (SRI), a U.S. Defense Department contractor. In 1972, these functions were transitioned to the Internet Assigned Numbers Authority (IANA) under the oversight of Jon Postel at Information Sciences Institute (ISI) at the University of Southern California. As the network evolved from the seeds of its founders, ARPANET was gradually disbanded. In 1995, the last restrictions to commercial Internet traffic were removed.

In 1998, the National Telecommunications and Information Administration (NTIA), an agency of the U.S. Department of Commerce, began a process to create a sustainable governance model for the IANA functions; this process culminated in the creation of the Internet Corporation for Assigned Names and Numbers (ICANN) in 2000. On January 30, 1998, ICANN issued for comment a policy "Green Paper" entitled: "A Proposal to Improve the Technical Management of Internet Names and Addresses." The proposal was widely disseminated to encourage suggestions and comments (NTIA 1998). The resulting ICANN model is a unique "multistakeholder" governance model for the centralized components of the Internet where governments participate alongside corporations and individual Internet users to create the policies that govern the Internet in a bottom-up fashion. ICANN technically remained a U.S. government (USG) contractor until the signing of the Affirmation of Commitments (AoC) in 2009 that transitioned ICANN from a USG contractor to a party to what is essentially a Memorandum of Understanding between the USG and ICANN about the principles of multistakeholder Internet governance.

The Internet is a U.S. creation, and the USG has been leery to relinquish all control over the basic Internet coordination functions. Transition from direct control through a contractor to the IANA function and now to the AoC model shows a willingness on behalf of the USG to "internationalize" the governance of the Internet, but to what extent the United States wants and is capable of exerting unilateral control over ICANN is a debatable topic.

It is easy to see an analogy between Internet governance and the global phone system. The reason you can direct dial internationally is because of the committee of cooperating telecommunications companies within each country, who in pursuit of their individual missions to connect their citizens to the world, had a shared global objective of ubiquitous phone communications. These companies formed the International Telecommunications Union in 1865. In 1947, the ITU became a part of the then-new United Nations (UN). The UN/ITU is a top-down, government-driven governance model. In contrast, the ICANN/AoC model is an "international multistakeholder governance model" that favors bottom-up policymaking. World governments participate in the ICANN model through the Governmental Advisory Committee (GAC) which is just one of several advisory committees that set Internet policy within ICANN. Some claim that the ITU/UN model is the correct model for Internet governance, while others claim the ICANN/AoC model is optimal.

The key cyber security policy issue is the Internet governance model and, in particular, the modality of participation by world governments. One of the most unique features of the Internet is that it is shared globally; any Internet-machine can talk to any other Internet-connected machine, and typing http://www.cnn.com in Kansas, Singapore, Berlin, and Moscow all take you to the same place. The technical reason for this global interoperability is the existence of the central coordination functions. If governments disagree on the central coordination functions and begin to use different standards/procedures, the Internet may fragment into multiple or partially connected pieces. Some governments prefer this approach for reasons related to censorship, national sovereignty, and countering U.S. dominance.

6.1.1 Net Neutrality

One word that is frequently used by professionals working in a wide spectrum of jobs related to the Internet is *content*. Content is a generic term for whatever information may be carried by bits and bytes through the wires and disks at any given point in time without distinction. The ownership, meaning, or origination of *content* is not assumed unless explicitly used to modify the word, as in "user content" or "voice content." The design of communications protocols has always been independent of the content of transmission sent. From a strictly technical perspective, it is unnecessary for Internet service providers (ISPs) to examine content in order for content to move through networks.

Ever since the advent of commercial ISPs in the mid-1990s, there has been concern that those who manage large portions of the Internet will unfairly prioritize, manipulate, and/or censor communication for economic or political gain, or both. Recent mergers and acquisitions have led to greater vertical integration of content providers, data service providers such as phone and TV service over the Internet, and ISPs, creating opportunities for favoritism at the data transit level. Proponents of Net Neutrality feel that ISPs should be barred—by law—from manipulation and prioritization of their data transit services that advantage their content and/or data services over competing services. Opponents feel that free markets will adequately address the issue and no new regulation is needed.

In order to fully appreciate the scope of net neutrality, it is important to recognize that different policies will have different technical enforcement points. For example, policies on routing between countries can only be enforced by cooperating telecommunications carriers and/or international treaty, while policies concerning domestic-only transit may be enforced through interstate and intrastate commerce regulation.

The policy statements in this section range from the establishing responsibility for establishing secure communications protocols to requiring ISPs to offer cyber security services. The reasons for controversy illustrate how cyber security efforts and net neutrality positions often seem to be at odds (Table 6.1.1).

6.1.2 Internet Names and Numbers

As discussed in Section 6.1, within the ICANN registration process, there are two corresponding sets of strings that Internet-connected entities register through ICANN. These are Internet names and Internet numbers. The current communications protocol limits the number of addresses to 4,294,967,296, or 2^{32}. Addresses are typically communicated by dividing the 32 bits into groups of eight and displaying each 8-bit set in decimal format, for example: A.B.C.D. There is no theoretical limit on the number of names, although currently the number of globally available top-level domain (TLD) names are limited by ICANN. To be found on the Internet, an entity must register at least one of each, and then must join them together and publish the result in an Internet-accessible Domain Name Service (DNS). Firms that allow registration of names within TLDs are called "Internet Registrars."

DNS is the technical system that allows human-friendly names, like http://www.whitehouse.gov, that stand for IP addresses, like 209.183.33.23, to function on the Internet. While the DNS is a massive and globally decentralized system, there is one shared global resource that is required for the proper functioning of the Internet on a global basis. This system is called the "DNS Root Server System." The Root Server System is arguably the single most critical component of Internet infrastructure. Most people

Table 6.1.1 Cyber Security Policy Issues Concerning Net Neutrality

Policy statement		Explanation	Reasons for controversy
6.1.1.1	The operation of the DNS Root Server System shall be performed under contract with some entity or entities.	Presently, the DNS Root Server System is run on a volunteer basis.	The volunteer approach has served the Internet exceptionally well, and ensures a democratic representation from interested stakeholders willing to invest resources in the success of an international communications system. The criticality of the DNS Root Server System requires more formal oversight to ensure agreed-upon policies can be enforced. The United States or ICANN should formally delegate this authority to an accountable party. Allowing the U.S. government to make decisions for the Internet root server administration process is an unnecessary projection of U.S. power and risks fragmentation of the Internet into multiple unconnected or semiconnected national networks. Similarly, contracting with ICANN or a standards body is similarly difficult because these entities exist as corporations subject to national laws in the jurisdiction in which they are domiciled.
6.1.1.2	The Internet Center for Assigned Names and Numbers (ICANN) shall be required to allocate a percentage of its revenues for security and resilience.	Since the Internet has had no single point of administration or control, it has been difficult to shape the Internet that is secure and controlled. Some feel that the present IANA and DNS root functions are antiquated	All nations rely on the Internet and a secure and resilient backbone. ICANN develops security protocols that ensure its control of the DNS system so that the system cannot be filtered or censored by repressive regimes with local control over telecommunications carriers. Because the Internet has historically had no single point of administration or control, it would be enormously difficult to shape the Internet to add controls that some countries may not want. Countries resistant to central control may instead use the control technology to create national borders. Although many stakeholders want a more secure Internet, others may want the opposite, an Internet that is open to allow control over what each nation's citizens may or may not see or say. Increasing the level of control would restrict the ability of countries to remain open and freely accessible.
6.1.1.3	ICANN shall turn over responsibility for Internet name and number space to the International Telecommunications Union (ITU).	This policy would put Internet administration in the hands of the same division of the United Nations that establishes agreement on telephone service issues.	The ITU has a long history and tradition of being involved in global telecommunications efforts and can be a significant global force to improve cyber security. Not only will this help the developing world to use cyberspace to improve their economy, it will help other nations by establishing security policies as it did for stabilizing phone services between nations. The ITU is good at connecting various national telecommunication systems, not at unifying them. If ITU was in charge of the Internet, there is a risk that the Internet could morph from a single global network into a collection of national Internets. The Internet name and number system should remain a multistakeholder governance model to ensure the involvement of nonprofit groups, individuals, and interested corporations. The ITU, as with any bureaucracy (especially a part of the United Nations) can be slow to move and adapt to new technologies or international conditions. Moreover, since each nation only gets one vote, countries devoted to censorship of their own populations could take over the Internet development agenda. The UN government-centric model makes it impossible for individual Internet users and corporate interests to participate in an ITU-driven Internet governance model.

(Continued)

Table 6.1.1 (*Continued*)

Policy statement		Explanation	Reasons for controversy
6.1.1.4	ISPs shall offer connectivity services equally to all individuals for any lawful use without discrimination.	This policy is referred to as "net neutrality" because it requires companies to offer the same services to all equally.	This policy should make it difficult if not impossible for Internet communication to be partitioned according to any political, social, or commercial agenda.
			This policy will protect e-commerce services from being cut off from customers due to their choice of ISP.
			There is no evidence that ISPs intend to segregate traffic. This policy does not allow ISPs control over the marketing of their own resources.
			This policy has the potentially unintended consequence that ISPs will be limited in their ability to inspect network traffic, and thus restricted from providing potentially valuable security services.
			This policy is typically recommended to be enforced only at the carrier level, when in fact it is the local and peer connectivity service providers who currently have limited sets of service offerings.
			The Internet of today is no longer an experiment, but is a business operated by profit-seeking firms. It should be allowed to function in a manner that generates profits for those companies that operate and maintain it, while providing goods and services at a level that customers are willing to pay for. Economic supply and demand should drive Internet operations, not mandatory access to all locations with no regard for cost or consumer demand.
			If enforced at all, policy would result in regulatory oversight that would present significant costs to ISPs and so create a barrier to entry for small business.
6.1.1.5	ISPs shall require substantial proof of identification from all customers, and log all Internet connectivity from each customer so it can be available for potential law enforcement measures.	ISPs currently do not actively dissuade anonymous access. This policy would require them to strongly identify all users, similar to a bank's requirements to Know Your Customer.	Anonymous access to the Internet facilitates cyber crime by allowing individuals to remain anonymous or hide behind false identities.
			The Internet has long been accepted as a place where anonymous free speech can be conducted. Requiring positive identification of all users will severely impact the ability for citizens of all countries to express themselves in a manner that has no attribution.
			Any systematic identification and log requirements would undoubtedly be abused by law enforcement, especially in countries that restrict free speech and other personal liberties. Anonymous Internet communications played a significant role in the Middle Eastern revolutions of 2011.

| 6.1.1.6 | ISPs shall offer security services to filter malware and other criminal activities. | This policy would require all ISP to make methods of detecting and preventing the transmission of malicious software available to their clients upon request. These services are often referred to as "Clean Pipe" and/or "Deep Packet Inspection." | This requirement would give ISPs the right to inspect all content sent or received by their clients.
This requirement would slow all Internet transmission as all content would be required to be inspected. It would not catch all malicious software as zero-day threats and social engineering attacks would not be part of the filters.
This requirement may end up in filtering out unusual protocols which may be necessary to operate unusual systems such as industrial control system, which could have devastating consequences if it interfered with the command and control features of those systems.
This requirement could be abused by including nonmalicious software or communications in the list of malicious software to be filtered. Political or commercial competitors could effectively be removed from the Internet.
This requirement would save all Internet customers from expensive and time-consuming malware and antivirus activities.
Liability would be unclear in terms of how much responsibility ISPs would have for missing malware or criminal behavior.
This requirement could lead to general filtering of any content deemed "unsafe" by a governing body, including political speech, music, or video downloads, photographs, and other censored content. |
| 6.1.1.7 | ISPs shall filter at their client connections to ensure that source address in incoming traffic is within some legitimate network prefix range allocated to the corresponding customer. | This policy would require that customers own the address space that they request their ISP to route. | This policy would prevent hosting services from offering Internet Gateway services and thus create a barrier to entry in the ISP marketplace.
This policy would require the establishment of a trusted repository of allocated IP address space (commonly called "prefixes") that includes the owning organization and the ISP that connects that organization to the Internet.
This policy would ensure that any entity that routes to the Internet is accountable to identify the origination of the traffic they actually route. |

(Continued)

Table 6.1.1 *(Continued)*

	Policy statement	Explanation	Reasons for controversy
6.1.1.8	All organizations that route Internet traffic shall register their route "policies" with third-party routing registries; these shall be continuously audited for compliance with ICANN agreements, and entities shall be accountable for compliance with declared and audited "policies."	ICANN participant agreements require adherence to route "policies" where the word "policy" modifying the word "route" is used to refer to the technical implementation of a standard, as described in Chapter 1, Section 1.3.4. This is a requirement for transparency and consistency in technical configuration of routes within their sphere of control.	The Internet operates smoothly without this level of control, organizations are responsible for correctly announcing their own route policies, and if they do not, they should be entitled to take the corresponding security risk that their number space could be announced by others. This policy would force registered entities to comply with ICANN agreements, which would reduce the probability of disruptive routing events. An example of the event that would be averted is the time that Pakistan Telecom announced a route for a subset of YouTube's registered address space which contained the YouTube DNS servers, and the route change diverted the majority of YouTube traffic to Pakistan. The policy would reduce the flexibility of registered entities from dynamically changing their route policies as needed to respond to changes in the Internet marketplace. There is no way to enforce compliance with this policy, so it would be superfluous. It would create overhead for compliance organizations while not preventing route hijacking by noncompliant ones.
	All organizations that route Internet traffic shall filter out announcements of unallocated and private address spaces based on publicly available information. These are filters that should be the same everywhere and applied globally.	The requirement not to route the private address space is currently in the ICANN handbook. This policy would extend it to all unallocated space.	This policy would ensure that no traffic sourced from private or unallocated addresses would be able to traverse the Internet. Although address space could still be anonymously appropriated, it would be associated with a legitimate address-space stakeholder who should be motivated to control the routes to their own number space. Several organizations maintain updated "bogon" (short for bogus networks) lists that can be used as a starting point for filtering private and unallocated address spaces. This is a commonly accepted practice at most ISPs which this policy would simply expand. To enforce this policy would require that lists of allocated address space be available from authoritative servers at every Internet access point. There is no mechanism for either identifying authoritative sources or replicating databases of address space, and establishment of this process would likely be fraught with errors that would inadvertently disconnect network segments.

are surprised to learn that the physical computer servers that comprise the DNS Root Server System are owned and operated by volunteers without contracts with any party. This is an artifact of the early days of the Internet when it was implemented more as a cooperative than a critical component of the global infrastructure. However, the present model has worked well in that the owners/operators appear to take their responsibility seriously and no major issues with these systems have ever materialized.

For example:

192.168.101.1   http://www.mycompany.com
192.168.101.4   http://mail.mycompany.com

With a publication like this, a company establishes that the computer named http://www.mycompany.com can be found at the Internet address "192.168.101.1." This publication allows other entities to query a DNS server by providing a computer name as input to the server, and receiving the computer number as output from the DNS server.

The numbers in this example are analogous to the telephone numbers that old movies and sitcoms were required to use to make sure that they did not inadvertently broadcast any individual's personal phone number in a fictional context. Those fictional phone numbers always started with "555" and the prefix "555" was not used by any actual phone number. In the Internet, there are a few sets of similar "unallocated" numbers (Rekhter, Moskowitz et al. 1996). They allow companies to number their internal network on a way that should never be routed on the Internet. Another reason why this is necessary is because there are not enough Internet addresses for everyone that wishes to connect. Hence, major companies and ISPs use a technique called Network Address Translation (NAT) to maximize the number of people that they connect with unallocated address space, and allow multiple computers to appear on the Internet using the same address.

However, the present model has worked well in that the owners/operators appear to take their responsibility seriously and no major issues with these systems have ever materialized. Many also feel the distributed and volunteer nature of the root server operators also presents positive governance features in that these servers are not under the oversight of any one entity or government (RSTA ongoing). A new version of the network communications protocol, Internet Protocol Version 6 (IPv6), would expand the address space to allow 2^{128} addresses.

A major concern with Internet names and numbers is that of either accidental or intentional diversion of Internet traffic to unauthorized destinations. For example, the translation from Internet names to Internet numbers can be subverted by a cyber attack called DNS poisoning. DNS poisoning refers to the corruption of a DNS server so that it stores an incorrect address for a given computer name. The incorrect address is usually a malicious site designed to look just like the website on the computer named in the query. DNS poisoning allows attackers to divert legitimate user traffic to malicious sites without their knowledge, and without touching the user's computer, simply by attacking the DNS server that the user queries for addresses. The security of both the user desktop and website of the company whose traffic is diverted may be impeccable, but nevertheless, both experience damage.

DNS was not designed with security in mind and is vulnerable to poisoning, man-in-the-middle attacks in which DNS queries are intercepted prior to reaching the server, and other subversive tactics. The Domain Name System Security Extensions (DNSSEC) were created to address these concerns. The process uses public-private key cryptography to authenticate DNS records with the authoritative source. Public key cryptography allows data that are encrypted with the private key of a DNS server to be decrypted by anyone with its public key, and vice versa. For DNSSEC to work effectively, a DNS server public key must be distributed in such a manner that users can verify its integrity. Then users can encrypt queries that can only be decrypted by the target DNS server, and DNS servers can encrypt responses with a private key. The public-private key cryptographic algorithms are designed to assure anyone holding a DNS public key who successfully decrypts a DNS response that the response must have come from the server holding the private key. Often referred to as a digital signature, the public-private key technology allows the key holder to sign data with the private key in such a way that allows the public key to be used to verify the digital signature. If the signature matches, the data are assumed to have been sealed by the sender. Note that because the public key is known to anyone, digital signatures do not facilitate confidentiality, merely data provenance and integrity.

As illustrated in Figure 6.1, DNSSEC takes advantage of the hierarchical nature of Internet domain names to distribute public keys. Although it is not required by software, technically all domain names end in ".". That is,

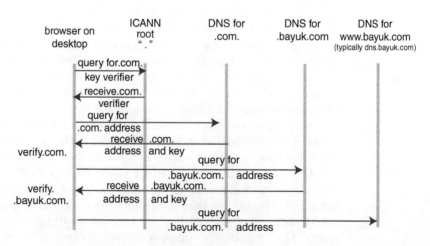

Figure 6.1   Message sequence diagram for DNSSEC.

".com" is really ".com." by design, so the "." is the root of the key hierarchy. Enterprises are assumed to be able to get a good copy of the root key and store it safely on their own DNS server (the protocol refers to this as a "trust anchor"). ICANN holds the public key for "." and for each top-level domain (TLD) issued on the Internet. These keys may be used to verify records at the next level of the hierarchy. Private keys for each server are used with a cryptographic algorithm to create a verification record for a given domain in the level below it, and the verification record is stored in the DNS record for the domain's DNS server. Output from a DNSSEC verification algorithm can be "yes, the address is verified," "the address is bad," or "it cannot be verified because some keys are not available." An authoritative DNS server that is DNSSEC-enabled will produce standard DNS records and DNSSEC cryptographic signatures for each record. The parent DNS server (.com in the case of example.com) will provide a cryptographic DNSSEC record to identify the real "example.com" thus eliminating the possibility that someone could be running a fraudulent "example.com" domain. The requestor can verify the integrity of a DNS record, say, www. example.com, by requesting DNSSEC records from example.com, .com, and the root (".") and cryptographically verifying the entire chain of signatures.

Despite its obvious utility, DNSSEC is a recent development and is not yet widely used. The DNS root was signed in 2010, and the largest TLD (".com") allowed publication of signatures for child domains ("example. com") in September 2010. There is processing overhead involved in using cryptography. Many sites have not established keys. Moreover, even if it was widely used, the process still relies on operating system and software security, and so there are still many malicious ways to bypass or subvert the process.

Cyber security policy issues with Internet names and numbers center on the adoption of technology to combat the bypass of DNS and routing protocols and to enforce agreements between ICANN, TLD registries, and registrars. The first few concern DNSs, the second few address issues related to routing traffic to the correct Internet numbers once they are identified by DNSs. The table ends with a few policies on potential regulation (Table 6.1.2).

6.1.3 Copyrights and Trademarks

Even if all Internet name to number routing was always accurate, there will still be users who are directed to websites that do not belong to the company they intended to visit. This occurs when companies do not register all the possible Internet domain names that seem straightforward representations of the company name. For example, a company named "product" may have registered product.com but not product.net. A competitor may register product.net and purchase the search term "product." Then when users search for the word "product" they see the

Table 6.1.2 Cyber Security Policy Issues Concerning Internet Names and Numbers

Policy statement	Explanation	Reasons for controversy
6.1.2.1 All DNS names shall be associated with individuals or corporations who are accountable for services provided under them.	The system that stores and makes information available about the owner of a domain is called Whois. The accuracy of the Whois is of critical concern to law enforcement, which often needs to locate the owner of a domain engaged in criminal activity. However, the accuracy of Whois information is suspect because domain name registrars do not always have the incentive to validate the information they receive.	Domain name registrars often have low margin business models. Extensive authentication and validation of users wishing to purchase names may increase domain registration costs. The scope of the Whois accuracy problem is not fully known and has not been formally studied. Some are concerned that strong authentication and validation of domain name registrants may present free-speech issues.
6.1.2.2 DNS server operators shall be licensed, and failure to maintain proper security controls shall result in loss of license.	This policy would require that any entity who publishes Internet name to number translations is subject to regulation.	Expectations for future reliability of the Internet will be greatly influenced by the success or failure of implementing secure and more robust DNS. Any server on the Internet may run services that translate Internet names to numbers. This policy would impose requirements on those who advertised such services to observe secure protocols for verifying the authenticity of name to number mappings. Operators of domain name services that are vulnerable to attack are complicit in Internet crimes they enable. There should be penalties for answering queries for domain name addresses with inaccurate network addresses. This policy would introduce needless bureaucracy that may be a barrier to entry for small businesses wishing to engage in Internet services. This policy may decrease the probability that Internet users would not be subject to DNS poisoning attacks. Issues of licensing and regulation with respect to the Internet raise serious jurisdictional issues. The Internet is present in all jurisdictions on Earth; regulating components of the fundamental naming and numbering infrastructure—which must be available in all jurisdictions in order for proper functioning of the Internet—may be impractical or impossible.

6.1.2.3	Operators of border gateway protocol routers shall be penalized for routing traffic to locations that are not registered for them.	Companies that are entrusted with transmitting traffic between network entities signed agreements with ICANN to submit that traffic in accordance with published routes, but there is currently no penalty for noncompliance.	The security and continued functioning of the Internet will be greatly influenced by the success or failure of implementing more secure and more robust Border Gateway Protocol (BGP). Entities who take responsibility for routing Internet traffic should be accountable for both their mistakes and facilitating criminal activities.
			Any replication of allocated address space to distributed databases would introduce delay in Internet connectivity. This would slow the pace of Internet commerce.
			The database of Internet addresses has not always been fastidiously administered. Allocation records may be incorrect. Automated filtering may inadvertently disconnect entities with small allocations.
			As any entity connected to the Internet may establish routes using the border gateway protocol, this policy would be very difficult if not impossible to enforce. No one entity has jurisdiction over all entities on the Internet, and penalties in the form of exclusion from routing would require 100% cooperation from the entire Internet community.
6.1.2.4	Government telecommunications regulatory agencies shall recommend and enforce effective and efficient means of securing telecommunications infrastructure.	This policy would require telecommunications regulators to be proactive and proscriptive in recommending cyber security improvements to the telecommunications infrastructure.	This policy acknowledges that regulatory agencies have insight into issues faced by telecommunications operators, and also objectivity that is not found within the companies themselves, so they are best suited for the task of recommending cyber security measures.
			Regulators should state objectives for cyber security rather than recommend means for achieving it. The experts on how to achieve objectives will always be the owner/operators.

result "product.net." They assume that they have found the company they are looking for and proceed to the product.net website. Though perhaps unethical, such practices are not always illegal. Even if they are illegal, there is no guarantee that the perpetrator will be caught or prosecuted. If caught, they may just be banned from using that search term and proceed to prey on a different competitor's customers. In extreme cases, companies who were late to the Internet may have had their company names intentionally registered by "domain squatters," which is a derogatory term used to refer to people who register domain names for the purpose of selling them to the highest bidder. ICANN has extensive policies and mechanisms to address domain name-related disputes.

Another form of domain squatting is to register domain names that are very similar to the takeover target, such as misspellings of the domain name, or adding numbers or seemingly innocuous community of interest identifiers to the end of the domain name, for example, a competitor or criminal trying to lure a company's customers may register "prodoct.com," "product1.com," or "product-ny.com" in an attempt to make their site appear legitimate. Where this type of domain squatting is conducted with the criminal intent, the typical pattern is to make the site look just like the login page of the target site, and use this page to collect the names and passwords of customers who mistake the criminal site for the real one. Such sites are typically also guilty of copyright violation as they display logos and other proprietary trademarks from the target domain. Competitors may also falsely advertise their own products under a logo belonging to a competitor.

Security technology for the purpose of warning a user that a site may be a counterfeit has been around since the late 1990s. As described in Chapter 1, it started when the browser vendors then changed the message delivered to the user when a root certificate could not be found for a given web server to say that the site was not secure and the user was taking a risk by visiting it. The user still had the ability to add root certificates to their browsers, but the security warning scared them, so most companies gradually gave in to the pressure of client concern and gave up running their own certificate authorities. The certificates purchased from the security vendors would periodically expire and leave sites unable to encrypt traffic, creating emergencies for company web server administrators. This customer service issue for security certificate vendors prompted them to create processes by which certificates had to be quickly and easily administered and delivered. These processes are often infiltrated by Internet hackers to generate and/or steal both root and server certificates that allow them to impersonate company web servers in the SSL mutual identification process. Even where impostor sites do not do a good job of perfectly imitating a site, users get so many pop-up warnings from legitimate Internet sites, many are inclined to accept any and all warning messages simply to get their jobs done (Herley 2009).

Copyright and trademark infringement is a cyber security threat not just because of lost business, but because the business transacted at such sites is mistaken for their own business practices. They sometimes become aware of the counterfeit site only after being sued for product liability and finding that the supposed customer has purchased a counterfeit product. Very popular companies have established divisions in their law departments with the sole mission of addressing such Internet fraud. Cyber security services advertise the ability to find a company logo wherever it appears on the Internet in order to combat such fraud.

Note that instances of name space squatting are not limited to domain names. In public addresses since leaving office, Colin Powell has cautioned that the "Colin Powell" entry in social networking sites is often not him, and urged his audience to register themselves in all currently popular sites simply to ensure that no one else takes their name (Powell 2009). The large communities who both trust and are loyal to social networking name spaces have made them a target for domain squatters both competitive and criminal. They have the same power to mislead as domain names themselves.

The cyber security policy statements in this section start with domain name issues. These are followed by content-related statements. The last few describe social networking concerns (Table 6.1.3).

6.1.4 Email and Messaging

Company impersonation has never been so blatant as it is in email. Even though the Morris worm exposed just how insecure the protocol was, there was no concern that the email servers would be impersonated. The actual exchange between two email servers is displayed in Figure 6.2. In the example of the communication between two email servers, there is clear text content and there is no authentication required. The protocol allows for the information to be typed into a command line, so it is not even necessary to have email server software to impersonate an email server using this protocol. Although some servers may require the presentation of a key for authentication or may restrict connections to a prespecified IP address, as long as any one server in the email relay between a sender and receiver supports a text-only-based command string as illustrated in Figure 6.2, then any individual on the Internet is spoof-able. Although email impersonation may happen from a person's own inbox due to malicious software running on their computer, simply having the email address of a person is enough to enable an impostor impersonate them to an email server, and this is what is illustrated in the example below. This ease of impersonation is why a person may occasionally be contacted by friends who say, "you sent me an email about X" and the supposed sender has no clue what they are talking about.

Table 6.1.3 Cyber Security Policy Issues Concerning Copyright and Trade Issues

Policy statement	Explanation	Reasons for controversy
6.1.3.1	It shall not be possible to own an Internet domain name without providing evidence of legitimate claim to the domain name requested.	This policy would place the burden of claim to a domain name on the registrant at the time of registration rather than waiting until they may be sued by the rightful owner.	Enforcement of this policy would require an evidence evaluation process, and thus unnecessarily delay the progress of e-commerce for 99.999% of the traffic for honest Internet registrants, without thwarting a determined attempt to deceive the evaluation process. This policy would limit opportunities for domain squatting and hoarding.
6.1.3.2	Registrants shall be limited in the number of sites they can own that are not active with legitimate e-commerce activity, and no company or individual shall be able to register domain names for the purpose of selling them.	This policy would end the practice of registering domain names in order to hoard them and sell them to others with requirements for e-commerce activity on those domains.	This policy would limit a lucrative business opportunity among creative individuals who envision what domain names will be popular in the future and offer them for sale to those who may benefit from their creativity. This policy is easy to bypass in that individuals would find a way to display legitimate-looking websites for the domains they registered while it would have the unintended consequence of preventing legitimate companies from hoarding domain names that were similar to their own, such as misspellings.
6.1.3.3	Sites that display content watermarked by another company shall be immediately removed from the Internet.	This policy would provide companies with a technical security measure to mark their content in a way that would allow automated detection and also an irrefutable conclusion that that any other company who displayed it was unauthorized.	Sites that display content that has been watermarked by a company with legitimate claim to the content should be held accountable for copyright violation without requiring expensive legal efforts on the part of the victim. The only way to take down Internet sites at the ISP level is to filter the IP address. There are some security services that provide lists of domain names that are malicious, but they typically do not include copyright violations, just crimeware repositories. As any site can reappear at a different address, and also a different domain name, this policy is not enforceable. Any filtering of Internet sites creates substantial free-speech and due-process issues.

6.1.3.4	No trademark or logo shall be displayed without the express permission of the owner.	It has become common practice for Internet sites to display logos of other companies. For example, a logo may illustrate a news or blog story, or a vendor may display a customer logo as part of an announcement that the company has bought their product.	This practice associates a company with the offending site without their permission and often damages their brand. Intellectual property lawyers are constantly incited to send cease and desist letters for inappropriate logo usage. This policy would save countless hours in unnecessary legal process. The practice of using logos as shorthand for a company in communication media is a timesaver for the information consumer. It is not normally intended or interpreted as endorsement by the company, so this policy is completely unnecessary.
6.1.3.5	Theft of digital certificates shall be subject to the same legal status as left of trademark or logo.	Digital certificates allow encrypted communication using keys that can be verified to have been issued by or sold to a specific company. Realistic Internet impersonation of a company's website often requires use of these certificates.	The only reason anyone would steal a digital certificates is to impersonate another company, so even simple possession of someone else's certificate should be evidence of intention to commit company impersonation. Digital certificates routinely are copied from computer to computer and service providers who manage multiple websites will often possess many certificates belonging to clients or potential clients.
6.1.3.6	Any policy that concerns a company or individual right to Internet name space shall also apply to name spaces in social networking sites.	This policy would include social networking name space in any policy that established restrictions on Internet name space infractions on copyright, trademark, and/or identity issues in general.	As social networking becomes more ubiquitous, the ability to maintain control over one's brand, whether corporate or individual, becomes more elusive. This policy would ensure that abuses identified and corrected in policy concerning Internet domain space are not revisited from scratch for the social networking domains. Social networking domains are privately run and have a wide variety of options for participation. There is no reason to assume that intellectual property issues that apply at the Internet level apply to all social networking sites.

```
$ telnet mail.company.com 25
Trying 192.168.142.13
Connected to mail.company.com.
Escape character is '^]'.
220 mail
SMTP/smap Ready.
helo
250 Charmed, I'm sure.
mail from:spoofvictim@anothercompany.com
250 <spoofvictim@anothercompany.com>...
Sender Ok
rcpt to: unsuspecting@company.com
250 unsuspecting@company.com
OK
Data
354 Enter mail, end with "." on a line by itself
malicious message text goes here.
250 Mail
Accepted
quit
221 Closing connection
Connection closed by foreign host.
$
```

Figure 6.2 Example email server communication protocol.

Advertisers embrace the openness of email server communications because they can identify customers using these open protocols. For example, if a company email server answers commands as in Figure 6.2, then an advertiser's automated program can attempt to send email communication to and eventually reach the whole population. They can do this by replacing the word "unsuspecting" with every possible spelling of a user name at that company. When errors occur, they simply cease the attempt and move to the next guess at a name. Moreover, it allows an advertiser to approach potential customers using "From" addresses with creative domain names that catch attention while there is no need to actually register them. When advertisers send email to a large quantity of potential customers without discriminating which of the potential recipients may actually have interest in their product, this is called "spam." Spam is a canned product that can include any variety of meat. It was highlighted in an old comedy sketch as the only thing on the menu, despite the fact that it occupied multiple distinct menu items (Monty Python 1970). In the early days of the Internet, users would use the word "spam" to describe content they had no wish to see, and excessive unwanted multiple postings elicited "spam" as the reply from angry users. The term spam now generically refers to any unwanted email content (Furr 1990). Both for profit and not-for-profit Internet watchdogs keep records of spam in order to identify perpetrators with the goal of reducing unwanted noise (Spamhaus ongoing) but, and any Internet user knows, these efforts are largely unsuccessful.

Another category of unwanted email is called phishing, a phonetic play on the word fishing. It refers to baiting, or luring, Internet users to click on links that take them to malicious websites. The malicious sites may be domain squatting look-alikes that collect user names and passwords. They may download malware. They may be fraudulent scams to trick users into transferring money from their bank accounts. When a specific set of high net worth individuals are targeted by phishing emails, it is called spear-phishing, in analogy with whales as the target. There are as many types of phishing attacks as there are Internet criminals.

Hence, both legitimate and illegitimate businesses routinely send excessive unwanted email, and the blatant ability to spoof email communication has been tolerated by the Internet community. There is very little incentive among e-commerce-related vendors to restrict it and no ability for a company or individual to do anything about it without cutting themselves off from potential customer or friend email communications. Most companies pay for Internet services in units of bandwidth, or the number of ones and zeros that can traverse a telecommunications line at the same time. The more email traversing the line, the more bandwidth a company needs. Telecommunications equipment providers also charge more by bandwidth. So if a company expected to need 100 GB of simultaneous bandwidth, both the ISP and the router vendor make more money. Hence, there has not been a great deal of effort among Internet vendors to cut down on unwanted or even criminally motivated phishing.

However, as spam is also used by criminals, and identity theft is rampant, some consumer rights organizations have provided some incentive to track and shut down known spammers (Spamhaus ongoing). In 2008, a company in the spam business was investigated by security researchers and eventually closed, with the immediate result of a 40% decrease in the number of unwanted emails worldwide (Vijayan 2008). Subsequently, the U.S. Federal Trade Commission has taken action against spam. However, the spam business is still thriving, and there has been no systematic attempt, public or private, to improve the quality of email security going forward. However, there are some technologies available to companies that wish to secure email communications that are in their own controls (BITS 2007). One is Sender ID Framework (SIDF), which utilizes DNS to identify the authorized email server for a domain and does not allow email from a domain unless the sending server is identified in the DNS records for the domain when a valid signature is expected. DomainKeys Identified Mail (DKIM) goes a step further and allows an encryption key to be stored in DNS, so companies can set rules to permit, rejection, deletion, or tag unsigned or improperly signed messages from a given business partner. The third is Transport Layer Security (TLS), which is called an *opportunistic* protocol because it can be set to require the highest level of security that is available on the server with which it communicates. At the lowest level, it does not authenticate the sender, and does not require communication to be encrypted, but at the highest level, it authenticates the sender and encrypts the communications so it cannot be observed by third parties eavesdropping on Internet traffic between two email servers.

Like the word *content*, the word *messaging* is a technical term of the Internet trade. Any security techniques that apply to email can generally be applied to text messaging or Internet chat capabilities, and these capabilities are referred to colloquially as *messaging*. Messaging technologies rely on protocols between sender and receiver that rarely authenticate, but simply identify the sender via a "user name" string presented as part of the message stream itself.

The cyber security policies listed for email and messaging begin with the common requirements that email and messaging be recognized as under the umbrella of enterprise or mission security. These are followed by more systemic issues related to spam and accountability in general (Table 6.1.4).

6.2 Cyber User Issues

To connect to a network is to be a user of cyberspace. Approximately 30% of the world's population is Internet-connected (Miniwatts ongoing). In addition to traditional business relationships now moved online as described in Chapter 3, the Internet has spawned new e-commerce business models over the past two decades. These include Internet-only storefronts that are separate from traditional brick-and-mortar sales locations, Internet sales wherein customers pick up merchandise from a physical store, and the use of targeted advertising to mobile shoppers who are price-comparing online while still shopping in traditional business location. Although e-commerce advertising had originally only mirrored pre-Internet public relations and marketing activities, several new marketing models have also emerged that did not exist prior to Internet ubiquity. These are information services that gather information from one corner of the cyberspace and sell it to another. Sometimes referred to as "the user is not the customer" models, these range from online surveys to large networks of monitoring systems designed to track user habits of everything from food preferences to political beliefs. The primary customer for this information is the advertising industry.

Security issues for cyber users have mostly arisen from unintended side effects of the e-commerce race to participate in new markets (Khusial and McKegney 2005). E-commerce transactions flow between the shopper, the shopper's computer, the network connection between shopper and e-commerce web server, the e-commerce web server, and e-commerce vendor internal network, and the connections between the e-commerce vendor and the service providers they need to close the transaction, such as a credit card payment clearing company. All of these connections are created using software, and any of that software may have a bug or a flaw that allows an intruder to observe cyber user data flow or disrupt the e-commerce transaction. In many of these points of connectivity,

Table 6.1.4 Cyber Security Policy Issues Concerning Email and Messaging

Policy statement		Explanation	Reasons for controversy
6.1.4.1	All entities that participate in electronic commerce shall offer customers the ability to verify their email server via standard protocols.	This policy would require e-commerce companies to publish keys for their email servers in DNS.	Consumers have a right to verify that messages from service providers and other vendors have not been spoofed. It is irresponsible to communicate via email with customers and to offer this capability. Consumers do not generally have email server verification software and so would have to rely on their ISP or hosting service providers to verify email authenticity. This requirement is thus better left to market forces.
6.1.4.2	All email communications on behalf cf or concerning the organization shall utilize organization-supported email services.	This is a requirement that people use their own organization's email systems when conducting the business of the organization, and refrain from such communication over yahoo, social networking sites, personal cell phones, and other public or private communications services.	This policy keeps all communications in range of management monitoring. It minimizes the number of people with administrative access to internal staff administrators. This policy inhibits the communication ability of individuals who may not be able to reach corporate services due to travel or outages.
6.1.4.3	Delivery and read receipts on email shall provide proof of electronic information delivery.	Various contractual and regulatory clauses require organizations who serve notifications to provide proof that the individual to whom the notification was sent actually received it. A noncyber example is certified mail.	The ability to use electronic delivery and read receipts as proof of delivery cuts costs for organizations that are legally accountable for notifying individuals in a variety of domains, from banking and insurance to municipalities and law enforcement. Current standards for authenticating digital records require a combination of key management, cryptographic algorithms, and proof of organizational control procedures. There is no infrastructure that allows such authentication that is common across Internet email systems.
6.1.4.4	Individuals shall have the ability to place their email addresses on a list which would make it illegal for marketers to send them unwanted email.	This is the equivalent of a national "do not call" registry for email solicitation. This type of list is currently used for phone numbers. Marketing companies are required to omit phone numbers on the do not call list from phone marketing campaigns.	A "do-not-email" policy enforcement mechanism to protect email addresses from unwanted solicitation would significantly reduce the number of unsolicited advertisements currently received via email. This policy should make illegitimate spam easier to recognize. Enforcement of the policy would save both bandwidth and storage resources by reducing the number of unwanted messages. Email is an effective way to reach consumers, and consumers who have expressed preferences for products and services via various online activities would continue to be solicited under this policy. It may be difficult to draw the line on what constitutes interest, and therefore the policy would be difficult to enforce. A major source of revenue for some e-commerce businesses is the email address lists they can generate based on their observations of Internet traffic. The value of these assets would be would be significantly adversely impacted.

(Continued)

Table 6.1.4 (Continued)

Policy statement		Explanation	Reasons for controversy
6.1.4.5	Internet messaging services shall allow users to select a community with whom to exchange messages and exclude all	This is the equivalent of an individual "white list" for each potential email recipient. Only those on the list would be allowed to send email or messages to the recipient.	This policy would allow Internet users to control their own resources and minimize the number of unwanted messages. It would save both bandwidth and storage resources. As there is no generally accepted authentication method for email or messaging, anyone may bypass this policy by impersonating any user on the white list. It is therefore unenforceable.
6.1.4.6	Individuals using the originators of the shall be required to use only Internet domain names for which they are registered.	This would restrict the use of *From* addresses on email to those for which the sender has registered with ICANN.	Restriction of from addresses limits innovation in e-commerce marketing without providing any additional security as Add Grace Period (AGP) could easily be used to temporarily meet this requirement were it imposed. This requirement would provide some ability to trace the source of a message to its domain. Enforcement would require utilization of secure protocols and thus drive more accountability for spam and phishing.
6.1.4.7	Known senders of phishing email shall be prosecuted, and sentences shall be commensurate with the crimes enabled by potential information theft from phishing recipients.	This policy would impose identity theft penalties on those who send phishing email.	Phish email senders are a small part of a large community of organized crime. Though their crime may seem innocuous, it is a necessary prerequisite to a larger premeditated attack on an individual, and should be taken as seriously as the attack itself. The phishing email sender is most likely a business that send bulk email for a variety of clients, and cannot distinguish between legitimate and illegitimate clients, and should not bear the burden of identifying Internet criminals. Moreover, simply sending an email does not guarantee that a user will be taken in by the lure.

observation of data flow provides information that may be used for later attacks, such as observation of user names and passwords being used for impersonation and identity theft.

From a security perspective, there are four major players in the e-commerce environment: the customer; the retailer; the product vendor, wholesaler, or manufacturer; and the attacker. It is the attacker's goal to exploit one or more of the three other players for illegal gains. Using vulnerabilities in software, application configurations, hardware, and even user habits, an attacker will seek to exploit these vulnerabilities to the attacker's advantage. e-Commerce attacks are constantly occurring. However, major media reporting on cyber security issues is confined to high-profile issues. Only the most interesting cases of fraud with the most severe consequences for the victims ever make it to the front page. Nevertheless, there is as much day-to-day activity in the information security cyber criminal circuit as there is in the drug circuit. In the book *Zero Day Threat*, two *USA Today* reporters describe the phenomenon as the product of three archetypes: *exploiters, enablers*, and *expeditor* (Acohido and Swartz 2008). Exploiters carry out data theft and fraud. Enablers are businesses whose practices allow it. Expeditors are technologists who identify the root cause from a technical point of view, though they may be attackers or defenders. The book is full of vignettes about organized crime "exploiters" systematically stealing data from unwitting consumers by impersonating the consumer at "enabler" banks. The exploiters not only exploit the consumer, an identity theft victim, but also exploit low-level social misfits, such as meth addicts. They enlist the social misfits to withdraw unwitting consumers' cash out of automatic teller machines or to order luxuries on the unwitting consumers' credit cards. The stories sporadically include tales of victories of law enforcement "expeditors" who figure out how the exploiters did it. The moral of every sad story is that the enabler did not sufficiently protect data within its custody, while an evil genius controlling three or more layers of organized criminal structure above the social misfits is never actually caught. The consumer is left with damaged credit, as well as loss of time and money, while the enabler claims that "adequate" risk measures are in place to secure the enterprise.

This section divides cyber user security issues into six subsections: malvertising, impersonation, appropriate use, cyber crime, geographic location ("geolocation"), and privacy. Malvertising is an anagram of the words "malicious" and "advertising." Impersonation deals with various types of impostors on the Internet, from anonymous postings to account hijacking. Appropriate use addresses common Internet behaviors that some deem antisocial, and may not be criminal simply because they have not yet been formally considered by legislators. Cyber crime addresses the organized criminal activity that is pervasive in e-commerce. Geolocation of Internet users, both consumers and criminals, is very difficult to determine, and presents its own special set of policy issues. Privacy is one of the concerns that fuels debates on cyber security geolocation policies, but privacy is a much broader set of issues, and so it has its own subsection.

6.2.1 Malvertising

e-Commerce businesses that rely on advertising typically utilize "mash-ups" to integrate multiple software sources (e.g., maps and coupons) onto a single page. The common element is that they are designed to attract consumers in a desired demographic, the advertising "target." One method of reaching the target is to identify web pages frequented by the target and purchase ads directly on those web pages. The web page owner/seller may require that the ad be provided to them for placement, or they could simply link to a site provider by the ad buyer and direct the user's browser to access the buyer's web content directly. This easy access to the Internet consumer has attracted criminals seeking to install malware. Like any ad buyer, they purchase Internet advertising from media networks and exchanges.

Malware is easy to distribute because numerous websites require Internet users to accept a wide variety of downloads in order to operate, and advertising software frequently continues to run in the background and connect back to the source site to send user tracking information. Malware does the same thing, and thus appears to the user like any other nuisance advertising process running on their computer. Malware that allows a computer to be remotely administered by the malware operator is referred to as a "bot" which is short for "robot." The correct interpretation of the analogy is that the person who unwittingly installed a bot on their computer has turned their computer into an instrument for the criminal operator. Multiple instances of bots administered by the same malware operator are called "botnets." Criminals use botnets as soldiers in cyber attacks.

Another type of cyber criminal lurking in the advertising community is engaged in click fraud, which is an automated way to impersonate a user clicking on an advertising link. Internet content providers typically charge advertisers based on the number of users who visit their websites and click on the advertiser's link. The content provider receives the click, records it in their billing records, and forwards the user's browser to the address of the advertiser's site, including a code in the forwarded universal resource location (URL) that specifies which site the user came from. The advertiser's web server received the user request to display a web page that is associated with the content provider's code. Both sides count the number of these clicks, and the advertiser pays the content provider based on the volume of user traffic sent from the content provider to the advertiser site. In click fraud, an automated program imitates the activity of an end user, simulating clicks on the advertiser's site from multiple Internet locations. The advertiser cannot tell the difference between the automated program and a real user, so it pays the content provider for the clicks. Savvy advertisers examine the browsing habits of users from different content provider sites and are sometimes able to pinpoint click fraud, but it is very hard to definitely prove.

A less frequently reported but still significant profit margin e-commerce criminal activity that comes under the heading of malvertising is coupon fraud. Online offers for coupons generally includes security codes and individual identification information intended to ensure that coupon are requested only by legitimate consumers. However, criminals often copy or modify coupons to increase values, decrease purchase requirements, defeat or eliminate security codes, extend or eliminate expiration dates, and/or alter disclaimers, terms and conditions. Moreover, they also sometimes create complete fake coupons from scratch. These counterfeits are then sold on the Internet for less than face value.

The policy statements in this section begin with malware issues that mostly not only impact the consumer, but also may impact the advertiser from the perspective of reputation. These are followed by click and coupon fraud issues, which impact only the advertising community or their direct customers (Table 6.2.1).

6.2.2 Impersonation

Impersonation on the Internet is easy not just because it is easy to register a domain name and email address that is not at all related to anything you are labeled, but because it is very difficult if not impossible for others to trace where you actually are. The ability of the Internet to obscure the origination of traffic is taken advantage of by criminals to cloak their activities in the guise of authorized use. In this age of routine business travel, authorized users have patterns of access from different cities on a daily basis. The communications from such users will vary with the business purpose of the specific visit.

It is very hard for some people to distinguish between an Internet user and a person. A person had an identity. A philosophical treatment of the concept may call it a "self," "soul," or "mind." A more practical concept is human placement in society in relationship to others, born to a mother, residing in a locality, responding to a name, and holding various documents bearing that name. Assuming that we agree on the definition of a person, and call that identity, we call identity in cyberspace *digital* identity. Digital identity is a completely different concept than identity. At the core, digital identity is a string in a computer database. That string is made up of 1s and 0s. It may or may not be the same string that an individual uses to log in to a computer, the string colloquially referred to as "login" or "user ID." That digital identity is stored in a database so that the identity can be automatically associated with other strings. One of these other strings is often a password. A password is not identity; it is a method by which identity may be verified or authenticated. In the early days of computer security, it became obvious that passwords could be shared,

Table 6.2.1 Cyber Security Policy Issues Concerning Malvertising

Policy statement	Explanation	Reasons for controversy
6.2.1.1 e-Commerce marketing that includes redirection of individual computers to sites via links that they did not intentionally follow shall be illegal.	Organized cyber criminals often purchase online advertising in order to direct user traffic to sites that infect their computers with malware.	This policy would eliminate a weak link in protection requirements around defense-related information and make it harder for espionage agents to learn about department of defense activities. This would radically change the manner in which advertisers currently use the Internet and require reengineering of most Internet sites and advertising business models worldwide.
6.2.1.2 It shall be illegal to install and run software on machines owned by someone else. All legitimate software execution shall be recognizable to the average computer user.	Websites frequented by consumers frequently require software to be running on the user desktop in order for the site to display properly. These sites often will run the software on the user's machine with minimal notice to the user that new software is being introduced to their system.	This type of policy would enlist the e-commerce software industry into helping the consumer manage his or her own desktop, and lay the framework for consumer awareness of the difference between legitimate and illegitimate software installs. This policy is aimed at helping the user tell what programs they intended to install and which are malicious. Although advertisers may claim this software is executed to enhance their ability to tailor ads to consumer preferences, organized crime uses these same mechanisms to trick users into installing malicious code.
6.2.1.3 Internet coupons shall identify the authorized consumer by name, address, and a unique identification number.	This policy is designed to ensure that Internet coupons are downloaded by legitimate consumers as opposed to resellers.	If manufacturers or retailers offer discounts via coupons in newspapers, no personally identifiable information is required to use them. This requirement for identification for Internet coupons represents an unnecessary invasion of privacy. Advertisers offering discounts should be able to verify that those who took advantage of the discounts are legitimate customers.

6.2.1.4	Internet advertisers charging for clicks shall be subject to regulatory standards and audit.	Click fraud is rampant, and establishing government oversight of the advertising community would be expected to deter such fraud.
		There are currently no barriers to entry in the advertising business. This would create a professional community who took fraud seriously.
		The advertising industry should judge the worth of individual advertisers based on revenue generated from aggregate clicks from a site, not from number of clicks. Regulatory guidance is not required, and should not be a substitute for astute business practices.
6.2.1.5	The Internet advertising community shall establish standards which would make it easy to spot and stop malvertising.	This policy would require the Internet advertising community to work together as is more typical of requirements for critical infrastructure industries such as banking or energy.
		Criminal advertising, click fraud, and coupon fraud are enabled by current advertising industry practices. This policy put the burden of a solution to these problems on the community that created them.
		The Internet advertising community is perhaps the least technical community on the Internet, and no amount of regulation is likely to create a circle of advertising security experts.
6.2.1.6	All consumers shall be trained on cyber security measures.	Consumers affect their own security when they choose passwords and click on links. This policy advocates teaching them how to make choices that will decrease the probability that they will be cyber crime victims.
		Simple cyber attacks can be thwarted by training users. For example, password-guessing attacks can be thwarted by training users on how to choose a hard password.
		Organized cyber crime uses highly sophisticated techniques to which even security experts fall victim. Training consumers is a waste of money and provides them with a false sense of security.
		It is unfair to expect a consumer to have to be technical enough to pass training to use the Internet. This blames the victim for the crime about to occur, energy is better spent in deterrence and prosecution measures.

and simple possession of a digital identity did not always correspond to the identity of the individual behind the keyboard. Strong forms of authentication were developed and classified into three factors:

- What you know
- What you have
- What you are.

A password is something you know, and if you know a password, this lets you into most computer systems. But some systems require a second or third factor of authentication: what you have, which may be a handheld token such as a smart card, or what you are, which is a biometric measurement like a fingerprint or a retina pattern. The more factors of authentication a system requires, the stronger the authentication. Most systems admin users have only the lowest possible factor of authentication, so the strength of correlation between the digital identity on the computer and a real person's identity is very low. A login string that identifies a user, in combination with an authentication factor, are generically referred to as "credentials." When viewed in that context, it seems more obvious that credentials are things that may be used to impersonate people, and that some types of credentials make such an impersonation attempt harder than others.

Prior to the use of the Internet for e-commerce, companies that required consumer agreement to a transaction demonstrated that agreement via a written signature. When these transactions were originally converted to the Internet, transaction information would be entered in an online form that would be printed and faxed to the counterparty. Security software companies anticipated requirements for digital signature to authenticate transactions on the Internet that required a signature. The most promising of this technology was a cryptographic technique described in Section 6.2 as public key cryptography. Split keys would be created for each user using public key cryptography. The user public key would be placed in a directory available to anyone who wished to verify a signature. The private key would be kept by the individual, their "digital pen" for use with a digital signing algorithm. The technology allows documents signed with the private key to be verified with the public key. In many implementation of digital signature for email, private keys are kept in a file on the owner's desktop. This technology provides something more than what you know, but is still dependent on a file that is sharable, so it does not actually count as a second factor of authentication. That is, two people could have the same file at the same time, so one could still impersonate another. Of course, one may forge a handwritten signature as well. The act of using a private key file in conjunction with the algorithm was called "digitally signing" a document.

However, when the Digital Signature Act of 1999 and the Electronic Signatures in Global and National Commerce Act were passed in 2000, neither required any proof of identity over and above simple login and passwords, and so the pressure for cryptographic algorithms whereby a private key and/or second factor of authentication were somewhat abated. This opened the door for a wide variety of online e-commerce transactions. It also lowered the bar for e-commerce transaction impersonation. Identity theft has been the number one complaint received by the U.S. Federal Trade Commission since 1999 (FTC 2011).

Another complication of impersonation concerns the age-old practice of slander. Slander on the Internet is so prevalent that it has given rise to new business models for e-commerce reputation maintenance and recovery. There is no accountability for slander cloaked in Internet anonymity or false identity. There are no negative consequences and only customers to gain by posting false accusations that are difficult to disprove.

As digital identity is just a string in a computer, there does not even have to be a person associated with it. In fact, most technology comes out of the box with a digital identity built into it. This is typically a default administrative user but may also be a user specifically configured to demonstrate the technology features of a product. These out-of-the box digital identities are called "generic IDs" because they do not belong to any one person. Often, generic IDs remain configured with the default password supplied by the technology vendor for the entire lifetime of the product. These IDs are well known to criminal elements and are often used to impersonate technology administrators (Table 6.2.2).

6.2.3   Appropriate Use

In the software industry, end-user license agreements (EULAs) are used to specify the terms and conditions under which software is licensed to those who purchase it. These agreements typically limit the authority of the user to copy the software and limit the liability of the vendor for any faults in software operation. These agreements are typically presented in an automated fashion while a user is installing software. Their terms are vague and sometimes one of their terms is that they can change the terms at any time and the user is still bound to them (Hoglund and McGraw 2008). Where possible, software vendors try to enforce these EULAs with automated techniques for license verification.

One common method of software license verification is for the software to "phone home," which is a colloquial expression used to refer to the capability of software to access the software vendor's website. Phone home features check attributes of the software installation with the vendor's records of purchase. For example, if a purchaser has installed the software on more machines than permitted via the EULA, the software may disable itself. Phone home features are also used to check for patches and updates, in which case the software may automatically update itself, or prompt the user to update the software. More insidious use of phone home features are used by spyware to upload data observed on the user's computer. Phone home features are not just limited to traditional computers and

Table 6.2.2 Cyber Security Policy Issues Concerning Impersonation

Policy statement	Explanation	Reasons for controversy
6.2.2.1 All Internet communication shall be attributable to an individual.	This policy would require identification and authentication as a condition for Internet connectivity. No anonymous access would be allowed.	There is no reason anyone should be able to use a communications network anonymously. As cyber attacks may be launched from any Internet location, this policy would allow immediate identification of the source of any attack.
		Internet sites are currently places where groups of similar interest allow anonymous membership promote free speech and uninhibited discussion without fear of retribution. This policy would destroy those freedoms.
		This policy makes sense both socially and economically only for highly critical networks like military or industrial control systems. It should be set at the enterprise, not the Internet level.
		Anonymous access allows personal and political rivals to commit slander without attribution.
		There are many situations where an individual needs to access the Internet only for a few minutes, such as to print out a boarding pass at a hotel or to check a reference in a library. Prohibiting anonymous access would have the unintended consequences of prohibiting all such conveniences.
		Internet connectivity protocols identify only computers by routable address, and many nonroutable addresses may share the same routable address. It is not possible to enforce this policy without issuing every individual their own address, and there are not currently enough available addresses for that.
		This policy would require a new bureaucracy to issue Internet IDs in the form of public–private key pairs. Individuals without access to a private key would be restricted from participating in e-commerce, for example, if their private key was corrupted or if they were refugees.
		This policy requires a global identification system which does not currently exist, so there would be no way to implement it.
		This policy should have an associated implementation strategy of implementing IPV6 worldwide and requiring every individual to register and use a unique address.

6.2.2.2	Assuming a false identity on the Internet shall be prohibited.	A false identity is signing up for a service or on a website with a name that does not correspond to a real person. This differs from anonymous access in that there is a trail of activity associated with the false name itself while anonymous access does not have the label of a name with which to correlate the activity.	Misrepresentation of identity is deceptive and manipulative. There is no justification for such communication. Fear of consequence for publishing one's views is adequate justification for assuming false identity. It allows otherwise repressed individuals freedom to communicate on subjects of interest, which may be necessary for their own mental or physical health. If this policy were enforced, individuals who are persecuted or stalked, whether their persecutors be political or personal, would have to reveal their Internet identity and personal contacts in order to use the Internet, so it would in effect prevent them from doing so at a time when they need it most.
6.2.2.3	Possession of credentials that correspond to another person's digital identity shall be forbidden.	This is a form of impersonation, called *account hijacking*, which differs from false identity in that the credentials used corresponds to a real individual, but not the one who signed up for the service which issued the credentials.	This policy would prohibit markets in Internet logins and provide law enforcement with means for prosecution before such logins were used to commit crimes like identity theft. Credentials cannot be stolen because the owner does not actually lose them. Accounts are not hijacked, simply borrowed. Credentials are often shared on purpose for economic reasons, as when people share access to download sites they use infrequently so that each can download their share allocated to one account. This policy would have the unintended consequence of making each user purchase their own account to such e-commerce sites. Though it would benefit vendors, it would limit the rights of consumers. Credentials are often shared on purpose, as when an executive delegates tasks to an executive assistant. Unless and until technology evolves to allow this use case, such policies will generally be ignored for the sake of convenience.
6.2.2.4	It shall be illegal in all jurisdictions for a person to use the personally identifiable information of another individual to sign up for an Internet service or website.	This is a form of impersonation, which differs from using a person's digital identity in that the real person corresponding to the information entered did not sign up for the service or website themselves at all.	Though this policy may already be in effect when it comes to financial services such as taking out loans in someone else's name, there are other situations where malicious users will sign up using someone else's information in order to create a complete identity in order to anchor it to another real person, such as when a criminal use children's social security numbers and create complete Internet identities in order to travel internationally. This policy is needed to prevent people from social engineering an individual's social and political connections by signing up as them on social networking sites. These social engineering techniques are often used to gather information with which to launch cyber attacks, and so enforcement of this policy would prevent cyber crime. Individuals often delegate Internet access on purpose, as when a celebrity delegates Internet presence to an agent. As long as this practice is prevalent, it may be used as justification for violating policies like these.

(Continued)

Table 6.2.2 (Continued)

Policy statement		Explanation	Reasons for controversy
6.2.2.5	International and national standards organizations shall issue standards for identity assurance ratings, and these shall be required labels on e-commerce websites.	International and national standards organizations currently publish security standards for a wide variety authentication technologies, but not currently in the format of consumer-readable ratings. Rather, they are implementation guides for system owners.	This policy would establish a much-needed standard that would help e-commerce businesses determine the veracity of various security software vendor claims for utility in securely identifying users. Like food labeling, requiring publication of the content of security technology would help educated consumers distinguish between secure and unsecure sites. The intended side effect would be a market preference for secure e-commerce. Many websites publish security seals, which generally mean that they have purchased a given security software product or service, but there is no standard that would give such seals any independent validation of security utility. This policy would provide guidelines for interpreting website security claims. This policy is the domain of the Federal Trade Commission, not international and national standards organizations such as the National Institute of Standards and Technology. Websites may present security claims without implementing them properly. Without an enforcement provision, this policy would be meaningless, and the effort to enforce security standards on all websites is beyond the scope of any government.
6.2.2.6	Use of email addresses for sending credential information or personally identifiable information shall be prohibited.	As described in Section 6.4, email is not a secure method of communications; nevertheless, it is generally used to send sensitive information.	Email is typically transmitted in clear text and may pass through several relay machines prior to reaching its destination. It is typically stored unencrypted. Sending personal authentication information via email is equivalent to public exposure of personally identifiable information. The issue is not the use of email but the unsecure nature of email. Rather than adopt this policy, policies for securing email should be investigated. Decisions concerning the risk of information theft should be left to individual or corporate discretion. Use of an insecure protocol for resetting passwords reduces the security of the authentication itself to the easiest way to eavesdrop on email.
6.2.2.7	Generic IDs required for software operation shall be accessible solely by the purchaser/owner of the software.	Generic IDs typically allow administrative access to software, and this policy would prevent vendors from delivering software provisioned with predefined passwords for generic IDs.	Delivering software with access passwords that are known to the entire community of software users is equivalent to delivering it with a known security vulnerability. Predefined passwords make products initially easy to use. Customers who wish to increase their security have the option of changing these passwords.

124

servers, they are standard operating procedure for mobile devices, and are typically incorporated into software that supports industrial control systems.

The opposite of a phone home feature is a command and control feature. A command and control feature allows a central administrator to control software on multiple computers. Each controlled computer is configured to *listen* to the *network*; that is, *network listening* is a technique that software uses to be alerted to Internet queries. Network listening features combine the Internet address of a computer with a subaddress, or *port*, that can be assigned by a computer operating system to a software process. A typical computer has 64,000 ports that can be distributed among software processes, and the controlled software will select one that is not used by any common programs. Malware command and control features are sometimes referred to as RATs, an acronym for remote access tool that conveys its malicious purpose.

These features are described for the purpose of emphasizing that the ability to install phone home or command and control features on an individual's computer without their knowledge presents a policy issue under the heading of appropriate use. These features are installed not only by software vendors whose software was purchased by the computer owner, but also by advertisers, e-commerce vendors, and industrial control system integrators. As these programs often are installed without the user's knowledge and/or run automatically on user's machines, the circumstance presents an issue concerning unauthorized use of computing resources. So even if personal data are not collected by phone home or command and control software, there are cyber security policy issues to consider separate from the data privacy issues presented by these features.

Other issues in this section concern appropriate use policies within an enterprise, given that it seems appropriate to expect that computers owned and operated by an organization should, in some sense, serve the enterprise mission. Appropriate use is a technology-neutral term but may need to adjust over time. Some nations—and not just those that censor the Internet—may draw a finer line between appropriate use and cyber crime than others. In this section and the next section on cyber crime, we draw the line according to mainstream U.S. culture, where political speech is legal, though it may sometimes be inappropriate, bordering on illegal, for example, if it incites discrimination or violence. By contrast, pornographic content depicting children invariably indicates cyber crime, so it is covered in the next section (Table 6.2.3).

6.2.4 Cyber Crime

Cyber crime refers to any criminal act which is conducted in cyberspace. These include infringement of both personal and property rights. Personal rights violated via cyber crime are typically freedoms of speech or religion, invasion of privacy, or issues relating to luring of minors. As discussed in

Table 6.2.3 Cyber Security Policy Issues Concerning Appropriate Use

Policy statement	Explanation	Reasons for controversy
6.2.3.1	Any software installed on computers without the express consent of the owner shall be considered trespassing.	It is common for Internet sites to install software on user's machines without their knowledge.	There is no difference from the point of view of many consumers between malware and adware. Both consume computer resources and invade privacy. There are legitimate business purposes for running inconspicuous software on consumer desktops. For example, sometimes, technology product features (e.g., printers and other peripherals) do not work as expected or are of limited utility unless there is corresponding software on the user desktop. It is more convenient for the user for this helpful software to be installed automatically than to bother them with pop-up windows and choices they do not understand. When a software company is contracted to provide software support for critical software with high availability requirements, such as in industrial control systems or e-commerce payment systems, it should be up to the software support service vendor to devise the most appropriate way to provide that support. Using data from the live software installation is a frequently used option because it can assist a vendor in determining software issues that may be site-specific. e-Commerce advertisers rely on data automatically collected from consumer machines in order to identify potential customers for targeting marketing campaigns. This is an information service for the consumer as the products are ones predetermined to be of interest, given the consumer's record of Internet activities. Express consent is a concept that requires further definition. A pop-up window question is often clicked away by a user who does not even notice it, much less consent to any text that appeared in it. Yet these types of mechanisms are commonly used in place of more appropriate mechanisms for requesting user consent.
6.2.3.2	Software companies shall be prohibited from implementing phone home features by default.	This policy would prevent the coverage of user permission for phone home features as part of a typical EULA.	Computer owners have a right to control all communication to and from their computers. If software companies show a benefit to consumers from phone home features, then they should be able to sufficiently motivate consumers to actively install them instead of installing them without the owner's knowledge. Enforcement of this policy would restrict software companies from seamlessly installing updates often needed by users to make maximum use of purchased software; these include critical security patches. Because software can be stolen by being copied, the phone home feature is the only way that vendors know whether their software has been pirated. It gives them control over granting licenses.
6.2.3.3	Software companies shall be prohibited from exercising command and control over consumer products.	This policy would prohibit the remote access to user desktops by software vendors.	There is no justification for sending commands to a computer that is owned by someone else, no matter what software is installed on it. Software support processes often query the computers that run the supported software to determine status in order to plan proactive maintenance.

6.2.3.4	Software installed for one product shall not install or attempt to install other products.	Often a software product install will actually install a package of software that includes products other than the one the user has chosen to install.	Vendors often try to expand their presence on a user's machine by placing all of their programs in menus, and if the user tries to use the ones they did not purchase, it prompts the user to purchase a license. This is an unsolicited advertisement that never goes away, creating an annoyance and a waste of computing resources. This policy would restrict software companies from making consumers aware of the benefits of enhancing their productivity with additional products that are compatible with the ones they have already selected.
6.2.3.5	Software shall not be installed in such a way that it runs without the user's express knowledge.	Often a software product installed will configure a system to start the software automatically every time the computer restarts and/or the user logs in.	Simply because a user chooses to install a product does not mean that they wish to run it every day. Software companies who use this method of install waste computing resources and slow down other software that the user may need more. Users often forget how to start software and having it run all the time relieves them of the responsibility to record and remember such details. There is no technology that would allow users to make choices about what should be running and when on all the computing devices they own. Once they install software, they expect it to be there, and would likely think if it was broken if it was not always running.
6.2.3.6	All computer operating systems that allow phone home and command and control features in software running on that operating system shall give users a choice of whether to enable them.	This policy would allow software companies to use such features, but only if the user could configure them.	This policy would allow software companies to contract directly with users on how these features would be used. The ability for the user to disable them would mean that only those features that benefitted users would be accepted. Any user-configurable item can also be configured by malware. This policy would not make it any safer for users to be protected from such features. They should just be entirely disabled.
6.2.3.7	Enterprises who allow staff to use computers for personal reasons shall set guidelines for appropriate use.	This policy acknowledges that when corporate users use corporate computers, they gain capability that may be inappropriate.	Where corporate users use corporate computers in an inappropriate manner, the corporation is enabling the behavior and should be accountable. Unless corporations encourage inappropriate behavior, they should not be held accountable for stopping it any more than the policy physical behavior in the workplace.
6.2.3.8	Individuals using computers that they do not own shall restrict their usage of those computers to the express purpose for which their access was granted.	This policy is similar to the previous one in that enterprise computers should be used in the service of the enterprise, but it places responsibility on the user to understand where lines are drawn.	By default, the property of others should be respected, and this policy would prohibit joyriding, the practice of using computers for purposes that benefit an unauthorized user at the expense of the owner. Computers that are accessible are assumed to be available for whatever capabilities are accessible. The burden should be on the owner to limit capabilities rather than on the user to restrict their activity. For corporate staff to have to change computers to perform a quick personal task causes more employer expense in time wasting than the expense generated from the small diversions from work that accommodate the small tasks.

(Continued)

Table 6.2.3 (Continued)

Policy statement	Explanation	Reasons for controversy
6.2.3.8	Individuals shall be banned from disclosing personal information about others online without their consent.	This policy would outlaw "doxing," which is disclosing embarrassing or otherwise damaging personal information about someone on the Internet from sharing personal details on the Internet. Hactivists have been known to target civil employees such as police and fire fighters by extrapolating embarrassing details from their social networking pages out of context.	There is typically a lot of peer pressure from friends and family to contribute to social networking sites, but any disclosure of personal details may put the lives of people in positions of public trust in danger. This policy would provide such individuals with protection without admitting fear. Doxing is a perfectly legitimate form of journalism. This policy is far too broad and restrictive of free speech. Each individual should be in charge of their own reputation, and though it may be a good idea to provide social networking guidance to people in positions of public trust, this policy is unnecessarily paternal.
6.2.3.9	The Internet shall not be used to incentivize discrimination.	This policy is aimed at reducing the ease with which the Internet may be used to spread slander.	This policy may have the unintended consequence of restricting many forms of criticism, and criticism is one of the most important functions of the Internet. This policy would be a deterrent to those who foment discrimination by strategically placing false rumors in social networking sites. Everyone has their own thresholds for what is inappropriate versus playful or suggestive of discrimination. This type of policy is too broad and can only be adjudicated on a case-by-case basis if it can be shown that harm has occurred.
6.2.3.10	Nations shall create consistent narratives designed to explain political policy and actively propagate them on the Internet.	Narratives are the equivalent of storytelling and help people to understand and appreciate cultural issues.	This is the equivalent of spending tax dollars on an ad campaign. Other countries use public relations narratives to successfully promote commerce. Terrorist adversaries are adept at spreading false narratives, which are not currently countered. The conscious effort to develop and spread friendly narratives should be a core competency in cyber security policy.

the previous section on appropriate use, there is a dividing line between cyber debate and cyber bullying that not everyone draws the same way. Inappropriate use can be seen as a spectrum, where in one end, there is the woman who impersonated a teenager to harass a rival of her teenage daughter, in the middle are the college students harassing their gay friend, and at the other end is an outspoken radio show host disparaging minorities. Though all are generally thought to have crossed the line of inappropriate use, there is no universal agreement that all cases deserve criminal prosecution. Because the law lags behind the myriad of ways that criminal acts may be conducted in cyberspace, an act does not necessarily have to be illegal to count as cyber crime. Cyber criminal acts may be illegal in some jurisdictions but not in others. While these issues evolve, case law and community involvement will help to define cyber crime against persons.

Cyber crime against property includes, but is not limited to: of disabling, destroying, disrupting, or appropriating assets. However, not all cyber criminal acts are new kinds of crime. They may just be traditional crimes that are enabled by or made more effective by automation. For example, credit card theft originally described the physical act of stealing a credit card and using the stolen card in a physical retail establishment. Today, credit card theft is typically accomplished by stealing the data associated with an individual card, and using that data to make online purchases. The only physical object that changes hands is the drop shipment of the merchandise purchased with the stolen "card."

When crimes such as card theft are conducted using specialized software that provides economies of scale in mass thievery, it is *organized cyber crime*. Specialists in the steps required to conduct crime provide services for hire, creating an underground economy. For example, see Figure 6.3. Figure 6.3 describes the relationships between various players and products in the organized cyber crime industry (BITS 2011). Figure 6.4 provides some perspective on each player. They are not all taking equal risks from participation in cyber crime activities. Many may claim to be legitimate merchant, such as gun dealers who are not accountable for the crimes committed by their clients. The Zero-Day vulnerability market is fueled by hackers looking for security bugs and flaws in software that the software owners are not yet aware of. They sell those vulnerabilities to people who design software that can exploit the vulnerabilities to break into systems. Each exploits is a single malware unit, and these units are combined into kits that allow criminals to infect computers to create botnets. Those botnets are rented for criminal activities that have earned the acronym CAAS, which stands for *Crime as a Service*, The services include everything from password harvesting to denial of services attacks.

Organized cyber crime may also generally refer to any situation where automation is used to facilitate Internet fraud. According to some experts, online gambling games of chance are more typically rigged than not, and online gambling companies would rather pay trivial fines when caught

Figure 6.3 Crimeware marketplace.

Figure 6.4 Crimeware risk-profit tradespace.

than stop raking in the tons of guaranteed profits generated by their software's interaction with overly gullible online gamblers (Menn 2010). Even online games of skill can be defrauded by players who reverse engineer the software and reap rewards that were not earned via skill but rather from cunning. Those who reverse engineer software used to run games can often use this knowledge to cheat just as or more effectively than counting cards in a poker game (Hoglund and McGraw 2008) (Table 6.2.4).

Table 6.2.4 Cyber Security Policy Issues Concerning Cyber Crime

Policy statement		Explanation	Reasons for controversy
6.2.4.1	The Internet shall not be used to incentivize violence against persons or property.	This policy is intended to deter people from using the Internet to direct violent behavior.	Poetic and rhetorical language often uses analogies and idioms to express opinions and beliefs. Not all violent language is intended to incite violence, and there is no way to prove criminal intent in this area.
			The use of Internet messaging to quickly gather large groups of people to a certain location for criminal purposes, known as *flash mobs*, is a violation of the personal liberty of those who are the intended victims of the gathering, and the rights of these individuals should outweigh the rights of free speech among criminals.
			Simply because someone responds violently to a written word does not make the author liable. Only the perpetrator is responsible for their own violent acts.
6.2.4.2	Individuals who are stalked, bullied, blackmailed, and/or harassed on the Internet shall be able to declare that the behavior is harassment under the law.	This policy would give an individual the right to declare Internet behavior as harassment, rather than leave it to subjective interpretation.	A typical response to charges of cyber bullying or harassment is that the perpetrator did not understand or anticipate its effect on the victim. This policy creates a situation where continued harassment after the victim's declaration is undoubtedly criminal.
			This policy would let any public figure stop all Internet journalism concerning his or her activities.
6.2.4.3	Individuals who use false identities or anonymous access to commit cyber bullying shall receive mandatory jail terms.	This policy would add penalties to convicted cyber bullies who did not identify themselves to their victims.	Those who cloak their identity to harass others have obviously premeditated their crime and are aware that their behavior is inappropriate.
			Not all instances of cyber bullying, even premeditated ones, are commensurate with punishment of jail time.
6.2.4.4	Individuals who use false identities or anonymous access to report false crimes or emergencies, as well as those who witness such events without reporting them, shall receive mandatory jail terms.	Anonymous Internet as well as phone access is often used to divert emergency response teams to false emergencies, leading to false arrests and diluted resources available for real emergencies.	This type of inappropriate use of the Internet disregards the need for response to genuine human tragedy, and individuals who commit such offenses are likely to exhibit other sociopathic tendencies, so should not be allowed to remain in society.
			This type of inappropriate use of the Internet is typically done by juveniles, and mandatory jail time may be an inappropriately harsh punishment.

(Continued)

131

Table 6.2.4 *(Continued)*

Policy statement		Explanation	Reasons for controversy
6.2.4.5	Financial institutions who are convicted of allowing online criminal money laundering shall be barred from offering the exploited financial services online.	This policy would prevent financial institutions from repeating transactions known to be used by criminals to hide profits and move them into legitimate investments.	As financial institutions make more money from deposits of criminal profits and expensive financial transactions that are used by criminals to hide these profits than they may be expected to lose if caught, they have little incentive to discontinue these practices when simply fined. Money laundering can never be actually stopped. Financial institutions are already audited against money laundering regulations and as long as good faith efforts exist to prevent it, they should not be held liable for the crimes of others.
6.2.4.6	A central registry shall be established of children's websites that are uninhabited by adult predators.	This policy would require websites aimed at children to meet standards for identification of all participants.	Current open ability for adults to reach out to children on any website, whether under false identities or not, enable unmonitored cyber crime. This policy would provide parents with a way to allow uninhibited communication between children online. The technology to enforce this policy is prohibitively expensive, and unless funded by communities or government, would likely be limited to an elite few who could afford participation.
6.2.4.7	The use of steganography to hide pornographic pictures shall be prohibited.	Steganography is software that combines the content of two pictures in such a way that only one can be seen by typical picture viewing software, while the other may be extracted easily with steganography software.	As the use of steganography may one day provide benefits to society, this policy should not be phrased as legislating the use of technology. If there is a reason for a policy to limit the process of hiding pornographic pictures, it should be stated more generally. Hiding pornographic pictures with technology may actually have benefit in that it will shield them from the view of those who may be offended by them.
6.2.4.8	Existing international organizations—such as NATO, ASEAN, OAS, EU, and AU—shall include cyber crime as part of all their deliberations and treaties.	This policy would encourage international organizations to embrace solutions to cyber crime, just as they would for any problem that requires international cooperation to resolve.	Even when cyber criminals are identified, it is often difficult to prosecute because many nations provide safe harbor for their citizens. These are political and diplomatic issues and should be solved by politicians and diplomats. International organizations sometimes work at the level of least-common denominator—the most bland statement that all nations can agree to, which may end up leaving status quo and respect for each other's laws. Such an agreement would be a step backwards as some investigations have already seen field-office level cooperation between nations. These organizations should play a key role to eliminate the sanctuaries for malicious actors as well as to improve the understanding of politicians and bureaucrats of the implications of cyber crime.

6.2.4.9	Nations shall become signatories to the *Convention on Cyber Crime* and encourage other nations to do the same. Nations should then implement the Convention by passing additional required laws to criminalize cyber attacks.	The Convention on Cyber Crime, originally from the Council of Europe, is an international treaty to harmonize laws that nations should pass to criminalize malicious activity on the Internet and set reasonable minimum internal standards for nations (such as responsiveness to requests for law-enforcement cooperation) (CETS 2004).	As more nations join the Convention, there are fewer sanctuaries for malicious actors to hide. The Convention is often seen as a "European" standard or treaty which might incur patriotic resistance for nations to become signatories.
6.2.4.10	National governments shall consider publishing unclassified, regular periodic threat assessments to national cyber security.	This would require national agencies to combine their findings annually into a consolidated report at an appropriate classification level. It should especially cover threats to the critical infrastructure sectors, the backbone networks, and industrial control systems.	Planning and protection require information. Such a report will be invaluable to establish a baseline of threats to help companies convince their management of the threat and secure resources appropriate to the threat. If poorly written, without a commitment to protect the private sector, much information in such a report would be either too high level ("Watch out for Chinese hackers") or too low ("patch your system with the x, y, and z patches").
6.2.4.11	National governments shall identify and cooperate with sectoral, regional, and local cyber security-related organizations. Where needed, governments can support the best-of-breed groups with funding or other direct support.	There are a great many cyber security-related organizations, many are voluntary. These range from ISSA or ISACA, to Information Sharing and Analysis Center (ISAC), and even ShadowServer Foundation and SANS Internet Storm Center.	Many worthwhile groups might (or already have) foundered for lack of short-term funding or other government cooperation. There are not enough organizations at the local level to provide cyber security expertise to those who need it. This policy will provide expert assistance to local efforts to secure information assets and fight cyber crime. There are many cyber security-related organizations, and some often are no more than a local club of like-minded enthusiasts or a front for a particular company's technology.

(Continued)

Table 6.2.4 *(Continued)*

Policy statement		Explanation	Reasons for controversy
6.2.4.12	Cyber security threat and vulnerability information shall be shared in a well-defined way that maximizes privacy and minimizes liability.	This policy would require that vulnerabilities be reported despite obvious disincentives for companies to share information on poor cyber security. This policy is meant to remove those impediments to information sharing.	Without easy access to information on threats and corresponding vulnerabilities, it is impossible to adequately assess cyber security risk. Well-defined procedures to share threat and vulnerability information will benefit the community as a whole. This policy will provide an easy way for companies to avoid blame for negligence in software product development as well as in information handling procedures. It will discourage liability avoidance using secure practice as companies will instead participate fully in information disclosure only after security vulnerabilities have been exploited. Existing national vulnerability reporting sites adequately cover current information-sharing requirements. As soon as vulnerability information is shared, the malicious community devises exploits for them that further erode victim's security. Vulnerability information should be kept confidential.
6.2.4.13	Nations shall create a national computer emergency response team to provide a 24/7 point of contact, assist companies in that nation by sharing best practices and other means, respond to significant incidents and vulnerabilities and provide situational awareness for cyberspace.	This policy will give a focus for security allowing fast recognition of events, coordination within the country and with other countries, and faster response to incidents.	Not only it is now an international expectation that nations will have the capability to conduct these standard functions, but each of these will significantly improve security and response. Though an important function, a national CERT needs personnel, training, funding, and other resources. To be effective, nations will need to ensure other such teams exist for key areas, such as industrial control systems, the domain name system, or other key technologies.
6.2.4.14	Nations shall ensure their law enforcement, prosecutors, and judges have sufficient expertise and tools to be able to investigate and respond adequately to reported cyber attacks and prosecute cyber crime.	There are many organizations involved in enforcing cyber crime, from local police (at the metropolitan, county, or state level), national police, prosecutors at all levels, and judges at all levels.	Passing laws to criminalize malicious cyber activity is not enough. For them to be effective, all parts of the law enforcement system must have the training and tools to ensure the laws are enforced and effective. If done well, this is a long-term (and potentially expensive) effort to help local and national police, judges, and prosecutors understand this new area of crime.

6.2.4.15	Nations shall be prepared to treat cyber attacks from a technical, criminal, or national security perspective, depending on the specifics of the attack.	This will give nations greater flexibility in their response, while including all cyber law enforcement in the potential for national defense measures. Attacks can be any one of these three things and nations need the mind-set and capability to see and respond appropriately.
		Nations lacking resources will need to divide their limited personnel, technology, and funding between each of these three perspectives to deal with attacks.
6.2.4.16	National government shall consider providing assistance to victims of widespread cyber attack, such as they might for damage to be caused by natural disasters.	Victims of cyber attacks are no less impacted by damage than by physical damage to the same computers. This policy would allow for the government to assist impacted businesses and individuals with emergency support such as loans to restore business environments. This policy has far-reaching and unknown economic impact on government and may be misused to pursue claims for every new malware. This should be reserved for only catastrophes and where there is a gap between existing insurance policies. Such assistance should not be for malware (even if very significant and damaging) unless the damage becomes equivalent to that from a physical natural disaster. This policy puts massive cyber attacks on the same footing as hurricanes and floods.
6.2.4.17	The International Telecommunications Union (ITU) shall focus efforts in cyber security on capacity building for nations. These should include developing computer emergency response teams, advising on security (especially for backbone networks), training and education, assistance on national strategies, and similar efforts.	New populations in Asia, Africa, and Latin America are coming online for the first time... and should find a clean cyberspace waiting for them. The ITU has a long history and tradition of being involved in global telecommunications efforts and can be a significant global force to improve cyber security. Not only will this help the developing world to use cyberspace to improve their economy, it will help other nations by policing new malicious actors and threats from these rapidly connecting nations. The ITU has many possible paths to become involved in cyber security. This policy would put that organization in a key role for capacity building, particularly for developing countries, an important development and security priority.
		The ITU, as with any bureaucracy (especially a part of the United Nations) can be slow to move and adapt to new technologies or international conditions. Moreover, since each nation only gets one vote, countries devoted to censorship of their own populations could take over the development agenda.

6.2.5   Geolocation

A major inhibitor to successful investigation of cyber crime is the inability to identify the physical location of an individual user. Though it is clear that user activity on a given computer is associated with an Internet address to which the computer is connected, the source address of an attack is rarely a computer that is physically located in the same place as the human attacker. Cyber criminals cloak their activity by obscuring their physical location. Perhaps by tacit analogy with physical crime, wherein the owner of the location or weapon is not responsible for criminal actions within it, ISP and hosting service providers are not held accountable for computer crime within their networks. If the analogy extended to aiding and abetting, different kinds of users may be accountable for the same crime. Enforcing account-ability for consumers, software developers, network administrators, and social networking identities requires different forensic capabilities. These include, but are not limited to, the ability to identify the source of a network connection at both the user and computer level, the ability to determine what physical path supports a network connection, the ability to know the provenance of software updates arriving from the network, and the ability to determine what changes software may effect on a given computer (Land-wehr 2009). None of these capabilities are in place on the Internet, and are only with great difficulty enforced on highly critical private networks.

There are so many vulnerable computers on the Internet that they keep catalogs of them, as a salesperson would keep a client contact list. By maintaining credentials for multiple vulnerable computers, an attacker can change the path by which they launch an attack every time they launch one. Figure 6.5 provides an example. In order to trace the attacker using the path in Figure 6.5, the victim would first have to gain access to at least one of the machines in the botnet and hope that they would be able to

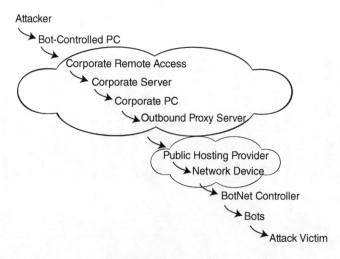

Figure 6.5 BotNet attack path.

find the botnet control server. Depending on how the botnet was configured, an investigator working on behalf of the victim may have to observe
network traffic going into and out of the machine, reverse engineer the
botnet software and find its configuration files, or use operating system logs
(normally not configured on vulnerable machines) to see evidence of past
connections from the botnet controller. From the botnet controller machine,
an investigator would have to perform similar steps to determine that the
attacker had accessed that computer from a network device belonging to
a hosting service provider. Depending on the relationship between the
attack victim and the service provider, an investigator working on behalf
of the victim may have to call a lawyer to file a subpoena to produce the
records of activity on the network device for the time of the attack. Even
if the hosting service provider is friendly and knowledgeable, once it is
evident that their own records show that an attack originated on one of
their servers, which had been compromised, they may be reluctant to share
this information unless compelled by a court order. They in turn would
identify the source as a much larger corporate enterprise. As this enterprise
was vulnerable at several network interfaces, both internal and external, it
is not likely that they have the expertise or the security logs required to
track down a multiple-hop network connection within their border. Even
if they are, they are just as unlikely as the service provider to admit it, and
the investigator working on behalf of the victim may have to issue another
subpoena. The information provided by the corporate enterprise would
identify the source as a bot controlled by the attacker, which itself is
unlikely to have logs and would require reverse engineering.

If the ultimate source of the attack ends up being a wireless user, the
difficulty of identifying a physical location is either increased or decreased,
depending on the capability of the user mobile device. If the device is a
laptop, the source would be typically be a wireless access control point,
which is a device that communicates on wireless protocols with end users,
and connects them to the Internet via a land line. An investigator working
on behalf of the victim would have to go to the location of the wireless
access point and eavesdrop on the connections, looking for the wireless
signal emanating from all computers in the area until it correlated one with
the network address of the attack source and homed-in on the attacker
location. However, if the user is on a mobile phone, these are often
equipped with global positioning system (GPS). This is a satellite-based
service that allows the device to query for its geospatial latitude and lon
gitude coordinates. These are often automatically queried and stored on
the device in order to be available to applications that require such information, such as applications that provide maps and driving directions. The
only difficulty in identifying the physical location of a user with GPS services enabled is the accessibility of these records remotely plus the fact
that the user is mobile.

Cyber attackers count on the difficulty and complexity of such investigations to cloak their Internet activities. Even if such an investigation was

successful, by the time it concludes, the attacker could have completely packed up and moved operations to a different physical location (Table 6.2.5).

6.2.6 Privacy

In order to use Internet services, information must pass in both directions between the service and service provider. The technical mechanisms that provide the data exchange pick up certain types of information by default from both sides. Internet and mobile application service providers thus get some of the information they process "for free." As this information was not requested from the user, but provided without their knowledge, it has spawned a new type of e-commerce business model, one wherein the customers are not the users.

Privacy is the ability of individuals to protect information about themselves and have the ability to release it selectively. Information security is the protection of information from theft, unauthorized change, or denial to authorized users (i.e., confidentiality, integrity, and availability). The discussion of cyber crime in this section illustrates that this ability may be critically important to prevent identity theft and stalking, but that is not the only reason an individual may seek control over his or her own data. For example, data concerning personal spending or browsing activity may present evidence of habits or personality traits that may subject an individual to discrimination. Even if individual behavior is not evident in an individual's data, one person's data are often correlated with social networking groups that they frequent and this association may introduce cause for discrimination or embarrassment. Smart Grid technology with inadequately secured Smart Meters that record behavior in the home environment are exacerbating privacy concerns. Some security professionals and advertising executives are comfortable repeating the phrase, "privacy is for pornsters and mobsters." But this terse dismissal of the need for privacy is insensitive to the plain fact that people do not always openly discuss everything about their personal lives, and the collection of extremely detailed data on one's cyber activity is equivalent to engaging in that level of open discussion. The advent of e-commerce businesses where the user is not the customer has motivated large-scale data collection services that not only gather correct information about individuals, but use heuristic algorithms to make informed guesses about attributes of an individual (Cleland and Brodsky 2011). Many service providers engage in detailed attempts to personalize user web browsing experiences by collecting information about their behavior and using it to determine what information to display to them. In so doing, they not only collect enough information about an individual to consider it a privacy violation, but they also use it to tailor a user's experience on the site to limit their views of system features to those that the site programmers have determined that an individual with that kind of attribute profile is most interested (Pariser 2011). When these

Table 6.2.5 Cyber Security Policy Issues Concerning Geolocation

Policy statement		Explanation	Reasons for controversy
6.2.5.1	Purposely hiding one's physical location, or helping others hide their physical location, on the Internet shall not be criminalized.	This policy would allow anonymization services, as well as the installation of proxy services on bots, to mask the source of Internet activities.	Only criminals need worry about their physical location being identified. Law enforcement should have the right to identify the source of any Internet location as it may be the source of a cyber attack. There are many legitimate reasons to hide one's physical location. These include eluding stalkers, spouse abuse, and political or religious prosecution. Anonymization services provide needed solutions for problems faced by these individuals.
6.2.5.2	Those who allow their networks to be used by cyber criminals shall be guilty of aiding and abetting any crime committed.	This policy would require all networks owners to identify all users and police their borders for unauthorized use.	When companies or individuals allow criminals to occupy their networks, this both shelters them from investigation and equips them with cyber artillery. The risk of unauthorized network access already presents a cost–benefit trade-off to network operators. Where unauthorized users consume network resources, their own business suffers. The decisions about how much security is good enough for their purposes belong to them. The cost of securing all the software on one's network would put many network operators out of business. This provision should be modified to reduce the impact of negligence, and instead refer to those who willfully and knowingly allow their networks to be used by criminals.
6.2.5.3	Network operators who use proxy services shall internally track user activity for immediate use in law enforcement reporting.	This policy would require enterprises to quickly account for all Internet activity.	This policy would make it easy for law enforcement to quickly ascertain the identity of a cyber intruder whose source appears to be a legitimate enterprise network. Even enterprises who have this ability today cannot execute quickly. The sheer number of internal network activity logs makes it impossible to sort through without forensic analysis.
6.2.5.4	Wireless network operators shall implement geolocation technology designed to pinpoint the location of each wireless user.	Troubleshooting equipment for wireless networks includes signal triangulation and other technologies that could enable operators to locate users.	This policy would make it easy for law enforcement to quickly ascertain the location of a cyber intruder whose source appears to be a wireless network. This technology is immature and difficult to manage on large wireless networks.
6.2.5.5	Geolocational informatior coordinates for any mobile device shall be available to law enforcement.	This policy would require mobile devices to allow access to geolocational information files, such as GPS coordinates, on mobile devices upon request.	The ability for law enforcement to track criminals would be significantly enhanced by enforcement of this policy. Any ability for geolocational information coordinates to be delivered from a user's device without their knowledge is an invasion of privacy and creates opportunities for misuse of the information for stalkers and other criminal or unwanted followers.

personalized menus are often laced with advertisements, they are referred to as online behavioral advertising. People are becoming increasingly dependent on services that are not commercially marketed to end users, such as search and global social networking. Hence, they are limited in their use of the Internet unless they submit to the collection of personal information. Such sites are increasingly bold about lifting data that has little to do with the service provided, such as when Twitter was caught uploading contact lists (Sarno 2012).

The policy issues in this section thus center on transparency and accountability for the handling of personal data, both identifiable and not. It starts by addressing privacy issues at the nation-state level and ends with issues of individual choice that present privacy trade-offs (Table 6.2.6).

6.3   Cyber Conflict Issues

Cyber conflict is a generic label for conflicts and coercion in cyberspace where software, computers, and networks are the means and/or the targets. It covers a broader scope than cyber warfare, and includes all conflicts and coercion between nations and groups for strategic purposes in cyberspace where software, computers, and networks are both the means and targets. Cyber conflict includes nation-states actively contending with each other in cyberspace for national security purposes. Not all cyber conflicts rise to the level of armed force, such as large-scale cyber espionage. Cyber conflict is not restricted to nations and businesses, but may be between any individual, loosely connected social networking groups, and organizations of all shapes and sizes. Where people engage in cyber conflict for political purposes or to defend ethical beliefs, this is called hactivism. A key point to remember in any discussion of cyber conflict is that it is not a discussion about computers, but about people.

Cyber conflict is often conducted for strategic purposes, as when nation-states actively conduct missions in cyberspace in order to contend for technical superiority (Adair, Deibert et al. 2010). These conflicts may or may or not rise to the level of armed force such as large-scale cyber espionage or cyber war. This term of cyber conflict allows a broader discussion of how nation-states and other organized groups with large cyberspace operations contend in cyberspace while reserving the term "warfare" for only the most significant attacks between nation-states. This term helps simplify concepts of warfare, espionage, and other attacks as it is broad enough to include many other hostility-motivated activities, but still specific enough to allow room for growth and discussion of the essence of violence conducted within or assisted by cyberspace. A legacy term for cyber conflict is *electronic warfare*, which was more restrictive as it was typically used to refer only to situations where cyberspace was both the means and the target of attack.

This section covers one of the key drivers of cyber conflict—claims to intellectual property in cyberspace. Conflicts over intellectual property

Table 6.2.6 Cyber Security Policy Issues Concerning Privacy

Policy statement		Explanation	Reasons for controversy
6.2.6.1	National governments shall pass laws to ensure companies do not use customer data in ways other than those required to execute the transactions or provide services, unless the customer has opted-in to such sharing.	It is common for companies to sell data about their customer base to marketing companies and/or to tailor the user experience based on collected or purchased data on personal attributes.	This type of Do-Not-Track option is an essential part of a consumer's right to privacy. This policy would not only enforce privacy but also help prevent the spread of data to additional entities where it may be compromised by attackers. Since the customer never did business with the compromised identity, the customer's information should not be exposed to such risk. Sharing information provides benefits to many customers as it allows specially targeted offers in the customer's interest and customized navigation.
6.2.6.2	Nations shall include significant privacy protections in all of their cyber security initiatives.	Cyber security initiatives are often focused on identifying and tracking activity. This policy would require these initiatives to adhere to privacy policies.	Well-designed security initiatives can enhance privacy as well, as hackers and other malicious actors are no longer able to gain access to private information. Privacy is a more pressing concern for some people than security, depending on the situation. Occasionally, there will be trade-offs between security and privacy, and societies will have to make the best possible trade-offs between these two laudable goals on a case-by-case basis.
6.2.6.3	International organizations shall help nations to harmonize information classification efforts to better tackle differences in privacy laws between nations.	Different countries define privacy laws differently, as each nation has its own laws, traditions, and balances.	Global standards might allow improved understanding of privacy requirements, improve privacy for citizens, and allow economies of scale in information handling procedures for multinational organizations. Such harmonization may be impossible as the differences between, say, the United States, China, and even allies consider economic impact on their e-commerce businesses so even harmonization among allies may be unbridgeable without significant effort. A single, global privacy standard is likely both impossible and unwanted; however, international organizations might be able to help agree on basic principles or classifications that can smooth harmonization.
6.2.6.4	National governments shall review existing laws to determine how they apply to cyber security and determine if there are any gaps and if any need to be updated (such as to be more technology neutral).	This would require laws related to cyber security to be reviewed at the national level. Some laws may need to be updated; others may be found to offer novel solutions to problems of cyber security.	This policy would allow security rules to protect privacy to be set by social scientists rather than technologists. A good example of a law that should be critically examined in a cyber security context is the U.S. Defense Production Act and Telecommunications Act of 1934. The findings, conclusions, and recommendations resulting from such a review should inform legislative staffs to introduce new laws or amend old ones. Often, reviews of old laws have led to conflicts between privacy advocates and security practitioners.

(Continued)

Table 6.2.6 (*Continued*)

Policy statement		Explanation	Reasons for controversy
6.2.6.5	Privacy policies posted on website shall be required and compliance shall be demonstrable.	As policy is distinct from process and procedure, simply stating a privacy policy does not imply that there are technical safeguards in place to enforce it.	Privacy policies are today's snake-oil. In order for them to have any value as a consumer evaluation tool, they must be regulated. Privacy policies are not contractual in nature but are statements of a company's security posture. Terms and conditions of software use are governed by end-user license agreements.
6.2.6.6	A suitable Internet administrator shall provide a method for individuals to sell data about themselves, and no other personally identifiable data market shall be permitted.	Although many facilities exist to collect and sell personal data, no facility exists that would allow them to profit from it.	There are a wide variety of ways that individuals can be profiled on the Internet, and none should be allowed without considering recommendations from a privacy advocacy group such as the Electronic Frontier Foundation (EFF). Information on Internet site usage is collected by e-commerce vendors, and rightfully belongs to them. As long as individual attribution is not made using names or (email) addresses, such information is a valuable asset, and owners should be allowed to sell it.
6.2.6.7	Each website that collects information about users shall make the fields collected available for user selection or allow them to opt out.	This policy would subject all Internet sites to Grahm-Leach-Bliley Act (GLBA)-like financial privacy rules, where the data can be used only for the purpose of providing services directly to the customer.	Opt-out policies implemented for GLBA were often made cumbersome and difficult to interpret. Privacy notices motivated by Health Insurance Portability and Accountability Act (HIPAA) are generally ignored as the alternative to signing them is to seek an alternative health-care provider. The default in these policies should be to prevent the collection of information unless formally approved, not to require action on the part of an individual to opt out. Any service that is offered on the Internet should allow a user to opt out of personal data collection, and if companies claim that the lack of advertising revenue makes this policy unaffordable, they can instead choose to charge the users a fee for the service.

6.2.6.8	Consumer protection agencies shall prohibit unsolicitec personalization.	This policy would require that personalization be treated as personally identifiable data, which currently focuses mostly on financial issues.	As website visitors do not pay for the service, they are not customers of the website and so are not considered website consumers. Setting priorities for consumer protection agencies with respect to privacy with respect to personalization would require greater transparency, user-settable controls, enhanced security, limit data retention, and methods for user consent and/or disclosure.
6.2.6.9	Consumer devices shall not be configured with phone home features.	Products such as cell phone, e-readers, and games typically gather information in order to provide the manufacturer or service provider with data on user interaction with the device or data on the device.	This policy would allow consumers to use devices without concern that their personal information may one day to be used to their detriment, even if only to avoid an onslaught of advertisement to their email address. There are many customers of consumer devices willing to allow their service providers to monitor their behaviors in exchange for more personalized services going forward. It would make more sense simply to require software vendors to disclose the data fields that are incorporated into phone home features.
6.2.6.10	Users who willingly connect to unsecured wireless services shall have no expectation of privacy.	Wireless services are often provisioned in such a way that users who connect can see each other's traffic. This is also the case in some land-based service offerings, though users are not explicitly warned of that possibility as they are when they connect to wireless through industry standard methods.	The rapid adoption of network services has made it difficult to meet network bandwidth demands. The widespread use of security features that would prevent users from eavesdropping on each other would slow the proliferation of service delivery. Given that network connectivity is rapidly becoming a requirement for individual livelihood, it is unethical to provide services that require users to make a choice between livelihood and privacy.

may be overt or covert, in which case they are classified as cyber espionage. The most extreme form of cyber conflict is cyber war.

6.3.1 Intellectual Property Theft

Although the copyright and trademark issues discussed in Section 6.1.4 are issues concerning intellectual property, those are closely related to a company's Internet presence and thus are issues on par with Internet names and numbers. Also, many aspects of cyber crime as discussed in Section 6.2.4 relate to theft of intellectual property. In this section, we consider threats to intellectual property used for competitive advantage such as patents and trade secrets.

The term *Advanced persistent threat* (APT) refers to an organization that is well equipped to study a cyber infrastructure in multiple dimensions, including network, application, human, and physical, with the ultimate aim of identifying and extracting information and/or undermining critical aspects of a mission, program, or organization. As described by the National Institute of Standards and Technology (NIST), "The advanced persistent threat: (1) pursues its objectives repeatedly over an extended period of time; (2) adapts to defenders' efforts to resist it; and (3) is determined to maintain the level of interaction needed to execute its objectives" (NIST 2011). Recent headlines show that many large global firms are subject to these attacks (Jacobs and Helft 2010; Drew 2011; Schwartz and Drew 2011; Markoff 2012). Several major cases have been thoroughly investigated, and it has been revealed that significant digital assets have been misappropriated and used for either commercial gain or subsequent attack planning (Alperovitch 2011). Yet there have not as yet been any unrepudiated attribution or successful prosecution that would indicate justice has been served in these cases. Rather, we are left to conclude that hackers in our midst regularly harvest intellectual property with the purpose of duplicating manufacturing lines, profiting from the distribution of stolen entertainment, damaging data integrity, and/or damaging physical equipment.

Many APT attacks begin by social engineering, that is, the act of persuading knowledgeable staff members to divulge information about how to access enterprise networks (FS-ISAC 2011). Social engineers working on behalf of APTs contact staff via social networks and impersonate friends, family, and coworkers, as well as assume false identities such as customers trying to test passwords. They may also engage in in-person social engineering, meeting a staff member on a business trip or other public place, and pretending to be a friend and confidant. This stage of the attack, also referred to as reconnaissance, is the first of a pattern of seven distinct stages. This complete picture as seen by security analysts is (Cloppert 2010):

1. Reconnaissance—social engineering and network scanning, infiltration with phone home malware designed to gather enough information to complete steps 2–4.

2. Weaponization—selection and placement of malware designed to evade security controls identified in step 1.
3. Delivery—propagation of weapon package to attack target identified in step 1, for example, via phishing email.
4. Exploit—execution of code that takes advantage of vulnerabilities identified in step 1 to plant weapon on target.
5. Installation—use weapon to install command and control malware.
6. Command and control—malware connects to malware operator website to retrieve commands.
7. Actions on intent—malware performed actions directed by malware operator.

The stages of the attack can iterate and evolve continually. APT attacks, when discovered at one location, had been traced in logs going back over 18 months. Because the malware "weapon" is specifically designed to evade existing security controls, there is little chance that there will be enough activity logs gathered to make it possible to determine exactly what intellectual property had been accessed by the attackers over the course of their site penetration.

Policy issues related to intellectual property overlap with all e-commerce policy issues described in Section 6.2. Impersonation is used to facilitate social engineering, malvertising is used for delivery, appropriate use addresses the weaponization that often makes use of crimeware, and geo-location issues make investigation extremely difficult. Additional policy issues concerning intellectual property have to do with more systemic issues that create a cyberspace environment where intellectual property theft resists forensics analysis and therefore prosecution. Policy issues range from nation-state objectives for technical superiority to enterprise objectives for awareness (Table 6.3.1).

6.3.2 Cyber Espionage

When copying and pirating are motivated by nation-state goals for dominance, the definition of the activity morphs from intellectual property theft to espionage. "Cyber espionage," like other kinds of espionage, is typically considered a legitimate activity for a sovereign state. Spying has long been an activity for states to conduct against one another. All issues relating to protecting intellectual property would apply to cyber espionage, whether or not the intellectual property in question belongs to a nation-state. This is because, given the size of global corporations, and the dependency of governments on their private sector for critical infrastructure and services, as well as considerable tax income, attacking a private sector company may indeed be part of a nation-state cyber espionage campaign (Table 6.3.2).

Table 6.3.1 Cyber Security Policy Issues Concerning Intellectual Property

Policy statement	Explanation	Reasons for controversy
6.3.1.1 Preservation of national intellectual property shall be a key diplomatic objective.	This policy would require intellectual property issues to be at the forefront of international diplomatic relations efforts.	Lack of a formal diplomatic response to get to the bottom of the numerous confirmed intellectual property thefts committed in cyberspace amount to tacit acknowledgment that the only solution is economic or physical conflict. Diplomatic efforts in this area are in their infancy, and innovative approaches are required to bring about peaceful resolution. As most intellectual property theft is profit motivated, it is performed by individual companies, and their governments have very little control over their activities.
6.3.1.2 Existing international organizations—such as NATO, ASEAN, OAS, EU, and AU—shall play a key role to coordinate investigations relating to cyber theft of intellectual property.	This policy would encourage international organizations to embrace solutions to intellectual property theft, just as they would for conflict in any of the other domains.	Many of the problems of cyber conflict are not technical. They are political and diplomatic and should be solved by politicians and diplomats. After a major cyber attack, these groups may be able to help prevent escalation and assist politicians to find key areas to difficult technical questions (such as attribution of the attack). International organizations sometimes work at the level of least-common denominator—the most bland statement that all nations can agree to, which may not be helpful during a cyber conflict.
6.3.1.3 Economic alternatives such as barring perpetrators from international marketplaces shall be considered as a first method of deterrent.	This is a policy to impose financial penalties for known cases of intellectual property theft.	Such deterrence is irrelevant. It is currently beyond forensic capability to make a nonreputable claim that any given company has benefited from intellectual property theft, and even if they do, they have already been rewarded in the marketplace by their customers. Such coordinated effort against a competitor would amount to antitrust, which is a worse problem for consumers than intellectual property theft. All honest firms have a stake in ensuring that intellectual property theft is discouraged. Peer pressure within industries should be pursued before being dismissed.

6.3.1.4	Business intelligence services shall be regulated and their activities monitored to ensure that they can produce legal claim to the information they provide to clients.	Business intelligence companies often search the Internet for information about competitors of their clients.	As hostile nations will not adopt regulations that prevent them from APT, this type of policy puts friendly nations at a competitive disadvantage. There is a fine line between business intelligence and intellectual property theft. Both activities have the overt objective of finding out as much as possible about a competitor's plans and products.
6.3.1.5	Scanning systems and networks belonging to others for vulnerabilities without their express permission shall be forbidden.	Scanning networks beyond one's own perimeter is a critical capability in planning a cyber attack.	Network scanning is normally performed in order to find vulnerabilities in the target systems. Those vulnerabilities are then exploited during an attack. Similar to intelligence gathering, unauthorized scanning of company or organization networks should be treated as criminal plan. Because of the Internet's lack of attribution and the difficulty in performing tracebacks, apparent source Internet addresses of scanning computers must not be assumed to be the actual IP address of an adversary's computer. This policy would be difficult to enforce.
6.3.1.6	All publicly traded companies shall be required to take measures to reduce staff susceptibility to social engineering,	This would require companies to consider it a fiduciary responsibility to shareholders to make sure intellectual property is protected.	As insider access is the most common cyber weapon delivery method, fortifying this periphery would strengthen the enterprise as a whole against intellectual property theft. Although training every company employee would present a prohibitive expense, an effective and ongoing social engineering awareness and anti-phishing program with a particular focus on senior executives and technologists who possess administrative credentials should suffice to satisfy the objective of this policy. Any systematic corporate training program for all staff will never be able to keep up with new and innovative cyber security threats. Companies are better advised to concentrate on technology protection measures that do not allow users to make decisions that would jeopardize intellectual property.

Table 6.3.2 Cyber Security Policy Issues Concerning Cyber Espionage

Policy statement		Explanation	Reasons for controversy
6.3.2.1	Aggressive and sustained cyber espionage intrusions that have a collective scope, duration, and intensity shall be considered "threat or use of force" per the UN Charter that allow the target country to take countermeasures.	However, it appears that for the past years, at least one nation has engaged in intrusions for espionage that has been especially aggressive.	This policy will allow espionage at lower levels, in line with normal international practice while trying to keep such behavior under aggressive and dangerous thresholds. As this threshold will be determined by norms of behavior, it does not require international treaties.
			The fact that spying is considered a privilege of nation-states is at the root of the cyber-espionage problem as well as the issues concerning theft of international property. UN Charters should instead concentrate on ways to deter spying on all fronts.
			Though these intrusions may not yet be so aggressive to be have passed a threshold of a "threat or use of force" it should be a policy that there is a specific threshold which will allow targeted nations to take actions that would normally be considered illegal under international law.
			This threshold could theoretically limit freedom of action for all nations, so it should be set sufficiently high so that the possibility that particularly aggressive and sustained cyber espionage intrusions may raise the level of a threat or use of force would be very improbable.
6.3.2.2	National government shall secure their own cyberspace.	This policy makes it clear that governments must secure their own systems and networks by all means: identifying threats and vulnerabilities; patching; locking down servers, desktops, and networks; and many more efforts.	Governments control incredibly important data, which they mandate that citizens provide. They have little credibility, however, if they give it less protection than their regulations force on the private sector for the same type of data.
			It is difficult and governments have proven they lack the ability to hire and retain a talented corps of specialists to protect their systems. Governments are already over budget, so an additional priority may mean stopping doing other work that has its own proponents.

6.3.2.3	Military leadership shall ensure there are programs to safely share information with, and between, companies in the Defense Industrial Base (DIB).	The DIB is an important element to modern military capability which in the United States has seen extensive cyber intrusion to steal DoD information.	This policy is in line with best practices in other sectors, such as finance, and helps coordinate to find and prevent intrusions into companies that maintain information on traditional weapons manufacturers, as well as service providers and others who have access to military information. Military encouragement of providing safe communications conduits between DIBs must be careful to ensure that companies do not take advantage of the opportunities to collaborate against the government on prices or programs.
6.3.2.4	Where there is a market failure to secure and defend against attacks, nations shall create targeted regulation to close these gaps.	This policy is not espousing that there is currently a market failure, though this may in fact be the case, just that should there be such a failure that regulation would be appropriate. Such regulations could be just for specific common carriers, like Tier-1 telecommunication companies, or for all Internet Service Providers, or indeed even for all organizations using the Internet.	Regulations are the ways societies deal with common problems that are not met by the markets. As such, these would be continuous with the traditional behavior of nations, and not new or radical. While this policy may be advisable in the event of market failure, regulations must come with conditions, such as to be specific to identified gaps; be minimally invasive; be technology neutral; and allow the regulated organization latitude on how best to meet their obligation. Such measures could include auditable cyber security risk assessment detailing functional specifications for systems and networks. As cyberspace can be considered a commons, any regulations would best be coordinated between nations—at least those that have the most cyberspace infrastructure and be in the interest of all nations. Also, of course, regulations, if poorly designed or implemented, could restrict communication between peoples and be far worse than the security problems the regulations were meant to remedy.
6.3.2.5	National governments shall ensure all staff (not just those involved in IT or cyber security) are trained to comply with basic cyber security skills.	This policy would require every government job function to have security responsibilities defined.	All government employees handle sensitive information and so all play a role in protecting it. This policy would make the level of compliance with existing national security policy visible to policymakers, and so inform future legislation. Such training would have to be simple—perhaps too simple—as there are so many existing compliance training requirements. To matter, such training would have to be monitored and noncompliance penalized, which would run afoul of many union rules.

6.3.3   Cyber Sabotage

Sabotage describes actions that are bounded often in time (during war), actor (by nonstate guerillas or state commandos), and result (destruction rather than espionage or crime). Cyber sabotage is a phrase that reflects the damage potential from cyberspace terrorists. Any kind of enterprise may be targeted by saboteurs, from individuals to nation-states. It is not uncommon for disagreements among hackers to evolve into the cyber equivalent of gang wars, wherein rivals destroy each other's information. Such activity may even escalate from the cyber to the physical world, as hackers ransack each other's homes in acts of vengeance against cyber attacks. Cyber gangs also stalk unsuspecting victims, as when groups of hackers with similar political viewpoints join forces to destroy or defame enterprises that conduct activities to which they are in opposition, or simply publish opinions that oppose their views.

When cyber attackers bond over similar political or ethical causes, they are classified as hactivists. Objects of hactivist attacks may be corporate or non-for-profits. They may even be individuals who are targeted on the basis of involvement in activities related to their job function, as when business partners of pharmaceutical firms were targeted by an animal rights group because the firms conducted product safety tests using animals (Kocieniewski 2006).

Where the target of cyber sabotage is a nation-state, hactivists and nation-state military cyber warriors may be indistinguishable. During a denial of service attack against the country of Estonia in 2007, hactivists rallied to the cause of increasing the strength of botnets used to deliver the denial of service attack (Clarke and Knake 2010). In this case, e-commerce in the nation was virtually shut down for a week, and although many hactivists claimed to be joining the attack for patriotic reasons, no nation-state took responsibility for the overall effort. In this case, only e-commerce was the target, but nation-state threats aiming to exploit cyberspace vulnerabilities may target any component of the national infrastructure, including, but not limited to, the operation of industrial control systems, the integrity of banking transactions, or the readiness of military equipment. As described in Chapter 3, potential damage from sabotage of cyber components of these systems may include physical harm because of the extent to which industrial control systems control physical processes. The policy statements in the following table concern nation-state cyber sabotage issues (Table 6.3.3).

6.3.4   Cyber Warfare

Military interest in cyber security predates the "cyber" era, as it is rooted in earlier doctrines like automation, intelligence and counterintelligence, operational security, computer security, and electronic warfare. Hence,

Table 6.3.3 Cyber Security Policy Issues Concerning Cyber Sabotage

Policy statement		Explanation	Reasons for controversy
6.3.3.1	International humanitarian law shall apply to conflict in cyberspace.	International humanitarian law (also known as law of armed conflict) is the traditional law used by nations to determine when it is legal to engage in armed conflict and what methods are considered ethical and legal. As cyber sabotage has potentially harmful consequences for humans, humanitarian ethical rules apply.	Because international humanitarian law is widely accepted (though of course with disagreement on specific cases), having it as a root of laws pertaining to cyber conflict makes sense. National governments and militaries must continue to determine how best to apply these laws to cyber conflicts. It is likely that problems with attribution will make it difficult or impossible to root cyber sabotage in international humanitarian law. Other avenues for deterring cyber sabotage should be considered.
6.3.3.2	Hactivists shall be considered a form of free speech.	Hactivist attacks by definition are not designed to steal, but simply to draw attention.	Hactivists are often surprised to be treated as criminals because their attacks are not designed to steal but simply to inconvenience. Their lack of harmful intention should be considered before classifying their activities as crimes. Disruptions in business or government services caused by hactivism may result in unintended consequences such as economic effects on customers or suppliers of the target. These innocent bystanders should not be subject to such intentional disruptions. In cyberspace, any negative attention directly causes inconveniences that require considerable expenditure of technology resources to address, as well as potential for lost profit due to inability to conduce e-commerce during an attention-getting cyber attack. Hactivists are therefore no less criminal than hackers for hire who may maliciously inconvenience their client's competitors.

(Continued)

Table 6.3.3 *(Continued)*

Policy statement		Explanation	Reasons for controversy
6.3.3.3	Government-classified sensitive information shall not be available to any one individual without the oversight of at least one other.	The intent of this policy would be to minimize the possibility for any one person to commit sabotage via information disclosure as it would require collusion.	This policy would reduce the probability that a person who has access to sensitive information would view it if they did not have a reason to, even if they were allowed to. It could have deterred the recent state department wiki-leaks scandal. The policy would imply that an agent working on behalf of the government would need to get permission to view information. This type policy was identified in the 911 report as contributing to the inability for government agencies to share information on overlapping investigations.
6.3.3.4	Firms with known adversaries who conduct transactions over the Internet shall employ security measures to protect against hactivism.	The social dimension of some organizations make them likely hactivism targets.	Not-for-profit companies generally champion social issues, and some businesses are routinely challenged by social activists in court or in the press. These companies are known to be subject to discrimination from some portion of the population. There is thus a higher probability that their sites will be attacked compared to Internet sites in general, so these companies should prepare for the worst in order to protect their users from potential economic harm due to cyber attacks. All organizations are already subject to due diligence requirements and regulations designed to ensure that their transactions are protected.
6.3.3.5	Nations shall define their critical infrastructure sectors and create mechanisms to coordinate with these sectors to create smarter policies for cyber and industrial control system security.	These infrastructures are those that a nation must rely on to provide critical services, the interruption of which will cause significant disruptions to the nation or cause many casualties.	Critical infrastructures require particularly strong and focused protection as their cyber defenses may not be adequate. To rely on government protection, they must cultivate a close relationship with government. This policy should lead to an engagement to ensure a strong flow of trust, then information, between the public and private sectors, and deter those who intentionally target private infrastructure to avoid confrontation with government. Emphasizing defenses for critical infrastructures can distract governments and defenders from other priorities, such as protecting military installations.

| 6.3.3.6 | As there may be gaps between "normal" attacks and attacks that rise to the level of use of force or armed attacks, nations shall assist organizations in their critical infrastructure sectors against such attacks. | A nation-state or hostile nonstate group might target organizations in the critical infrastructure sectors, even using enough resources to have the scope, duration, and intensity to consider a retaliatory use of force or armed attack. | No organization should be left on their own against sophisticated attacks against which they have no reasonable defense. Government should come to the aid of its citizens.

Such attacks would be far more dangerous than the typical attacks that even very well-defended organizations could be expected to defend themselves against. Accordingly, nations must be appropriately prepared to provide assistance. Depending on individual nations and organizations, this assistance could be added resources (like security professionals, added forensics, or new tools), improved response, or even counterattacks (if these would be legal under international law).

It may often be difficult in practice to determine the threshold for such assistance or what assistance would make a difference against sophisticated attackers. These attacks should not include minor events such as defacements or transitory denial of service attacks. For government intervention to be justified, the scope, duration, and intensity should generally be so stunning in scope that they are clearly recognized as atypical. It may also be difficult for governments to provide mutual aid if they are under the same attack. |
| 6.3.3.7 | Nations will develop detailed response plans for major incidents and link these, as appropriate, to plans for other kinds of incidents (such as earthquakes, hurricanes, or typhoons, or terrorist attacks). | Cyber incident response plans typically include identification of specific actions to be taken in the event of incidents. Response plans usually identify key responsibilities, actions, decisions, needed information for those decisions, and timelines for escalation. | Plans can never cover all possibilities, but the process of planning will help organizations think about possibilities, their organizational response, and needed decisions and actions. The more time organizations can spend on these plans and planning, the more they will be much more prepared for whatever eventuality may emerge.

Proper planning does take resources and management attention, which can often be very limited and detract from higher priority activities such as cyber defense planning.

These plans could guide response for intentional incidents as cyber sabotage, and at the same time minimize potential damage from criminal acts, natural disasters, or as acts of war depending on the scope, duration, intensity, and adversary for each incident. |

cyber security is still deeply entwined with all of these military topics which have confused practitioners and theorists for the past decades. One of the first reports to highlight the possible risks of computer automation was the Ware Report of 1970, at the dawn of the age of computing when remote terminals allowed people to access computers even though they were not in the same room (Ware 1970). Most of the threats and vulnerabilities with which the military was concerned in 1970 remain valid concerns: accidental disclosure, deliberate penetration, passive and active infiltration, physical attack, logical trap doors, supply chain intervention, software and hardware leakage points, and malicious users or maintenance people.

Military attitudes toward "information warfare" developed rapidly after successful technology-enabled offensive strategies, driving new doctrine, strategies, and theories, especially in the United States, where it was coined "RMA" for "revolution in military affairs" (Rattray 2001). Though the strategic objective to capitalize on cyberspace in general is clear, the U.S. Department of Defense views on cyber security changed several times over the subsequent 15 years. The doctrinal concepts thrashed from information warfare to information operations and information assurance (all of which generally treat cyberspace as one dimension of the information realm), offensive and defensive counterinformation, computer security (a more traditional view), and network operations and network security. Cyber-related security forces of varying strategic roles were scattered throughout the military's existing structures until the order for their consolidation into a single four-star command in 2010. Now, there is a central U.S. Cyber Command, as part of the U.S. Strategic Command. "Cyber war" today means war that happens to be conducted using artillery only found in cyberspace. This definition reserves the term "warfare" for the way it is traditionally used by states to refer to conflicts where force can be legitimately used by sovereign states. Nevertheless, the connection between cyber war and traditional war is increasingly obvious. Cyber warfare is in the process of being merged with the larger body of understanding, concepts, and laws. This definition does not match with the public use of the term "cyber war" which has been used to cover everything from online juvenile hooliganism to acts of organized crime to espionage. This definition is also in line with the current general consensus between international lawyers, although it is acknowledged that the general consensus between lawyers may change very quickly after a devastating cyber attack, especially if inflicted by one nation on another.

The Department of Defense focus on cyber war predominantly considers "cyber" as networks. Its doctrines sort through the difference between traditional battles and cyber battles. For example, in cyber battles, preemptive first strikes using overwhelming forces does not necessarily remove adversaries; trying to use cyber counterattacks to disable attacks in progress is complicated by issues of identifying targets, and the topology of the battlefield may change in progress (Denmark and Mulvenon 2010). As a result, a more recent military strategy aspires to these goals (Alexander 2011):

- Treat cyberspace as a domain for the purposes of organizing, training, and equipping, so that DoD can take full advantage of cyberspace's potential in military, intelligence, and business operations.
- Employ new defense operating concepts, including active cyber defenses, such as screening traffic, to protect DoD networks and systems.
- Partner closely with other U.S. government departments and agencies and the private sector to enable a whole-of-government strategy and an integrated national approach to cyber security.
- Build robust relationships with U.S. allies and international partners to enable information sharing and strengthen collective cyber security.
- Leverage the nation's ingenuity by recruiting and retaining an exceptional cyber workforce and to enable rapid technological innovation.

The policy statements in this section therefore range from strategic partnership initiatives to the decision by an individual country to launch a cyber attack. The first several policy statements describe policy cooperation issues. These are followed by cyber military operations issues. These are followed by policy issues with respect to the use of military force (Table 6.3.4).

6.4   Cyber Management Issues

Even if the military has unmitigated success in arranging its resources around its mission, the best laid plans to establish military cyber defense may be laid low by its unexpected dependence on civil infrastructure (Lynn 2010). The namespaces and numbering systems that provide the infrastructure for both public and private telecommunications are managed by private industry. The practice of technology as a field of professional discipline is quite young compared to other fields. Software architects do not have a guild or apprenticeship system as do architects of physical facilities. Technology consultants are not required to learn their trade through a series of peer-administered exams as do medical consultants. Buyer beware is the rule of the day. The field of technology practice has therefore, not unexpectedly, yielded a field of technology malpractice. Technology malpractice investigations are motivated by suspicion of management neglect of security issues (Rohmeyer 2010). For example, they provide evidence in legal cases of negligence brought by the U.S. Federal Trade Commission (Wolf 2008).

Nevertheless, a half century of practicing security professionals has seen the accumulation of a large body of knowledge in cyber security. Shared experience of similar technology architecture and operational processes has yielded both best practices and rules of thumb that should not be cast aside simply because there is no scientific basis for their universal

Table 6.3.4 Cyber Security Policy Issues Concerning Cyber Warfare

Policy statement	Explanation	Reasons for controversy
6.3.4.1 International arms control efforts shall be focused on limiting the proliferation of cyber security technology.	This is policy for cyber security by analogy with nuclear weapons policy, that proliferation should stop, and thereby the world will be a safer place.	The proliferation of offensive cyber capabilities would be extremely difficult, if not impossible to stop. They are difficult to define, are relatively inexpensive, and can be developed in any basement or computer lab. Any treaty to stop proliferation would be nearly impossible to verify or enforce. International arms control efforts should be focused on limiting the scope of permissible targets and use of cyber attacks and not generally the weapons themselves. Possible frameworks to do that include existing restrictions of the laws of armed conflict, or new constructs seeking to limit the use of cyber technology. The definition of the term "munition" or "weapon" in cyber security is not well enough understood for this policy to be effectively enforced. This type of policy was at the root of attempts in the late 1900s to limit the proliferation of cryptographic technology. That policy had the undesired consequence of making U.S. corporations easier targets, and so would this one. Cyber attacks can be conducted covertly, with difficult attribution, so if there is a prohibited attack, it might be difficult to determine whom to hold responsible.
6.3.4.2 Military leadership shall promulgate a declaratory policy to help set international norms and help set defense expectations.	A declaratory policy could include elements like no-first-use against broad societal targets, no use of viruses or worms, not having attacks appear to come from protected entities (like hospitals), and similar items.	Declaratory policies can be used to limit options. A declaratory policy improves transparency and helps guide development of capabilities and doctrine. If well-worded, they do not necessarily take away options. Rather, they rightfully restrict options that should never be considered. Declaratory policies allow adversaries to anticipate actions.
6.3.4.3 Military leadership shall develop and declare a national security strategy for cyberspace and supporting policies, and coordinate these with allies.	A national security strategy for cyberspace should highlight key decisions, and how they support agreed-upon goals. Issues to be addressed would be the balance between offense and defense, the role of key organizations, coordination of operations, and interaction with civilian authorities and the private sector.	Strategies are effective ways for top leadership to give transparency to their intent and provide guidance to their bureaucracy. National strategies for cyberspace can often be overclassified—causing unneeded concern from outsiders—and overmilitarize cyber conflict, seeing it as a problem militaries are best equipped to solve.

6.3.4.4	Military leadership shall coordinate operations with private sector organizations.	Cyberspace is dominated by the private sector as it is not in other domains. In space, air, and even in the open ocean, those domains are dominated by emptiness. Even on land, people will flee a conflict if they can. There are no such options in cyberspace where the "space" itself was created and owned by the private sector.	Private-sector organizations are critically necessary to ensure national cyber defense. If they are unconvinced by military strategies or technologies, they can intervene with national leadership to cancel or hamper unliked programs. As future cyber conflicts will likely be fought on their networks and systems, close coordination with them is critical for defense. The military has a propensity to classify everything and any mandate to work with the private sector is likely to end up with arguments on classification efforts that will compete with the private-sector's cyber security efforts to protecting profits.
6.3.4.5	Militaries shall widely coordinate between offensive and defensive cyber operations, between kinetic and cyber, between attack and exploitation, and with civilian counterparts.	Coordination with both its own supply chain and targeted asset owners is a critical factor for any military operations. These are cyber-commands civilian counterparts.	Each of these actions is needed because of the unique nature of cyberspace. Not only is it new and generally untested, but effects can cascade and impact unintended civilian systems. Any counterattacks may be seen as proportional by an adversary but be targeted directly at the host nation's critical infrastructure. Coordination with potentially numerous individuals from multiple organizations will necessarily slow down the tempo of cyber operations. The military's missions in cyber should not touch civilian infrastructure, simply military cyberspace. There is no need to coordinate with the private sector for the cyber command to fulfill its mission, as its mission is purely to protect military systems from cyber threats (Alexander 2011). Other areas of government have greater charter to provide cyber security assistance to the private sector (e.g., U.S. DHS). Many skilled cyber-defense operations centers are owned and operated by the private sector. If the military does not coordinate with them, they will lose access to desperately needed talent. Active defense causes great concern from the public, and especially privacy groups. If done poorly and incautiously, the temporary benefits will not outweigh the permanent loss of trust. Some government infrastructures may be dual use, supporting both civilian and military users. Military activity from these may be seen as disproportional by the target or world leadership. Also if targets cascade, the activity may actually be disproportionate and/or illegal. Either way, it may escalate the conflict more than planned.

(Continued)

Table 6.3.4 (Continued)

Policy statement	Explanation	Reasons for controversy
6.3.4.6 Militaries shall conduct realistic exercises of their cyber defense plans, including the public sector and other nations.	Tabletops are exercises that allow participants to walk through simple scenarios to give participants practice decision making, test them against a given response standard, or familiarize participants with response plans. Tabletops are also used to explore what concepts to determine what appropriate responses might be.	To be done well, exercises can require extensive planning beforehand. In general, the better quality of training and lessons require higher levels of planning and resources. Hence the cost–benefit of exercises may not outweigh the alternative, which is to study current cyber-espionage cases. The results of these exercises are needed as feedback into the national strategy, metrics, incident response plans, and military doctrine. These exercises should include small targeted tabletop games to explore specific aspects of response plans up to large-scale national war games including partners from across the country. Exercises allow participants to practice response, decision making, and coordination during peacetime, giving them a chance to make mistakes, learn their roles, and create "muscle memory" when the consequences matter less. These lessons can be learned relatively inexpensively, especially using tabletops. Tabletops exercises are heralded as ideal learning tools, but no commander who understands his or her job needs to gather a wide variety of valuable human resources to play a game in order to understand what needs to be done to defend cyberspace. Moreover, the most critical decision makers are typically absent from the exercises, and they are reduced to methods to generate data to fill reports with warnings of things the exercise developers already know about.
6.3.4.7 The military shall enhance the skill sets of its cyber workforce, to include not only the traditional cyber workforce of information technology specialists but also staff needed for missions related to the "contested domain" of cyberspace.	Often the "cyber workforce" is conflated with the "IT workforce." Militaries require cyber skills in mission operations that are unrelated to typical information technology support such as operators, defenders, military planners, Judge Advocate Generals, and intelligence support.	There should be no division between information technology support of the military and staff required to conduct cyberspace missions. Running military technology should be considered a mission on equal footing with other defense missions. Any other approach would leave information technology staff not responsible for cyber defense. There are different skills sets required to operate technology infrastructure than to conduct military missions in cyberspace. This policy allows militaries to fully understand the depth and breadth of workforce skills and appropriately allocate them. A focus on cyber assignments delegated to non-IT staff can overweigh the importance of those who conduct attacks, who are typically a small percentage of the total cyber workforce. This may create the false impression that their services are more important than cyber defense assignments.

6.3.4.8	Militaries shall ensure their workforce that "faces the adversary" most gets additional combat-related training.	All who have a primary role of attacking or defending against the adversary should have a similar combat mind-set to their kinetic peers.	Because of the prevalence of cyber attcks originating from inside, it is not possible to determine which section of the military cyber workforce will be most adversary-facing. All cyber staff should have equal ability to recognize and deal with adversarial cyber threats. As there is always more training required than the resources to provide it, training must be allocated to where it is most likely to be immediately useful.
6.3.4.9	Military leadership shall consider cyberspace as a new domain in which warfare can occur, just like the traditional domains of air, land, space, and maritime.	Like the other domains, it is a place with international, personal, and commercial interests, with its own geography. Unlike space and the air, it has very low barriers to entry.	Consider cyberspace as a domain helps not only to raise the importance of cyberspace, but makes it easier for nonspecialists to understand. An unintended consequence of military classification of cyberspace as a domain is that military operations may treat it as a warfighting domain, forgetting it is dominated by the private sector. Cyberspace is no more a domain than artillery is a domain. It is a tool to be used in the conquest for air, sea, and land.
6.3.4.10	Military leadership shall prioritize cyber defense over offense.	Cyber defense is the ability to stop adversaries from effectively using cyber offensive capabilities. Cyber offense (using nonkinetic cyber capabilities to attack adversaries in cyberspace) is also considered an important military capability.	Without a functioning cyberspace, nations may be unable to run their economy, make political decisions during conflict, or generate military force. Any or all of these might be disrupted by an adversary if defense is not considered the highest priority. This policy makes sense only for nations that operate critical infrastructure using cyberspace. Some allied nations in the world have so little dependence on cyberspace that their marginal dollars in the context of their community of allegiance are best spent on attack. Defense can be complex and expensive, while offenses can be a deterrent, and thus also contribute to defense. Theoretically, some adversaries can be deterred by a sufficiently advanced offense.
6.3.4.11	Cyber offense shall be treated as a valid, sometimes even preferred, military capability.	This policy would prioritize cyber attacks over more traditional physical attacks as a first consideration for all military operations.	Cyber offense is equivalent to nuclear weapons in that its use may disproportionally affect civilians. Cyber attacks on large-scale critical infrastructure may indeed have disproportionate effects. While cyber attacks may have unintended consequences, cyber offensives are probably more likely to be used as nonkinetic attacks that neither kill nor cause permanent damage. A cyber attack that disables an air defense site rather than the site being targeted with a kinetic iron bomb, probably will save the lives of site operators. Likewise, a cyber attack against an electrical power system could be configured to cause damage that is much more transient and reversible than a similar impact caused by kinetic attack. Where commanders have access to nonkinetic and nonlethal capabilities, it is more humane to use these attacks.

(Continued)

Table 6.3.4 (Continued)

Policy statement	Explanation	Reasons for controversy
6.3.4.12 Military leadership shall over time integrate their capability and forces for cyber conflict into their traditional warfighting doctrines and structures.	Historically, military cyber capabilities have been linked to intelligence, to special offensive programs, or to information technology reinforcement programs. This puts cyber security outside the normal understanding of missions operated by military organizations. This policy would establish the objective of reintegration.	Integrating offensive and defensive (and intelligence) operations allows integrated effects on the battlefield, cyberspace operations should be no exception. Specialized cyber organizations serve important purposes, but their capabilities need to become integrated into formal command and control and operational structures. It may be difficult for many diverse cyber security operations to become integrated because capability itself is exceptionally sensitive. Where a military organization is relatively immature at integrating cyber capabilities, forces consolidation will detract from the missions and defense programs for which the small cyber conflict units were originally developed, and leave those programs with a critical lack of cyber security support.
6.3.4.13 Military leadership shall prioritize developing rules of engagement for cyberspace that mirror those for other domains, but applied to the realities of cyberspace.	Rules of engagement specify when and how a friendly force may use force against others. In kinetic warfare, these can be relative straightforward or (such as during irregular warfare) very difficult. In cyber conflict, they will be difficult not only because it is a new domain of warfare, but because of the technical nature of cyberspace.	This policy may mean that the rules for engagement will likely begin by being very restrictive, as they should be until, over time, political leaders, commanders, operators, and lawyers become more familiar and knowledgeable with cyber conflicts and capabilities. Restrictive rules of engagement are frustrating to military operators or commanders who may feel they have capabilities useful to an ongoing fight. Where rules for engagement do not exist, the military may be conducting hostile and damaging cyberspace operations without the oversight or knowledge of their own government. Rules of engagement are what keep militaries on the legal side of international humanitarian law.
6.3.4.14 Military leadership shall be cautious about certain targets and capabilities: active defense, cyber operational preparation of the environment, and targeting foreign critical infrastructures.	Active defense usually means a capability to "hack back" systems involved in attacks. Cyber elements are intruding into foreign systems prior to an offensive attack. Foreign infrastructures will be depended on by foreign militaries and as such are usually legal targets.	In each of these areas, it is usually entirely legal for militaries to pursue these targets and capabilities; however, it should be done very cautiously. Cyber operational planning elements are a needed capability to prepare for offensive action, but could be escalatory, as adversaries may see the cyber elements as the opening shots of the attack itself.

6.3.4.15	Cyber attacks shall be considered a "threat or use of force" or an "armed attack" (according to the UN Charter) based on the scope, duration, and intensity of the attack.	These thresholds are keys for determining whether international actions rise to the level of force, conflict, or warfare and determine what actions a targeted nation or the international community may do in response.	This policy will ensure that only attacks that are equivalent in effects to those from kinetic weapons at the high-end of the use of military force will be considered armed attacks, while the threat or use of force is at the lower end. Where cyber attacks are intended to cause massive harm, but fail in their objective, these attacks should be considered acts of war. To treat them with less significance merely gives the enemy an unimpeded chance to improve its capabilities. The determination of whether war is an appropriate course of action should be made based on the effects of any attack rather than the modality of that attack.
6.3.4.16	Nations shall be considered to have responsibility over the elements of cyberspace located within their borders.	Though cyberspace is commonly thought to be borderless, it operates on physical infrastructure and organizations that are rooted in the physical world and located within the sovereign borders of nations.	This policy holds nations responsible for attacks coming from their territory. If they are not able to cease attacks coming from their territory, other nations can take countermeasures, especially if the attackers are under the overall control of the state. Nations accordingly should be held responsible for attacks of cyber warfare launched from their borders and be obliged to stop the attack if it is able. This responsibility should vary depending on the scope, duration, and intensity of the attack. If nations are not able to meet this obligation, targeted nations are entitled to take countermeasures (in line with the UN Charter and laws of armed conflict). If private groups are conducting attacks on behalf of the state, the state may be held responsible if it maintains overall control of the group (such as providing resources or guidance on targets and weapons) Holding nations responsible may provide cover for repressive countries to further clamp down on privacy and free speech. Also, the United States has so much of the Internet infrastructure (and many unsecure computers) that it will have to make a significant effort to stem the many attacks (often measured as fully one-third of all attacks globally) coming from its cyber territory.
6.3.4.17	"Cyber terrorism" should be considered as terrorist attacks that are conducted through cyberspace.	Actions like recruiting or spreading propaganda is not a terrorist attack and should not be considered "cyber terrorism" just because they happen in cyberspace. Only cyber attacks that disable, destroy, or disrupt cyber systems or information and that are intended to terrorize should be considered cyber terrorism.	Treating cyber terrorism this way greatly simplifies the concept by excluding a great number of attacks that have nothing to do with terrorism, but that often are given that label. By calling cyber attacks "terrorism," some organizations have been able to gain larger budgets as their management is more willing to spend money on terrorism than if the same actions are undertaken by criminal groups.

acceptance. This section explores some of the policy issues that routinely arise in managing cyber security. Cyber security has long been used to control assets tracked by computer systems, and so cyber security management is accustomed to apply checks and balances to ensure that their fiduciary responsibility for asset management is met. Cyber security management often begins with research into both technology capabilities and system requirements. It is dependent on the capability of an organization to buy, build, or outsource technology components, and so supply chain management is a critical requirement for success in technology practice. Often, cyber security management will attempt to delegate security functions to areas of cyberspace management that are most closely associated with the assets to be protected. However, these delegation attempts sometimes fail due to a lack of security skills sets in the delegated area. An often suggested solution to this problem is some type of certification and/or accreditation for security professionals. These requirements extend to suppliers of services and equipment that are incorporated into an enterprise cyberspace infrastructure. Checks and balances are required to hedge against cyber security risk. There is a large amount of research in cyber security practices that has enabled successful security solutions, and it has led professionals to adopt principles that provide guidance for security design and operation. However, as discussed in Chapter 3, more research and development is needed to cover both existing and emerging cyberspace usage scenarios.

6.4.1 Fiduciary Responsibility

Operations is a generic term in many technology and systems-based organizations to refer to the staff that maintains and monitors business process. In heavily technology-supported businesses, technology operations and business process are intractably intertwined. Even where two separate departments maintain and monitor the technology-enabled processes and business-level process independently, the Operations department is supported by screens and programs that are information-rich views of the same technology whose byte-flow and electronic circuits are monitored by the information technology department. For example, the technology department may configure employees to use systems while the business department will be responsible for configuring customer users. Operations, or "ops," as it is colloquially called, also generally include technology services support organizations like desktop software installation and help desk. Of course, there are always exceptions, and this depiction of mainstream technology operations is not necessarily applicable to industrial control systems (ICSs).

Nevertheless, as in any community where sizable assets are maintained by a few privileged and trusted people, operations administrators routinely face ethical dilemmas. In addition to controlling user access to systems, Operations is the caretaker of the assets themselves. In large systems-oriented organizations, large databases of personally identifiable information (PII) and information repositories of trade secrets are handled according to preset routine, in the same perfunctory fashion as systems containing cafeteria menus are handled. However, in a secure organization, the access control settings and monitoring processes for the sensitive information are more rigorous than the technologies and procedures implemented to support the menus.

Cyber operations in any sizable enterprise is typically a round-the-clock endeavor. Even where global marketplaces do not demand active support, automated system processes may be required to devote considerable computer resources in off-hours to crunch numbers to produce data for start-of-day consumption. The 7×24 nature of operations makes ops the obvious first point of contact for any message or alert which may indicate potential business interruption. Hence, security incident identification and response procedures are a routine part of operational process, even those that do not consider themselves responsible for security (Kim, Love et al. 2008).

The policy statements listed in this section all address issues that arise in accepting or performing information caretaker responsibilities. The first few fiduciary responsibility issues concern the establishment of management processes that are required to demonstrate that due diligence is exercised in the caretaker function. These are followed by specific expectations that data owners typically have of data caretakers. The remaining issues address the role of nation-states in establishing conditions for the smooth functioning of a technology industry requiring demonstration of fiduciary responsibility (Table 6.4.1).

6.4.2 Risk Management

Risk management applies to any kind of risk. Typically, a risk management officer or division will focus on credit risk, market risk, and operations risk. Technology risk is a subset of operations risk, and cyber security risk is typically viewed as a subset of technology risk. The human element in operation is considered more of a risk than the technology risk because despite all of the software flaws in computers, they are still typically more reliable than people at performing a job repeatedly and consistently. Even for systems under development, it is far more common for software engineers to sabotage a system or a project by intentionally exercising the authority in their own job function than to thwart security measures (Rost and Glass 2011). Given its low relative risk in the hierarchy of the things risk managers care about, security risk is often absent from any centralized enterprise risk management process. If any formal cyber

Table 6.4.1 Cyber Security Policy Issues Concerning Fiduciary Responsibility

Policy statement	Explanation	Reasons for controversy
6.4.1.1 Senior management shall appoint a Chief Information Security Officer to bear the responsibility of cyber security management.	The role of a Chief Information Security Officer is intended to provide leadership and coordination for the organization's information security strategy, policy, and operations.	If security advocates are placed high enough in management to be peers of Chiefs in other areas such as the Chief Legal Officer and Chief Financial Officer, the need for security in organizational process and procedure should get sufficient management attention to be successful. A culture of security is not created by the appointment of an individual. Where upper management appreciates the needs for security, it can be done in a variety of matrix management structures. Where they do not, such an appointment will place the individual in a position of responsibility without authority.
6.4.1.2 An organization appointed by senior management with appropriate budget and authority shall establish a program to authorize and document changes to critical digital assets, to detect changes as they occur, and to compare the detected changes to the authorization.	Many organizations approve changes, but do not confirm that only approved changes are implemented. This policy calls for change control to the extent that every detected change is verified as authorized or not authorized.	This policy requires that a level of detail be kept for every planned change that would allow an independent observer to verify that the change was correct. As many planned changed require considerable talent just to execute, it puts too much of burden on ops to compare a plan to an actual change. If plans cannot be specified to a level of detail necessary to verify change authorization, then the detail is likely not to be sufficient for informed approval either. This policy would add benefit to both processes.
6.4.1.3 Lack of tested technology business recovery plan for critical services shall be considered negligence for critical consumer services.	This policy would require that technology hosting providers and software services vendors maintain alternate computing facilities that may be configured to be used in the event of a main system failure, and also to test the failover from the main site to the alternate site.	Where consumers and businesses are encouraged to reply on vendors to operate technology processes that are business or mission critical, those services shall be supported as per technology industry standards. Unless business recovery processes are part of a service contract, customers of technology service providers should not expect them to be incorporated into services. To stay in business, a technology vendor need only offer the service, not maintain the integrity of user data. As described by Louis Black, not having a technology recovery plan is like inventing fire and not keeping a torch lit in case the main fire went out. Services that are completely lost would have to be reinvented.

(Continued)

This policy should ensure that access to sensitive information is not mistakenly granted to individuals who do not need it and that it is removed from individuals who no longer need it.

Requiring users to be registered and be individually authorized may delay access to information needed to perform critical functions.

	Requirement	Explanation
6.4.1.4	Wherever access control has been configured to protect cyberspace assets, the identity and organizational role of each user granted access shall be tracked to ensure that the access is revoked when the purpose of granting access is no longer valid.	This requirement is referred to as "identity management." It usually involves setting up a database of identity information, usually modeled on human resources and contractor data repositories, and using the database as an integral part of user authorization workflow and automated systems audit.
6.4.1.5	Process control systems that control hazardous processes and/or materials shall be very highly restricted.	Many automated systems control operations in which mistakes have safety implications (e.g., chemical mixing processes or heavy manufacturing equipment). Accidental or intentional changes in the programs that control such systems could have devastating results on the health of individuals in the proximity of such systems. The fewer people that have access to these systems, the less likely it is that they will be controlled by anyone with malicious intent. Process control anomalies happen for reasons other than cyber security attacks, and when they do, it is better to have open access to the process control systems in order to allow any individual capable to redirect the process.
6.4.1.6	An organization appointed by senior management with appropriate budget and authority shall ensure that appropriate cyber security awareness and training have been provided to all appropriate personnel on an accepted time interval.	Organizational cyber security programs cannot be fully executed by security staff because everyone in the organization who handles information may have the ability to impact information attributes such as confidentiality, integrity, and availability. It may not be obvious to a staff member how their behavior enhances or detracts from the cyber security program. Security training makes their responsibilities with respect to security clear and makes them accountable for their role in the security program. For businesses with ICSs, appropriate ICS awareness and training should be required. Many individuals have no ability to adversely affect information security and such widespread training programs are thus a waste of resources.
6.4.1.7	National governments shall ensure that sensitive information held by vendors be given the same protection it would be given by the government agency contracting with that vendor.	This is a common standard for commercial organizations which cannot pass along responsibility for regulatory compliance simply because technology services are outsourced. This policy would hold government agencies responsible for safeguarding information, regardless of whether it has been handed to vendors or not. Governments must ensure that service providers they enlist protect information at government-established standards. This could include PII (such as names or personal identification numbers such as U.S. Social Security Numbers) or intellectual property on government programs or projects (such as weapons development or acquisition). This policy would require not only sufficient protection of this information but also notification to the government if there was a security breech in the environment containing this information.

Table 6.4.1 (*Continued*)

Policy statement	Explanation	Reasons for controversy
6.4.1.8	National governments shall measure their own security using performance-based measures.	This policy would measure organizations against specific procedural and technical steps, such as success against periodic penetration testing and the time delays to patch major vulnerabilities, rather than just paperwork-only reviews.	Often, governments measure their security only by writing and reading reports (e.g., the Federal Information Security Management Act [FISMA] in the United States). A more realistic and effective measure would be to use stronger performance-based measures such as how difficult an organization is to hack into; how long their patch cycle takes; or response to specific stimuli. Many nations may not have the necessary infrastructure to scale up periodic penetration testing, exercises, or other means to give a standard measure of performance.
6.4.1.9	The nation's executive branch shall consider assembling a committee of cyber security experts from a variety of industries to advise on cyber security policy and assess cyber security programs. Such groups can also be established at other levels (especially department/ministerial).	This policy would encourage a nation's executive branch to reach beyond a small circle of current advisors and seek out assistance on cyber security strategy issues. Examples in the United States include the National Security Telecommunications Advisory Committee (NSTAC) and National Infrastructure Advisory Council (NIAC).	As the field of cyber security is very wide, lessons learned in its practice from a variety of domains will strengthen the ability of the administration to deal with the widest variety of issues going forward. Too often, cyber security experts leave government service but are willing to continue to serve on a voluntary basis. There must be very strong provisions to ensure such advisory groups do not become closed cabals of industry-government corruption or encourage anti-competitive behavior.
6.4.1.10	National governments shall codify a national cyber security strategy that includes public and private sector components, and involve coordination with key stakeholders. The strategy can include overlooked areas such as security for industrial control systems.	A national strategy lays out guidance from the national executive and should include policies, priorities, measurement, compliance, and access to funding. It can lay out priorities for research and development, defense, and stakeholder engagement.	A national strategy makes clear the national priorities and helps steer and encourage all national efforts. A poorly thought-out strategy can lead all efforts in a mistaken direction, overlooking possibly disastrous vulnerabilities or threats. It can also lead to inconsistent regulatory requirements.
6.4.1.11	Nations shall have an organization and senior leaders with enough influence and resources to drive the nation to improve its cyber security. This leader should also generally have budget authority and direct access, when needed, to the national executive.	A senior leader (such as a "cyber czar") with sufficient staff in countries is often key to making progress for cyber security.	Bureaucracies are resistant to change so a senior leader with the power to coordinate, convince, and coerce change is often essential. A senior leader outside of normal bureaucracies can often confuse chains of command. If one organization and one leader are seen to be the center, that may lessen the feeling of responsibility for other leaders and departments—especially if they lose resources to the new czar.

security management process occurs at all, it is typically done by those responsible for technology and management.

There are not many guidelines on how to perform cyberspace risk assessments, but there has been substantial work performed under the heading of information security risk assessment. Where information is considered as an asset, information security risk determines the potential loss due to damage to information. Damage to information is typically portrayed as loss or degradation of information confidentiality, integrity, or availability, though some have suggested that information security attributes be extended to encompass attributes that refer more directly to its value, such as utility and possession. Although there are many economic analysis methods available to a cyber security manager making risk assessment decisions, in its most basic form, the cost of a security measure is compared to the expected loss avoidance, and if it costs less to implement the measure, the measure is recommended to be implemented (Gordon and Loeb 2005). The hard part of this type of analysis is not to do the math, but to actually know what the risks are, and to know that the suggested measure, whose cost can be quantified, will actually perform as expected once it is installed. Security standards provide little to no guidance on this part of the process.

It is important to distinguish risk assessment as a management tool from either risk management or security management. After risk assessments are done, decisions are made based on the results. Where strategy is involved in the security decision-making process and the outcomes of those strategies are monitored, this is risk management. Where the programs, processes, and projects are created to act on risk management decisions, this is security management. Risk management results in objectives and guidance for security management. As such, risk management is at the heart of many debates on security policy issues. These debates include discussion of cyber security strategy, policy, and implementation, and include risk assessment, risk decisions, concepts for mitigation such as transfer, as well as measuring effectiveness and monitoring evolution.

Organizations in the critical infrastructure sectors are typically held to a higher standard of risk management, with systemically critical organizations being held to the highest standards of maintaining best security practices. This includes systems and networks whether they are connected to the Internet, or are completely privately operated networks for a limited number of identified parties, or proprietary networks within one organization, or industrial control systems which may have very limited network capabilities. Cyber security policy issues in risk management include organizational responsibility to understand and evaluate cyber security risk, segregation of duties utilized in risk and security management, and the government's role in assuring risk management practices for the critical infrastructure upon which communities depend for both cyber and physical services (Table 6.4.2).

Table 6.4.2 Cyber Security Policy Issues Concerning Risk Management

Policy statement		Explanation	Reasons for controversy
6.4.2.1	Organizations (whether public or private) shall be held responsible for defending themselves against "normal" cyber attacks, which are attacks which standard security practice would be able to stop.	Organizations (whether government agencies, companies, or nonprofits) must protect themselves from typical attacks. Organizations that are more critical have higher levels of responsibility.	This policy ties needed levels of protection to criticality, with responsibility assigned to those who hold the risk. Organizations in the critical infrastructure sectors will be held to a higher standard of defense, with systemically critical organizations being held to the highest standards of all of maintaining sound security practices. This includes systems and networks whether they are connected to the Internet, are private or proprietary networks or automated control systems.

Attackers have been increasing their sophistication and many organizations are now outclassed and unable to defend themselves without significant increases in funding and resources.

If there was an agreed-upon set of cyber security standards, then critical infrastructure owners and government agencies could be held accountable for implementing them.

Despite the ubiquity of cyber security standards, accepted practices in the application of cyber security risk assessment processes are not domain specific, and so still leave all major implementation decisions to subjective judgment of impact by system owner/operators (e.g., draft NIST 800-37r1). There is no reason to assume this exercise would have a different outcome.

In many security standards, "best practices" remain in the state where subjective owner/operator opinions dictate implementation requirements; it will be easy for targets of this policy to avoid its legislative intent. For example, recently, this practice led some energy system owner/operators to declare that none of their infrastructure was critical. It is not possible to establish via policy standards that do not currently exist. These types of requirements are best left to domain-specific regulators.

This policy would raise the bar of the minimum amount of cyber security that those who operate critical infrastructure upon which the Nation depends must implement, and provide the basis for holding them accountable for implementing a standard level of cyber security. |

6.4.2.2	All cyberspace systems shall undergo risk assessment.	Information security risk assessment strategies have been in place since the early days of the Internet. They are designed to ensure that threats are considered when deciding on control procedures, and that common vulnerabilities are identified and addressed.	This policy requires that every information system used by an organization is analyzed for security flaws. Risk assessments follow checklist approaches to security assessment, and new and innovative technologies and threats are often missed. Moreover, the fact that a risk assessment was done does not necessarily mean that vulnerabilities were fixed. These factors combine to provide the criticism that risk assessments commonly provide a false sense of security.
6.4.2.3	An organization appointed by and reporting to senior management shall have appropriate budget and authority to identify what mission critical digital assets, whether in applications, devices, and/or networks, are cyber vulnerable.	This policy places responsibility for conducting organization-wide cyber security risk assessment with senior management.	Without an inventory of assets to be protected, and the charter to conduct security risk assessments, security management is unguided and likely to be the equivalent of security theater. Cyber vulnerabilities should be identified by experienced professionals, and so the identification process does not require attention at the senior management level.
6.4.2.4	An organization appointed by senior management shall provide appropriate budget and authority to establish and maintain a cyber security program to secure digital assets throughout their corresponding systems life cycle.	This policy places responsibility for managing an organization-wide cyber security program with senior management.	Though risk assessment and vulnerability reduction processes may be in place, without an overarching security program, there is no verification or validation that security goals are achieved. As all cyber security processes are supported by the information technology program, the security program need not be separate, and in fact may be more effective if integrated within technology processes.
6.4.2.5	An organization appointed by senior management with appropriate budget and authority shall identify how to monitor the security of these assets during the installation, maintenance, upgrade, and change-out to assure a cyber secure system.	This policy places responsibility for managing an organization-wide cyber security operations and incident response with senior management.	Where there are joint resources assigned to incident response, those responsible for supporting critical system transaction processing will always claim the lion's share of technology resources. This often leaves inadequate resources dedicated to security response. As in the case of security program management, all cyber security processes are supported by the information technology program, the security operations area need not be separate, and in fact may be more effective if integrated within technology processes. If resources are not adequate to provide security, technology managers should be held accountable as they are for any other system deliverable.

(Continued)

Table **6.4.2** (Continued)

	Policy statement	Explanation	Reasons for controversy
6.4.2.6	National governments should encourage a market for cyber security risk management.	This policy would provide economic incentives to establish a market for cyber security risk management.	Cyber security risk management is not currently economically viable. Entrepreneurs with ideas for cyber security risk management businesses should be encouraged.
			If poorly implemented, the government might crowd out private-sector solutions or be too technology- or vendor-specific. Subsidies based on government definitions of cyber security risk management would detract from creating solutions that make sense to an emerging cyberspace marketplace.
			These could include ways to allow companies to transfer cyber security risk through insurance or catastrophe bonds, as they do for other kinds of hazards.
			This policy does not go far enough to ensure that private operators of critical infrastructure perform risk management activities. These should not just be encouraged but mandated, and this would create the necessary marketplace to comply with the mandates.
6.4.2.7	Government shall create a security metrics, or "dashboard," reporting system whose scope is the systems and networks operated by the Government.	This policy would require that systems and networks supported by the standards setting arm of the government be monitored and measured according to established standards.	The standards setting arm of the government requires accurate information about the state of security in the systems and networks which follow their standards. Requiring this information allows them to receive feedback.
			This activity is already supported by the standards-setting arm of the government (in the United States, the Department of Commerce, which includes NIST), and government systems are already uniformly subject to security management requirements (e.g., FISMA), which require management monitoring, and a "dashboard" policy is redundant.
			This policy would require first an inventory of systems supporting the government as a whole, and so would create transparency for its dependency on systems security.
6.4.2.8	New standards shall be established to calculate return on investment in information security, and these shall acknowledge benefits that emerge from control over assets.	Return on security investment is currently calculated based on loss avoidance, and loss avoidance calculations use probability of attack as a critical input. The benefits of security in the absence of threat are not quantified.	Return on investment risk analysis loss probabilities are based on historical data and loss avoidance, but there is no historical data on which to base probability judgments for cyber security. Therefore, new types of calculations are required to accurately reflect the soundness of security investment.
			Security investment is just one aspect of technology management and should be justified on the basis of the benefits it provides. No special treatment is required to ensure that benefits are considered.

6.4.3 Professional Certification

The process of certifying information security professionals is a growing and dynamic field. There are literally thousands of certifications available, ranging from hands-on examinations of product-specific knowledge, to subject area certification, to broad information security certifications. None of the popular cyber security certifications carry any form of liability or bonding beyond an expected adherence to a common code of ethics and conduct, nor are they equivalent to professional registration regimes. While the term "engineer" is often used in this career field ("software engineer" and "network engineer" are common examples), it is not in the same context as a registered or licensed engineer that is subject to a given government's regulations of the profession.

Normally, companies and organizations will train and certify their cyber security employees to some standard acceptable to the broader career field. But if internal employees are not used exclusively for cyber security operations, organizations and companies are not relieved of the responsibility for regulatory compliance when they outsource technology operations. Hence, they must find ways to demonstrate that the vendors with whom they have contracted are capable of meeting cyber security requirements. This requirement has spawned a plethora of checklists used by companies to determine whether the vendor security posture is capable of delivering a security operational process. For example, the DoD has established a certification program as a response to an audit finding that DoD contractors were performing security work without the requisite background. The director of the program maintains that any certification is better than none, as it gives the government a tool for oversight that can be improved going forward (e.g., DoD 2005). However, the certification required to perform the job function of a security engineer is one that can be achieved by passing an exam of technology facts and requires no demonstrating of security engineering experience. Nevertheless, a high school dropout who gains this certification on the job will be favored by policy by the DoD for a security engineering job over a successfully practicing engineer with 20 years' experience and advanced degrees in cyber security. One reason given for upholding the DoD standard is that certifications require continuous learning while advanced degrees are not evident of continuing education in security. However, the authors include Certified Security Information Managers (CISM), Certified Information Systems Security Professionals (CISSP), and Certified Information Security Auditors (CISA), and well understand that one can get ongoing education credit hours from the organizations that support these certifications by attending vendor-advertisement presentations, reading magazine articles, or watching news-oriented podcasts. Moreover, there are many fields within cyber security where staffs require additional training, but there are currently no certifications in that area, for example, secure software engineering. None of the certification's continuing education requirements have requirements to be related to the job function one is currently performing, and there is little by way of audit. Nor are we aware of anyone who actually had their certification revoked based on lack of ongoing education.

On the other hand, a certification can expire if one does not pay renewal fees, and this is the reason why policy should support companies who may be trying to get more value out of their education and training dollars than simply paying for certification tests. It makes more sense for a large enterprise to invest more in security staff up front for thorough technology education and then keep people trained for the job in which they are placed.

The policies in the section include professional certification standards issued at the individual, organizational, and national level (Table 6.4.3).

6.4.4   Supply Chain

In the cyber security supply chain, the most visible exposure to threat is often seen as external, such as an ISP, reference data source, or cloud computing application. The enterprise-to-enterprise communication that is required to run a technology operation in cyberspace has surfaced many issues with respect to organizational representation of information upon which others must depend to operate in harmony. It has also highlighted the lack of formal accountability for the veracity and integrity of that information. However, the supply chain also includes everything that technology practitioners do to support infrastructure and applications internal to the enterprise.

The depth and breadth of the cyberspace supply chain is difficult to quantify. It will differ depending on the type of system contemplated. It will always include some kind of software, but may also include software developers themselves. The types of hardware it may include range from mainframe computers to programmable chips. Almost all elements of the cyberspace supply chain have experienced known incidents of counterfeit or sabotage, and it is often hard to tell the difference, as a counterfeit part may malfunction and create unintended sabotage (DSB 2005).

That is, another very visible but often overlooked part of an organization's supply chain is the organization's own IT department. This department is often not fully integrated with an enterprise, but integrates itself with a suite of technology suppliers that it assumes responsibility to operate on behalf of the business. Weakness in internal supply chain, such as delays in onboarding new staff, account for a lot of negative audit findings due to workarounds by staff needing to use computers to get jobs done. Given a choice between violating security policy and being cited for poor performance, performance wins every time.

Moreover, technology managers are routinely plagued by software vendors who do not consider security requirements and usually disclaim

Table 6.4.3 Cyber Security Policy Issues Concerning Professional Certification

Policy statement		Explanation	Reasons for controversy
6.4.3.1	Individuals in positions of responsibility with respect to cyber security shall be certified to be competent in the field.	There are several cyber security professional associations who offer certifications to members who can pass a test and provide evidence of cyber security experience. This policy would require every cyber security professional to join one (sometimes even a specific one) of these organizations, pass the test, and remain a member.	It is critically important that individuals who have responsibility for security measures fully understand how their job function contributes to the overall cyber security landscape. Certifications provide the broad security background necessary to provide this view. There is no consensus among cyber security experts that people who have achieved any of the available certifications are more competent to do a cyber security job than someone with equivalent experience who is not certified. This type of policy favors individuals who can afford to pay for certification tests and annual certification fees. Whether or not there is any existing professional body of knowledge agreed upon to be necessary for cyber security professionals to understand is irrelevant to the fact that a certification process acknowledges the need for one and that cyber security professionals have to undergo some preliminary version of the desired test in the meantime while it is being developed. This allows the process to be established to receive the body of knowledge when it becomes available.
6.4.3.2	Nations shall encourage a professional cyber cadre to define and defend new job classifications for cyber security professionals.	Cyber defenders, planners, and attackers need specific high-level training for their highly specialized disciplines. The type of training required depends on industry, type of system, and role in cyber security program.	Investments in job requirement analysis will drive a more sophisticated workforce and cyber specialists. Current definitions of job classifications are just beginning to be enforced (DoD 2005). Allowing changes to the rules in progress interferes with enforcement efforts that are just beginning to take root. By loosening bureaucratic rules for recruiting and retention and establishing new job classifications for cyber security professionals, programs should particularly encourage definition of critical requirements that are underdeveloped, such as cyber security for industrial control systems.
6.4.3.3	National governments shall encourage (and in many cases require) all government personnel working in cyber security to be trained and certified. For areas like industrial control system cyber security where there is not adequate training nor programs, these should be encouraged. In general, nations should favor existing commercial certifications rather than develop government-only programs.	Certification and training programs—like those from SANS or industrial control system (ISC)[2] — establish well-known baselines and are widely available.	There is a large body of knowledge in cyber security that has been accumulated over the years, and requirements for training and certification would ensure that working professionals are accountable for applying it. As there is no agreed-upon standard cyber security curriculum, widespread adoption of a specific training program and guaranteed subsequent hiring programs may have the unexpected consequence of reducing the variety of cyber security expertise within government agencies. These concerns are even more exacerbated for ICS.

(Continued)

Table 6.4.3 (Continued)

Policy statement	Explanation	Reasons for controversy
6.4.3.4 Accreditation, training, and certification programs shall be established for all personnel working in industrial control system cyber security.	There is no standard curriculum for industrial control system cyber security nor are there any certifications or university interdisciplinary programs for cyber security of industrial control systems.	There is a large body of knowledge in cyber security that has been accumulated over the years, and requirements for accreditation would ensure that working professionals are accountable for applying it. However, the same cannot be said for industrial control systems. As there is no agreed-upon standard cyber security curriculum, widespread adoption of a specific training program and guaranteed subsequent hiring programs may have the unexpected consequence of reducing the variety of cyber security expertise within government agencies. These concerns are even more exacerbated for industrial control systems.
6.4.3.5 Management shall collect data on cyber security professional hiring and use it so determine cyber security hiring effectiveness.	This is a requirement for management due diligence to ensure that plans for cyber security hiring have been successful.	This policy forces managers who recruit and hire cyber security personnel to assess the effectiveness of their efforts. These assessments should lead to continuous improvement in cyber security staffing effectiveness. This type of policy should be a routine function of human resource management endeavors and should not be specific to cyber security. Creating special functions for cyber security that overlap with routine management unnecessarily overburdens cyber security managers with extra paperwork.
6.4.3.6 National criteria for evaluating cyber security accreditation, training, and certification programs to all cyber security accreditation, training, and certification programs used by government and critical infrastructure operators shall be established, applied, and published.	It is very hard to know which vendors are capable of meeting claims that they provide adequate cyber security training. This policy would create a guide for the average citizen or industrial organization to find a credible cyber security training firm.	This policy would provide much needed guidance to government agencies and critical infrastructure operators who are individually evaluating training programs. The multiple simultaneous evaluations of the same training programs is not cost-effective as it requires a technically credible government organization to identify who is credible in industrial control systems and that does not exist. Publication of an "authorized" list of cyber security training programs would be a disincentive for entrepreneurs poised to enter the cyber security training market, and eventually lower both the availability and the quality of available training options. Companies would have to pay premiums to companies on the list rather than seek out innovative training approaches. All hiring goals, metrics, and plans should be made public to encourage applicants—and allow public tracking of progress.

accountability for how the software works (Rice 2008). This places a large burden on technology managers who must chose among insecure software products and integrate them into a technology infrastructure for which they are responsible for maintaining quality of service.

This section starts with policy statements concerning software security quality that are typically encountered in the context of enterprise acquisitions. It then covers cyber security supply chain policy issues of national importance and builds on prior statements concerning Cyber Conflict in Section 6.3. These policy statements are followed by more general issues of supply chain effects on infrastructure (Table 6.4.4).

6.4.5 Security Principles

Over the years of security management practices, several studies have attempted to classify security technology practice into general security principles (Neumann 2004). The result is that there is a common body of knowledge of cyber security architecture patterns that, if observed in the requirements stages of technology engineering, serve to suggest well-known solutions to well-known security problems. Security principles are generic descriptions of security features that provide solutions to cyber security problems that are both common and well understood. For example, the principle of least resource, which dictates that users should have at their disposal the fewest amount of shared computing resources that they need to complete their tasks, and no more. Many of these principles were derived by the information systems audit profession, and have their origins in the service of the accounting profession, whose early assignments with respect to computers were to ensure that computer-generated computers could properly account for corporate assets (Bayuk 2005). Some evolved alongside and consistent with government standards for security such as the Orange Book and its successors (DoD 1985; ISO/IEC 2009a,b). Others emerged from the study of cryptography in computer science (Denning 1982).

Many of these principles have been codified by the information systems auditors, some as early as 1977 (Singleton 1994). These have been continually updated by the Information Systems Audit and Control Association (ISACA), global certification authority for information systems auditors, *Control Objectives for Information Technology* (COBIT) (ISACA 2007). For example, ISACA defines segregation of duties as a basic internal control that prevents or detects errors and irregularities by assigning separate individual responsibility for different steps in a multistep process for initiating and recording transactions that result in change of assets custody. This technique is commonly used in large IT organizations for software deployment processes so that no single person is in a position to introduce fraudulent or malicious code without detection. It is also commonly applied to secure financial transactions, and is also used in high security setting

Table 6.4.4 Cyber Security Policy Issues Concerning Supply Chain

Policy statement	Explanation	Reasons for controversy
6.4.4.1 Software vendors shall be liable for damage resulting from code malfunctions.	End-User License Agreements are typically worded to deprive customers of any rights to liability for production malfunction.	End-User License Agreements are currently contrived to deprive end users of any rights to liability for production malfunction. Software vendors should be subject to the same standards of product liability as any other industry. Software may malfunction for a variety of reasons, and many of these have nothing to do with the code. A user may install the software on a platform without the necessary resources for it to operate. Malfunction in these cases would not be the fault of the software vendor.
6.4.4.2 Software support shall not be fully automated.	This policy would require software support processes to always allow a customer to contact an individual to resolve support issues.	Software flaws are expected not just in delivered process, but also in automated support system. Any technology vendor that provides support must give customers a way to talk to a person in order at least to report support issues. For example, there are often flaws in automated support mechanisms. such as loops in customer support trouble-reporting systems that do not allow customers to submit details of their problems, or choices constrained to a list of technical problems that do not include the one experienced by the customer. Software companies price software according to the level of effort it will take to support. Where the level of effort is expected to be minimal the price is cheaper, and customers get what they pay for.
6.4.4.3 Software security standards shall be required to legally operate e-commerce Internet sites	This policy would establish minimum security controls on all e-commerce services.	Given the risk to consumers of potential malware, impersonation, and asset theft resulting from insecure websites, no website should be able to offer consumer services without abiding by established security standards. There are no established security standards that will guarantee safety from attack, and no enforcement mechanism that would provide assurance that any given website abides by them.
6.4.4.4 Nations shall use their acquisition policies to create incentives for IT companies to improve the security of their products.	National governments purchase tremendous quantities of IT equipment: hardware and software, networking equipment, desktops, automated control systems, and more. This gives nations leverage to negotiate improved security for those purchases.	If national governments, often the consumers purchasing in the largest quantities, negotiate for improved security, it will bring benefits not only to those national governments (in the form of improved security) but to companies in that nation and indeed to all consumers worldwide. If systems are more secure out-of-the-box then costs will be cheaper over their life cycle. It is difficult for national bureaucracies to change procurement practices and improved security can often make systems marginally more expensive at the onset (though cheaper over the whole life cycle).

6.4.4.5	All personnel at all suppliers of cyberspace components destined for military or industrial control system use shall be screened for potential security problems.	The global supply chain makes it possible to inject malicious software and hardware into the nation's critical infrastructure. This policy would require those who handle products destined for such environments to be rated trustworthy.	Screening for security problems are a minimum requirement. A full background check or a DoD security clearance might also be required for more sensitive programs. Since component makers of software, PCs and networking gear usually do not know the end user of their systems this policy would mean every maker would have to comply, which would be overly broad. Screening should only be necessary when a risk assessment dictates. Blanket policies such as these are unnecessarily expensive. Screening may expose employees to violations of privacy expectations, or could reveal historical information that could harm the employee's future employment potential in noncritical environments.
6.4.4.6	All cyber security regulations applicable to DoD networks shall be applicable to defense industrial base networks used to provide services to the department of defense.	Cyber security standards are routinely set for government agencies and this requirement extends those security requirements to companies that provide them with the products and services they use to carry out their missions.	This policy would eliminate a weak link in protection requirements around defense-related information and make it harder for espionage agents to learn about department of defense activities. This policy is too inclusive as it extends to all defense contractors, not just those that provide critical services or are in possession of classified information. Moreover, not all DoD security requirements are publicly announced, and this policy would require widespread sharing of these requirements.
6.4.4.7	The DoD shall specify the organizational management structure that defense suppliers should used to manage cyber security programs.	Secure management practices are just as important as security of computers and networks. DIB companies must adhere to management structures specified by the DoD.	Specification of security management structures in DIB companies and organizations will reduce the risk of management mistakes. Business leaders may feel that they should not be told how to organize their management structures, that what is important is to produce goods and services conforming to what is specified in a performance contract.
6.4.4.8	All cyberspace components destined for military use shall be made in country.	To greatly reduce the risk of embedded malicious code, devices destined for use in military applications should be manufactured domestically.	Most cyber hardware and software is produced overseas, potentially creating a security risk while also impacting the U.S. job market. This policy is entirely impractical and would run up DoD IT budgets drastically. Moreover it may not even buy much protection if the designs are made outside the country, by foreign corporations or by foreign nationals working for U.S. companies All countries are subjected to the "not made here" problem when it comes to hardware and software. The United States enjoyed a unique position for decades when manufacturing was largely done domestically. However, globalized supply systems have changed the economics of production, moving manufacturing to locations where labor and materials are cheaper.

(Continued)

Table 6.4.4 (Continued)

Policy statement	Explanation	Reasons for controversy
6.4.4.9	Cyber security suppliers shall be prohibited from sharing security intellectual property with hostile nation-states.	This is the type of policy that would add security products to the list of munitions prohibited from export to hostile nation-states (State 2010).	This policy would make it easier to pinpoint cyber security intellectual property leaks by restricting information flow between sets of security companies and hostile nation-states. This policy would prevent U.S. companies from protecting their global infrastructure in places where the need is greatest.
6.4.4.10	Where a third party information systems service is utilized to achieve business objectives, security requirements commensurate with the risk to business process of systemic failure of that service shall be contractually imposed and compliance monitored.	This requirement has its origins in accounting outsourcing such as payroll and benefits process, but is becoming more relevant as cloud computing services are used to perform critical business functions. Many industries are regulatory-required to include this statement and resources to enforce it as an essential component of internal security programs.	Though a business may not by virtue of outsourcing transfer its regulatory requirements via contractual relationships, service contracts that include security requirements and audit clauses allow them to provide appropriate due diligence while reaping the benefits of economies of scale and specialized expertise in service delivery that are available from specialized service providers. The major reason why a business contracts for information services is that it has no internal competency to perform them. Therefore, even oversight functions that seek evidence that contractual requirements are met are typically performed by staff with minimal understanding of the outsourced service who are satisfied with a checklist rather than an investigative approach.
6.4.4.11	Onboarding and other administrative processes shall be designed to facilitate rather than delay business function.	Operations management may be tempted to direct staff to bypass security procedures in order to quickly onboard a new and important client or high level employee executive.	Many security procedures in large organizations are so burdensome that they inhibit productivity for authorized users. Security procedures are required to ensure that and businesses should incorporate time delays into their onboarding processes rather than pressure security personnel to make quick decisions. Information security should rather benefit from the equivalent of a just-say-no campaign.
6.4.3.12	Cyber security access control mechanisms shall be rated for effectiveness, and this rating shall be required to be included in all cyber security sales literature.	This policy would require an authoritative agency to develop criteria to evaluate the strength of access controls such as logins and passwords.	Every system is different, so an access control that works for one may not work for another, which would render the rating meaningless. In physical security, as secure specifications are developed, they are adopted in the form of local codes and ordinances, which, if demonstrably effective, may be raised to state and federal standards. The same practice should be followed for systems security.

6.4.4.13	Software vendors shall allow third parties to review code for security flaws.	Current, many ICS vendors will not allow third parties to inspect their code for security flaws which makes security disclosures very difficult at best.	Software vendors would have to expose their Intellectual Property to third parties, as access to their code would be required to comply with this policy. Third party code review or penetration testing cannot be done without access to the code. The benefits of code review to users outweigh the threats to intellectual property from a small set of security testers, who could easily be screened and/or bonded.
6.4.4.14	Software security standards shall be required to legally operate –Commerce Internet sites	This policy would establish minimum security controls on all e-commerce services.	Given the risk to consumers of potential malware, impersonation, and asset theft resulting from insecure websites, no website should be able to offer consumer services without abiding by established security standards. There are no established security standards that will guarantee safety from attack, and no enforcement mechanism that would provide assurance that any given website abides by them.
6.4.4.15	Automated inventory systems in critical infrastructure such as health care shall be subject to regulatory audit.	Automation of inventory management allows "just in time" supply chain management, where inventories are kept to a minimum because suppliers can ship replacements just as the last item is removed from inventory.	Automated supply chain management systems often rely on highly vulnerable technologies such as radio frequency identification (RFID) chips embedded into labels of packages. Overreliance on these technologies as a replacement for actual inspection of inventory items could blind management to actual shortages. Inventory is a critical business asset and companies have considerable vested interest in the integrity of these systems. External auditors are unlikely to add value to business process oversight for their own critical assets. Although external auditors are unlikely to add value to business process oversight for their own critical asset, where not for profit companies or municipalities perform needed community services, consciousness of potential loss via theft is minimal. Inventories are not as closely watched. Regulatory oversight may be beneficial in these cases.
6.4.4.16	Diagnostic laboratories used to record and correlate food sample measurements and customer complaints shall be owned and operated by domestic entities.	This is a requirement to keep all the information used to make decisions about food safety within the jurisdiction of national borders.	As cyber attack patterns grow more sophisticated, all information that contributes to consumer safety should be considered a potential cyberwar or cyber terrorist target. Many food sources originate outside of the national cyberspace infrastructure and it is not feasible to transfer control of laboratory networks to firms for protectionist reasons because competing services are readily available in the country of origin.

such as missile launch scenarios. The same technique could be said for any operation that controls an asset or process critical to enterprise mission or purpose. This is what makes it a security principle.

A key contribution from the accounting profession is the principle of segregation of duties, which dictates that, for situations wherein a user controls valuable assets, every individual one of them should be restricted from changing ownership of those assets without the collusion of others, a principle designed to deter insider fraud. This requires automated processes that transfer assets to be broken down into subprocesses, and no one person being given permission to execute every step in the subprocess. A pure technology derivation of this type of accounting principle is the principle of least privilege which dictates that users should have the minimum access they need to perform a technology task and no more. Segregation of duties applies not just to technology processes, but also to management processes. The most significant of these is the process by which security is managed. Managing security is a two-step process: risk and operation. Once security risks have been identified, management makes decisions on whether, and if so, how to reduce security vulnerabilities. These vulnerability reduction programs should then be treated just as any other set of technology projects. Projects, by definition, are not persistent, and so any management of security measures that requires day-to-day oversight, such as user administration, is an operations rather than a risk management process. Where management has responsibility for risk management, and also security projects and/or operations, there is temptation to accept risk rather than spend resources to reduce vulnerabilities or verify that processes are working. On the verification side, this is obvious, and teams of auditors are normally deployed to ensure that security operations are well-managed in critical systems. However, on the risk management versus vulnerability reduction side, it is common to see the function assigned to the same individual. Hence, formal risk acceptance processes for security policy violations are common, even if the most senior managers in the firm have endorsed security policy.

System security features based on tried and true security principles are not accomplished by technology alone, but by combinations of people, process, and technologies conjoined with security-aware management practices. This section includes policy statements from security principles to illustrate the issue concerning their adoption. From the variety of examples, it is clear that the application of security principles is system and implementation specific. Principles that apply to one situation may not necessarily apply to another.

Cyber security policies listed in this section are based on management, technology, and operations principles, in that order, although it is clear that these are interdependent. These policies are stated generically to apply to any system, for example, e-commerce, industrial control systems, or mobile device frameworks (Table 6.4.5).

Table 6.4.5 Cyber Security Policy Issues Concerning Security Principles

Policy statement		Explanation	Reasons for controversy
6.4.5.1	Senior management shall play a hands-on role in setting enterprise security strategy, and security strategy outcomes shall be reported at Board level.	Tone at the top is an audit term used to explain that unless senior management takes a topic seriously, no one else in the organization will.	Security management often suffers from responsibility with no authority. Moreover, too often, critical systems such as ICS are not covered under information technology security programs. Senior management need not design security strategy in order to determine what it is worth to the firm and assign appropriate resources and budget. Security management is best left to specialists.
6.4.5.2	Information shall be classified and labeled. Handling procedures for each information classification type shall be developed commensurate with the risk of misuse of information of that type.	This is an organization-wide requirement for information classification, labeling, and handling. An example is the use of the labels Top-Secret, Secret, and Unclassified. Another example is Proprietary, Confidential, and Public. In such systems, all information with the same level is protected the same way.	Information classification requires those who originate data to analyze and make decisions as to security requirements. Information classification systems are often abused by classifying information at a high level that does not need to be classified at a high level. This becomes a way to hide information from those who would otherwise have access to it.
6.4.5.3	All information shall be classified according to its content and purpose, and dissemination limited to those in roles who require it to perform designated responsibilities.	This policy is referred to as "need to know" because it results in access controls that limit information to those who need to have it to perform a given task or job function.	This policy prevents sensitive information from being shared unnecessarily and so protects individual privacy. This policy prevents information sharing by putting a burden of proof that they need to know information content on someone who requests information, when that person may not know the information content.
6.4.5.4	An individual who approves the disbursement of electronic assets shall never be the same as the person who distributes approved disbursements.	This type of statement is referred to as a "segregation of duties" clause. It has its roots in finance, where invoice approvals where done by an individual who checked that good were delivered before giving permission to send a check to a vendor. The policy is meant to ensure that no one individual is able to disburse electronic assets.	Today's electronic transaction systems allow large quantities of assets to be transferred with very little effort or observation, and this policy requires that two or more people must overtly collaborate in order for electronically-controlled assets to be misappropriated. It allows management to enforce accountability for asset disbursement. The policy prevents individuals from executing transactions without the assistance of others, and so may create delays in the distribution of currency, goods, and services. Where staff resources are scarce, this policy creates unreasonable burden on management efforts to achieve efficiency in transaction execution.

(Continued)

Table 6.4.5 (Continued)

Policy statement		Explanation	Reasons for controversy
6.4.5.5	All personnel shall be screened for potential security problems.	Those who handle critical assets must be trustworthy. Screening services check for indications of a poor attitude toward security, including past convictions, outstanding warrants, and substance abuse.	Past issues with security are a good indicator f an individual's propensity to exploit a position or trust.
			Any screening is a privacy violation. More emphasis should be placed on current job performance than background history.
			Information used for background checks is widely available in some countries but practically nonexistent in others. This puts individuals in countries who have no background records in an unfairly competitive position for jobs.
6.4.5.6	Identity management and authentication for individuals who operate government and/or critical infrastructure systems shall be centrally controlled.	This policy would require a system that includes a database of individuals who have access to critical infrastructure, a method to authenticate those people, and a way to provide them with access into government and critical infrastructure systems.	A central function that tracks individual access to critical infrastructure would allow functions such as personnel background checks and strong access control to increase in standardization as well as take advantage of economies of scale.
			Any large-scale government project designed to provide access to private infrastructure deprives the private property owner of the ability to manage their own assets. Such actions are evidence of totalitarian regimes, not peaceful efforts to solve community security problems.
			The level of control provided by such a centralized authentication system would potentially itself introduce a large threat, as it may be exploited to gain widespread administrative access to critical infrastructure.
			This policy is reasonable only for IT systems. A typical ICS or mobile framework does not have a central point at which users are identified, nor a list of what functions system-wide a user should have access to. It tends to rely on IDs delivered with machines and so does not typically integrate with enterprise identity management systems.

		Among other things, this policy would allow all systems to conform to principles of least privilege. To conform to the "principle of least privilege" means that these systems will allow the minimum individual access required to perform a well-defined function. This would reduce overall infrastructure vulnerability due to a malicious utility employee.
6.4.5.7	Systems that maintain mission critical processes such as industrial control systems (ICS), shall utilize some form of software application whitelisting...	A *reference monitor* is a generic term in computer security that refers to a process that intercepts requests for system resources and consults a list of authorization rules to see if the requesting subject has access to the requested object. This policy is to maintain a reference monitor to be used to identify and authorize all software on critical systems..	This policy is reasonable only for IT systems. A typical ICS or mobile framework does not have a central point from which software is executed, much less identified, nor a list of what software a user should be able to access. There is an old adage: "to a carpenter, everything looks like a nail." As systems acquire more and more software-enabled features, they are viewed as part of cyberspace. However, non-IT systems such as ICS and mobile frameworks are fundamentally different and policies such as these assume a simplicity that does not exist and with which it would be impossible to comply.
6.4.5.8	Unencrypted data other than that required to monitor business process shall never be available to Operations.	Frequently, Operations has access to all data in an organization because they are responsible for its integrity. This may lead to inadvertent or intentional unauthorized data disclosure to Operations staff.	Even if all data were encrypted, there must be automated ways to decrypt it in order for it to be used, and since Operations would need a way to test those processes for integrity like any other, there is no real method of enforcing this policy. Segregation of duties with respect to data access may be established within Operations groups so that no one individual or support group would be able to see unencrypted data without collusion.
6.4.5.9	Where the same data is used by more than one department within an organization, authoritative data sources shall be established and each record shall be entered just once and shared with any other organization that requires it.	This type of policy is referred to as a "data origination and reuse" or "need to share" policy. It is usually used in large organizations that process large amounts of data and is usually meant to minimize data storage and human data entry costs.	Implementation of this policy may increase data integrity by minimizing the possibility of mistakes in cross-correlation of records between different departments in a single organization. Organizational boundaries within which data may be freely shared can be difficult to determine where sensitive data is concerned. Data records often contain multiple fields with different security requirements, and these can be difficult to separate when designing data sharing strategies. Different departments may have different requirements to authenticate data sources, and the level of scrutiny provided by the originating department may not meet that requires by a consumer department.

(Continued)

Table 6.4.5 *(Continued)*

Policy statement	Explanation	Reasons for controversy
6.4.5.10 Remote network access to unattended desktops shall never be allowed, even for the purposes of desktop support and maintenance.	This policy would require that desktops be technically configured to allow remote support only when express permission is granted by the desktop user.	This policy is required to maintain accountability for workstation activity. Where is it common for desktops to be commanded remotely by technology staff, the permissions assigned to the user to which the desktop is assigned may be compromised, and/or that desktop user may be able to repudiate network activity performed from the desktop. This policy inhibits the flexibility of technology staff to provide normally intrusive services such as trouble-shooting in an unobtrusive manner. For ICS, shared access is sometimes an operational requirement and could be monitored by biometrics or other means. This policy has the unintended consequence of not being able to make use of remote desktop technology as part of operations support procedures for critical infrastructure, where it is often necessary to provide an external specialist with access normally granted only to internal staff.
6.4.5.11 Operations shall monitor user activity to ensure that sharing of user access does not occur.	This policy would require that each user of a system be verifiably provided with a unique login identifier, that a profile of usage behavior be associated with each login, and anomalous behavior investigated.	This is a simple and effective way to detect whether users have given their passwords to others and makes it possible to pinpoint which users took what actions during investigations of system activity. This policy would facilitate efficient and effective identification of account hijacking attempts. Not all users should be restricted from sharing access. For example, a married couple may share the working spouse's login to their health benefits website.
6.4.5.12 Operations shall identify and report any nonbusiness use of systems resources.	As operations is responsible for maintaining business process, any cyber resources that are used outside of the proscribed operations process are not authorized.	This policy requires advance preparation of a pre-approved list of authorized use of resources. It deprives users and their management of needed flexibility to experiment with new uses of technology as well as ability to connect new devices to networks, download software, and experiment with technology services without being policed by low level staff. A system cannot be secured if its purpose is not well-defined. If this policy cannot be enforced, then it will not be possible to secure the system.

6.4.6 Research and Development

Although often lumped into the same heading, research and development are very different things. Research involves breaking new ground, bringing the latest theories and experiments together to hypothesize about a solution to a problem. The process of research is to formulate experiments that will prove or disprove such hypothesis. Development is about building systems for which there is some basis to believe that engineering processes using existing materials and processes will be able to be specified to meet requirements. Both are present hard problems that the U.S. Department of Homeland Security has categorized into a set of laudable but to date, unattainable goals. These include scalable resilient systems, enterprise-level security metrics, system assurance evaluation life cycle, combating insider threats, malware, and botnets, global-scale identity management, survivability of time-critical systems, situational understanding and attack attribution, attribution of technology provenance, privacy-aware and usable security (Maughan 2009).

Research is less immediately useful to businesses and military operations than is development. Hence, cyber security research issues often center on the efforts of academia to contribute to the growing body of knowledge in cyber security. Academic issues necessarily include ways to fund education of graduate students, who are expected to emerge from academic institutions as experts in cyber security technology. Academia has some very different characteristics from industry and government (Jakobsson 2009). First the demographics in academia are biased toward younger, more inquisitive, less risk-adverse users, users who are early adopters of technology. These are users who cannot get fired for negligence, and resist and question attempts at education aimed at conformity to policy. There is also considerable turnover in this community; every year some existing students leave and new students join ongoing research projects. Finally, controls are more lax in an academic environment. As a result, there is greater risk and less control. Unfortunately, since everything is interconnected, this situation can impact other sites. If academic networks and student machines get attacked and compromised, they can be used to launch cyber attacks. Corrupted computers in academia can be used as proxies and bots. This is the environment where most cyber security research takes place.

Moreover, cyber security research itself is limited to what current academics have identified as hot topics from funding sources. There is little, if any, references in cyber security research to systemic cyber security issues such as those found in industrial control systems. Most cyber security research is conducted in departments of computer science and little, if any, in engineering departments. Control theory that is studied in the engineering disciplines does not address security. Fortunately, not all businesses rely on academia to produce research. Many cannot wait for innovative technologies to emerge, so some have cultivated their own research institutions dedicated to studying issues of interest to the enterprise. While it is also rare that security issues are included in privately funded research endeavors, it is not completely unheard of (e.g., Bilgerm, O'Connor et al. 2006).

Development, on the other hand, is a practical necessity in most corporate enterprises. Even where all software code is purchased and customization is outsourced, technology staff is routinely charged with meeting business requirements by engineering solutions composed of existing technology building blocks. As observed in Chapter 3, there are readily accessible security standards which guide security development processes, and these are supported by a wide variety of vendor security products and services. Security issues in development tend to center around the process used by the development organization and whether it considers security requirements (SSE-CMM® 2003). Moreover, there are software development practices that are known to produce vulnerable code, and it is recommended that these be specifically avoided (McGraw 2006).

Policy issues in the practice of security research and development concern government support for research initiatives, both academic and private. The policy statements in the following table begin with high-level nation-state issues, which are followed by statements reflecting concerns for academic and research quality (Table 6.4.6).

6.5   Cyber Infrastructure Issues

This section contains illustrative examples of cyber infrastructure issues faced by private sector industries. The U.S. Department of Homeland Security's National Infrastructure Protection Plan (NIPP) acknowledges 18 such examples as the critical infrastructure and key resources (CIKRs) of the nation that are managed by the private sector (DHS 2009). Though some are more active than others, each of these sectors is required by the plan to participate in a public–private sector partnership efforts to secure the national infrastructure. The list of sectors include food and water systems, agriculture, health-care systems, emergency services, information technology, communications, banking and finance, energy (electrical, nuclear, gas and oil, and dams), transportation (air, highways, rail, ports, and waterways), the chemical and defense industries, postal and shipping entities, and national monuments and icons.

The section includes discussions and examples of information assurance policies in the illustrative domains of financial services, health care, and industrial control systems. Note that industrial control systems is not itself an industry sector, but a generic label for the type of automated equipment used in a wide variety of industry sectors.

Table 6.4.6 Cyber Security Policy Issues Concerning Research and Development

Policy statement		Explanation	Reasons for controversy
6.4.6.1	The Nation's executive branch shall assemble a committee of cyber security experts from a variety of industries to advise on cyber security policy and assess cyber security programs.	This is a requirement for a Nation's executive branch (e.g., the U.S. President) to reach beyond his small circle of current advisors and seek out assistance on cyber security strategy issues.	The breadth and depth of cyber security issues is beyond the expertise of any one individual. National leaders should have access to the most enlightened views possible. There is no need to establish a policy at this high a level. There are already multiple paths and processes by which national leaders solicit and receive advice on critical issues. Cyber security issues fall into this category.
6.4.6.2	National government shall help fund basic and applied research in cyber security risk, systems and software, in line with priorities established by the national strategy. As much as possible, such research should be collaborative, multi-disciplinary, and unclassified.	This policy would provide funding for cyber security research in software, testing, computer, and network domains. It should also include multidisciplinary studies of the national security impacts (with security studies, legal and international affairs departments) as well as industrial control systems (ICS).	Research and development funding not only produces new security technology that can be applied to today's threats, but motivates graduate students to study cyber security problems, and so contributes to the brainpower that will address future cyber security threats. Research and development funding from the government can sometimes crowd out problems that are considered more germane to the private sector. Moreover, if researchers are unaware of other research (such as if it being done as part of a classified project) funding can be duplicative and wasteful.
6.4.6.3	Government shall annually review all research and development investments related to cyber security.	This policy would require the production of an annual report describing how national research and development funds allocated to cyber security are spent.	Without a clear research agenda for cyber security, such assessment would be a subjective exercise as opposed to an informative report. At best, it would be a simple enumeration of information easily found elsewhere, and at worst, a witch hunt targeted at subjective evaluation of waste. Other areas of research of strategic interest to the national government are supported with dedicated university affiliated research programs. Cyber Security has reached the tipping point both in importance and the level of funding to adopt a similarly coordinated strategy.
6.4.6.4	Private sector companies shall be given tax incentives for pursuing cyber security research.	Private sector companies typically follow security standards and use existing products rather than devise their own innovative solutions. This policy is intended to motivate innovation.	This policy would increase the overall quantity of cyber security research by attracting participants to the market. Companies not currently engaged in cyber security are not likely to be attracted by a tax deduction. However, such a tax deduction may result in companies reclassifying existing research effort in related field such as customer tracking as cyber security identification mechanisms. This would result is overall reductions in tax revenue without security benefit. This policy may motivate private companies to spend on cyber security research but there is no guarantee that the nation will benefit as they may not share the results of their research.

(Continued)

Table 6.4.6 *(Continued)*

Policy statement	Explanation	Reasons for controversy
6.4.6.5	Shareholders of publicly held companies shall be given tax incentives for pursing cyber security research.	This policy is meant to increase the desirability of stock in companies that pursue security goals.	Investments in cyber security research should be judged by marketplace results, rather than simply spending which may not yield actual security benefits. This policy would motivate the private sector to fund research in cyber security. It could increase their market value and also stimulate economic interest in cyber security products.
6.4.6.6	National competitions shall be established to reward student talent for and innovation in cyber security. Other competitions can also reward outstanding universities and research institutions.	Competitions with cash prizes are intended to attract talented students to the study of cyber security issues.	Implementation of this policy should create a community of students interested in joining the cyber security workforce. This program might reward students for studying techniques that could be used malicious hacking, rather than defense.
6.4.6.7	Nations shall encourage awareness, education, and training for cyber defense starting with students in primary or middle schools and continuing through specific technical training for cyber defenders.	Cyber safety, cyber security and cyber ethics are currently the subject of pilot programs in the elementary and high school, this policy would move them into the mainstream curriculum.	This policy would promote critical thinking about cyber security at an early age, and by so doing influence future decision makers to incorporate ethical principles into systems of the future. Investments in training and education will drive a more sophisticated workforce and cyber specialists. This policy would raise the level of cyber security nationwide. The general populace would better understand how to protect themselves in cyberspace, while professionals in information security would have a more intuitive grasp of how to secure their systems and software. Education is a large-scale effort as many people deal with cyberspace and need varying levels of understanding. This means a potentially expensive and long-term effort. Moreover if awareness programs that are technology specific ("practice safe faxing kids!"),they would rapidly be out of date.

6.4.6.8	National governments shall make university scholarships available to students wishing to pursue studies in cyber security, in return for a period of government service.	This policy is intended to motivate students to study cyber security at the college level. Undergraduate college curriculums typically do not include cyber security specialization.	There are not enough knowledgeable cyber security professionals in the nation to fill the jobs expected to be required to safeguard national interests. A national scholarship program would provide a pipeline of qualified professionals. Graduates of undergraduate programs will not have much cyber security expertise. Cyber Security focus usually starts at the Masters level because the amount of foundational knowledge required to practice cyber security in any given domain requires undergraduate concentration in the domain itself. This policy would motivate the creation of cyber security curriculum and also motivate students to pursue cyber security work in government. It may also encourage universities to develop programs where none currently exist, such as cyber security of industrial control systems.
6.4.6.9	Academic communities shall pursue student chapters of cyber security industry associations.	Many industry associations cultivate student chapters, but the cyber security professional associations currently do not have much momentum in this direction.	Today's students are engaged in social networking. Cyber security awareness tends to discourage social networking. This type of program would bring together students working on cyber security in a cyber safe environment. Cyber security professional associations have experience requirements to which students should aspire and these are freely available on websites. There is no need for more formal awareness activity of this career path.
6.4.6.10	Research and development into cyber security systems, technologies, and operations shall be pursued to the extent necessary to fill gaps between management objectives to secure cyberspace and current capabilities.	It is often the case that management would like to control a cyber environment but lacks the methods, tools, and procedures with which to enforce control. This situation puts them in a position of responsibility without authority.	This policy empowers managers who are accountable for controlling assets with the means by which to do so in the long term, even if their current capabilities are lacking. Policies like this may be viewed as an open checkbook for all sorts of research related to cyber security without foreseeable benefit to the organization.
6.4.6.11	All software development shall adopt best practices for securing the software development life cycle.	This policy would require adherence to secure software coding practices as well as security testing.	Secure coding practices are known to reduce vulnerabilities in deployed technology products. Innovation requires constant change in organizational strategy and process. Secure coding practices are too static to adapt to the pace of technology growth.
6.4.6.12	All systems development shall adopt best practices for securing the systems development life cycle.	This policy is similar to the one above, but adopts whole of system approach rather than the security of a single software component.	Best security practices requirements that systems security requirements be considered early in the development process and integrated into product features. Security requirements should have no more priority than any other requirement, as a successful system will end up as a balance of qualities that are important to its stakeholders.

6.5.1 Banking and Finance

The banking and finance industry encompasses a wide variety of institutions with the common focus on products and services for managing money. These institutions include banks, credit card issuers, payment processors, insurance companies, securities dealers, investment funds, clearance firms, and government-sponsored lenders. The companies comprising the U.S. banking and finance industry account for more than 8% of the U.S. annual gross domestic product (FBIIC and FSSCC 2007). All other industries now use e-commerce capabilities for online fund transfers, mortgage research and applications, viewing of bank statements, sales of financial advice or guidance, and subscriptions for interactive consulting. As the sector manages money using information technology, it is constantly threatened by cyber attacks. Capable and persistent cyber criminals present increasingly organized and sophisticated approaches to commit theft and fraud.

Security has always been a concern of the banking and finance industry. The banking and finance industry is also adept at fraud detection and response. These concerns have driven the development of many technical Internet security controls. The industry has a thoroughly documented history of dedication to various public and private forums to provide defenses against attack, enhance resiliency, and sustain public confidence in trusted banking relationships (Abend et al. 2008). These volunteer efforts have proceeded in conjunction with steadily increasing regulatory oversight of the cyber security policy that has always concerned the banking and finance sector (see regulatory history at http://www.ffiec.gov, culminating in the ongoing; FFIEC 2006). Increasingly, there are also legal jurisdictions that focus on financial transactions that had not previously targeted financial services (Smedinghoff 2009). In addition, consumer pressures to respond to the increasingly sophisticated and organized threat landscape have driven the financial industry to set its own cyber security policies to address issues of concern to its customers (Carlson 2009).

Financial audit has long been the basis for best practices in security controls. Communities of information systems auditors were the first to compile standards for enterprise security programs and management strategies (FSSCC 2008). Regulators are likely to continue to focus on whether financial institutions have developed adequate strategies for planning, implementing, and monitoring controls for systems development life cycles. Regulators have developed detailed guidelines on topics such as training software developers, automated and manual code reviews, and penetration testing. For example, in 2008, the Office of the Comptroller of the Currency issued guidance on software application security (OCC 2008). Interface integrity in the service of security is something that physical security professionals refer to as Crime Prevention through Experimental Design (CPTED) (NCPI 2001). Secure interfaces require adequately secure infrastructure on both sides of the interface. Often, this requires unrelated, independent organizations as well as manufacturer, to design to specifications.

The financial industry has long been plagued by the cyber security crime of identity theft. Identity theft is not actually a crime against the bank, but against its customers. Banks are affected as customers in bulk are taken in and thereafter impersonated by criminals, who gain access to bank accounts and withdraw funds. As banks are used to fraud, this activity has been tolerated as the cost of e-commerce. Nevertheless, the pain that bank account takeovers cause consumers has caused bank regulators to issue a requirement that banks add a second "factor" of authentication.

However, most second factors chosen by banks were variations on the password theme in that they are still easily appropriated, either by being guessed by someone who knows certain information about an individual, or by an intruder who invaded a consumer desktop. Information security practitioners consider authentication strength to increase in three levels, generally characterized as something you know, something you have, and something you are. As described in the discussion on impersonation in Section 6.2.2, something you know is a password. Something you have is a physical component in the possession of an individual that is used to facilitate identity verification. Something you are is a measurement based on physical biology, called a biometric. Examples are fingerprints and retina scans. This policy requires the second of the three levels: something you have that would not be vulnerable to such guessing and eavesdropping threats.

The continuing threat to consumer confidence in financial institutions motivated bank regulators to issue a "red flag" rule. This rule requires a banking institution to monitor for potential critical activity on a person's account with the goal of detecting fraud in progress and preventing account takeovers. The rule requires that both customers and regulators be notified of fraud attempts thwarted by the bank.

Note that all policy statements in Section 6.4 apply to the cyber security policy decision makers of the financial industry. Where financial institutions offer online services, those in Section 6.2 apply as well. The policy statements in this section therefore range from regulatory issues to consumer concerns. They are familiar to the banking and finance industry. The first few concern regulations that apply specifically to the banking and finance sector, but could more broadly apply to any company that is a party to online monetary transactions. The next few concern the banking and finance industry as well as any company that spends a great deal of time and money on security regulatory compliance. The remainder are examples of financial cyber security policy concerning services that banks may or may not include in their own cyber security policy to achieve cyber security goals based on their own risks assessments, and these would not be directly influenced by external standards or regulation (Table 6.5.1).

Table 6.5.1 Cyber Security Policy Issues Concerning Banking and Finance

Policy statement		Explanation	Reasons for controversy
6.5.1.1	Regulations such as privacy of personal data (GLBA), and due diligence in detection of and response to threats (FACTA) to customer accounts shall apply uniformly to all institutions that handle consumer information.	Currently these regulations impose management and audit requirements only on financial institutions and this policy would extend it to retailers and other companies that handle sensitive information on consumers.	The unequal application of regulatory standards to financial and nonfinancial firms conducting similar lines of business is an ongoing concern, both in terms of competition and with respect to the notion that a break in the weakest link of a chain wreaks havoc upon the chain as a whole. Financial institutions are the only type of organization where actual consumer assets are at risk, and hence there is no need to extend security requirements to other industries.
6.5.1.2	Bank regulatory authorities shall increase minimum regulatory capital requirements where the cyber security risk profile of a financial institution indicates systemic security issues.	Regulators routinely set minimum capital requirements that banks should have in the event that unforeseen events require them to cover losses in investments made with accountholder assets. This would require them to maintain additional balances where investments were at risk due to cyber security issues.	The potential amount of money that banks may lose due to cyber security attacks has no upper bound, and this policy could require banks adequately prepare for the possibility of those events. Information security risk has long been a component of technology risk, which is itself a component of operations risk. These risks have long been under scrutiny by regulators and no new regulations are required to ensure this occurs.
6.5.1.3	Financial institution regulatory authorities shall not proscribe how security controls should work, and instead emphasize that financial institutions shall accomplish goals for transaction security for every consumer.	Although regulations do not specify the technical configuration of security measures, regulatory auditors have taken a best practice approach to regulation enforcement. The result is that banks must use regulatory guidance as checklists in order to pass regulatory security inspection.	Banking regulations are detailed to the extent of micro-managing financial institution cyber security risk reduction strategies. This stifles innovation with respect to security control measures and also relieves financial institutions of responsibility for independent development of transaction security strategy adequate to control fraud and misuse of consumer and business accounts. Best practices exist because organizations have been successful thwarting fraud and account misuse by implementing those strategies. Regulatory auditors who collect these strategies and audit accordingly are raising the bar for security hygiene within the industry.
6.5.1.4	Regulators shall provide clear guidance that will alleviate concerned with wireless security technology to facilitate financial transactions on mobile devices.	Consumers use just beginning to use financial services over mobile devices, and there is no special regulation that covers this communication of transactions.	Just as online banking introduced the threat of identity theft, the introduction of financial transactions over wireless media could introduce currently unknown exposure, which should be a subject of immediate concern. The technology used to conduct transaction over wireless media is sufficiently similar to that used for current Internet banking transactions that no new regulatory oversight is required. Regulators are not in a position to understand enough about wireless technology to proscribe safe usage. Banks should be accountable for transaction security for all transactions they support regardless of platform.

	Requirement		
6.5.1.5	Laws that require notification to financial customers when sensitive data is exposed shall be uniform nationally, and if possible, globally.	Currently, every U.S. state has its own data breach notification laws, and many non-U.S. countries have their own laws as well. These are often inconsistent.	Banks that may have locations in only one state nevertheless have customers who are residents of other states. This required small banks to expend considerable legal resources to reconcile and regulations just to plan for the possibility of a data breach, even if one never occurs. Data breach laws should be molded by the people whose privacy is at stake. As communities can only enact laws within their own jurisdiction, these laws are properly enacted at the state level.
6.5.1.6	Financial institution crime pattern analysis data including bank identification shall be made available to all consumers.	Although new reports of security breaches and identify theft are ubiquitous, legal requirements for crime reporting is confined to regulatory relationships and regulators do not share this data with the general public.	Financial institutions voluntarily share identity theft information through industry associations such as the Financial Services Information Sharing and Analysis Center (FS-ISAC), the Anti-Phishing Working Group (APWG), the Identity Theft Assistance Corporation (ITAC) (FDIC 2004). This data is widely published and available for critical review. While financial institutions may experience large-scale fraud and data breaches without informing the general public, there will be no incentive to make security a marketplace differentiator.
6.5.1.7	Consumers shall be allowed to restrict transactions that transfer balances out of their account to well-defined parameters that preclude money being transferred outside their accounts in ways that are unexpected.	Many banks provide "positive pay" services that require accountholders express pre-approval to execute transactions that transfer balances out of their account.	If all banks offered such services and consumers were aware of them, a great deal of fraud could be avoided. Consumers have a difficult time with even simple online transactions, and the extra security layer of express approval for wire transfers could discourage them from using the most convenient mechanisms for accomplishing online banking.
6.5.1.8	Where accounts are subject to identity theft, a physical authentication token shall be used to supplement authentication tokens that can be copied from a user's computing environment via software, or knowledge of the individual's history.	Banking regulators have recognized that passwords are the basis for most banking authentication and that this authentication method is not adequate to prevent identify theft.	Physical authentication that requires a person to have a personally issued physical token or biometrics device in order to execute bank transactions in addition to a password, pin, or a security question answer could significantly reduce the occurrence of identity theft which results in theft of online balances or credit. The infrastructure required to issue physical or biometrics identity tokens and equipment could be cost-prohibitive.

6.5.2 Health Care

The health-care industry encompasses a wide variety of institutions with the common focus on products and services for maintaining health. These institutions include hospitals, doctor's offices, diagnostic laboratories, medical equipment manufacturers, emergency care specialists, visiting nurses, and a host of other medical community professionals and services. These institutions use typical enterprise support systems such as accounting, administration, collaboration, and advertising. In addition, from the perspective of cyberspace operations, these constituents will utilize two types of mission-critical systems unique to the health-care industry: systems used to administer medical practice and systems used to administer medicine. By administering medical practice, we mean the tools and techniques of doctor's offices, hospitals, other care providers, pharmacies, pharmaceutical manufacturers, and insurance providers to ensure that medical facilities and supplies are available and medical staff are recruited, trained, and paid. By administering medicine, we mean the process of caring for human patients. We shall call these logistics systems and provider systems, respectively. Logistics and provider systems used by the health-care profession differ in both functionality and data content.

The primary function of logistics systems is to track patients and resources through the maze of organizational workflow that has been created in order to connect patients with health-care providers, facilities, and treatments. The organizational workflow streams from patient home computers through workplace benefits systems, insurance agencies, diagnostic, and treatment facilities. Data content in these systems is the information required by this organizational workflow to function. It includes data that many patients consider private, and information security with respect to such information is regulated by the Health Insurance Portability and Accountability Act (HIPAA) (HIPAA 2003).

The primary function of provider systems is to provide a patient with medical care. These include drug delivery pumps, automated sample chemical or viral analysis, diagnostic imaging tests, remotely monitored electrical implants, and a wide variety of other innovative devices. The information flowing through these systems may begin with the authorization from a logistics system, continue through physician prescriptions, include automated or manual analysis to identify treatment appropriate to given patient conditions, and incorporate test results and automated communication of those results to logistics systems, completing the information life cycle for a simple treatment. Moreover, a single patient likely to require any one provider system interface is likely to incur multiple records on a variety of provider systems.

Cyber security issues unique to logistics and provider systems often focus on interoperability. Interoperability is a major goal for the health-care industry because it is seen as an enabler of fast and accurate decision making with respect to patient treatment. Where logistics systems may be rapidly combined with provider systems, patient histories may be automatically factored into expert-system-based diagnostic and prescription algorithms, enabling more accurate and effective treatments. For example, the recently established National Health Information Network (NHIN) dictates information sharing to enable easy exchange of health information over the Internet (HHS 2010). This critical part of the national health information technology agenda will enable health information to follow the consumer, be available for clinical decision making and support appropriate use of health-care information beyond direct patient care to improve population health. The NHIN is not one organization, but is an abstraction defined by the U.S. government as composed of independently operated systems. These include information service gateways, Health Information Organizations (HIOs) operated by an information provider or consumer, such as a provider emergency medical response, laboratory systems, or doctor's offices, and NHIN Operational Infrastructure, a set of web services that stores information about HIOs and their data repositories in order to enable connectivity via security services and provide registry information on user capabilities. In essence, NHIN is a set of specifications for HIOs to query and provide data to each other, plus a repository of information concerning authorized HIOs. Where services for health information already exist, they would also be considered HIOs from the point of view of NHIN. These are referred to in NHIN documentation as Health Information Exchanges or Integrated Delivery Networks. The system has no data usage restrictions, but relies on HIO compliance with a Data Use and Reciprocal Support Agreement (DURSA) rather than any data-level security features or due diligence requirements to ensure that DURSAs are met with a feasible level of success.

However, such requirements for quick and easy information sharing also introduce at least two types of major security issues: privacy and integrity. If the NHIN concept is truly the next bar to be met in health-care information sharing, then a corresponding bar in cyber security must also be raised. Questions remain with respect to the evidence standard to which health care should be held accountable when requesting patient information from the system. For example, the question of what information needs to be shared in a disaster situation will vary with the type of event, and different emergency responders will need different information. For example, a physician involved in emergency triage needs different information than the State's Director of Emergency Management, or the U.S. Secretary of Health and Human Services (Toner 2009).

The point of the NHIN plan and others like it is that the health-care industry has not yet taken advantage of the technology revolution. Existing health-care systems and programs that are targets for information sharing that could lead to vast improvements in patient care range from automated chemical agent surveillance systems, to voluntary contributions to news sites. In between are patient tracking system and mandatory reporting requirements, and, for the most part, these systems are stand-alone systems and are not integrated (Toner 2009). These systems are both publicly and privately held. They include emergency operations and information fusion centers at the local, state, and federal levels whose purpose is to merge the various streams of information. The advantages to the health-care industry of free flow of information are palpable to the service providers trying to get head of the next wave of potential pandemic.

This press for quick and easy information sharing comes against a losing battle for security controls over the health-care information repositories that already exist. A recent survey showed that more than half of information technology professionals working in health-care organizations do not believe that their organization adequately protects sensitive information, and an even larger majority had experienced data breaches (Ponemon Institute 2009). While these statistics may be explained by the fact that those who answered the survey were most likely security-aware, as they had been targeted by surveyors funded by security companies, it also indicates that even those health-care companies who think their IT controls are adequate experience data breaches. Where internal control reports persuade executives that systems are secured to an industry standard that may itself be inadequate, the perception is that there can be no blame in inadequate security, because no one can be expected to exceed industry standards. This type of "not my fault" attitude is easy for a health-care company to assume in a world where even highly technically sophisticated companies that are attacked may leave health-care professionals feeling both helpless and blameless (McMillan 2010).

There is also recognition among technology professionals working in health care that much of the information/communications technology necessary for the realization of integrated systemic solutions to health-care data integrity issues exists. Barriers to information sharing are not currently security issues, but technology interoperability, data dictionary standards, and reliability concerns, as well as training issues at all levels of the health-care system. These and many of the same structural, financial, policy-related (reimbursement schemes, regulation), organizational, and cultural barriers that have impeded the use of systems tools will have to be surmounted to close health care's wide information/communications technology gap (Proctor 2001). Adding cyber security concerns related to privacy and data provenance significantly increases the complexity facing these professionals.

Nevertheless, policies for interoperability and data sharing ability should not be confused with standards for privacy and integrity. Interoperability standards (ASTM 2009; MD FIRE ongoing) are meant to facilitate communication, not to control information flow. When it is further recognized that the health care also uses industrial control system technology to autodeliver treatments that, if incorrectly administered, may be life-threatening, it is even more important to recognize the distinction and segregate policy decisions accordingly.

The policy statements in this section therefore range from regulatory issues to life and death concerns. They should be familiar to those working in cyber security within the industry. The first few concern what cyber security professionals refer to as "hygiene" issues. They discuss information security standards that have been known to be effective in reducing risk of data breaches when applied consistently to enterprise data. The next few concern cyber security risks introduced by interoperability requirements or lack thereof between various types of health-care data repositories ranging from medical devices to aggregate case databases. The remainder concern information sharing issues and potential interrelationships between policy goals for information sharing and policy goals of privacy and integrity (Table 6.5.2).

6.5.3   Industrial Control Systems

Despite their high reliance on automation, ICSs are not typically designed with access controls, their software is not easily updated, and they have little forensics capability, self-diagnostics, or cyber logging. While the lifetime of the equipment in an IT network typically ranges from 3 to 7 years before anticipated replacement and often does not need to be in constant operation, ICS devices may be 15 to 20 years old, perhaps older, before anticipated replacement, and run $7 \times 24 \times 365$. Moreover, patching or upgrading an ICS has many pitfalls. The field device must be taken out of service which may require stopping the process being controlled. This in turn may cost many thousands of dollars and impact thousands of people. An important issue is how to protect unpatchable, unsecurable workstations such as those still running NT Service Pack 4, Windows 95, and Windows 97. Many of these older workstations were designed as part of plant equipment and control system packages and cannot be replaced without replacing the large mechanical or electrical systems that accompany the workstations. Additionally, many Windows patches for ICSs are not standard Microsoft patches but have been modified by the ICS supplier. Implementing a generic Microsoft patch can potentially do more harm than the virus or worm against which it was meant to defend. As an example, in 2003 when the Slammer worm was in the wild, one distributed control systems (DCSs) supplier sent a letter to their customers stating that the generic Microsoft patch should not be installed as it would shut down the DCS. Another example was a water utility that patched a system at a *water* treatment plant with a patch from the operating system vendor. Following the patch, they were able to start pumps, but were unable to stop them (Weiss 2010).

However, as discussed in Chapter 3, the biggest threat to industrial control systems is not necessarily the remote access necessary to maintain the operation of the field devices. An example is the Idaho National Labs Aurora demonstration that physically destroyed a diesel generator by

Table 6.5.2 Cyber Security Policy Issues Concerning Health Care

Policy statement	Explanation	Reasons for controversy
6.5.2.1	All systems used by a health care company shall be operated in compliance with the Health Insurance Portability and Accountability Act (HIPAA) Privacy and Security Rules.	HIPAA specifies administrative, physical, and technical safeguards for covered entities to use to assure the confidentiality, integrity, and availability of electronic protected health information.	Information may be transferred internally within the organization via unexpected methods. Making the scope of the company HIPAA program the entire systems environment ensures that such unanticipated transfers do not result in unintentional exposure of electronic protected health information. Many company's office systems maintain information that is just as sensitive as electronic health information, for example, personally identifiable information about its own employees. The HIPAA compliance program is very expensive to operate and the scope of the regulation is very clear. Narrowing the implementation strategy to administrative, physical, and technical safeguards for only the systems that store and transmit electronic protected health information allows adequate protection without unnecessary cost, which would be passed to consumers.
6.5.2.2	Cyber Security regulation with respect to health care shall impose technology requirements for data protection based on information classification.	This requirement is motivated by privacy concerns. Although HIPAA addresses health care concerns, it does not fully cover sensitive health care data in every format in which it is currently used in all logistics and provider systems.	Any technology requirement may increase cost of service delivery, so unless there is a specific return on investment in terms of either overall health care effectiveness or cost reduction in logistics or provider systems, it does not make sense to legislate cyber security for health care data. Organizations are not currently motivated to secure data. Even HIPAA regulations allow data sharing beyond patient needs given patient consent. Patients in need of health care are too preoccupied to make informed decisions on long-term use of their health data and so should be able to rely on privacy without being asked to sign it away. Experience with the financial industry shows that even the most detailed technical security requirements cannot anticipate all possible security threats, and therefore cannot adequately address overall goals for security, so any low-level regulation is not likely to be effective.
6.5.2.3	Nonrepudation and accuracy of data shall be addressed by health care provider policy prior to confidentiality.	This policy acknowledges that there are multiple objectives for security policy and suggests that the ability to identify who modified data and whether it is correct should be the primary goal of a healthcare security program.	Healthcare resources are scarce and privacy should not be the overarching priority on how to spend security dollars, No one ever died of embarrassment, but they have died out by getting the wrong prescription. This policy assumes that security dollars are static. The same security control measures that protect integrity may be leveraged to ensure some measure of privacy.

6.5.2.4	Access to health care data shall be contingent upon evidence that such access is required to diagnose or treat a specific case.	Current proposals for health information data sharing do not include requirements relating to the specific purpose of data sharing. This policy would introduce the requirement.	Qualified health care providers should not be worried about justification for data access. It is enough that they be subject to audit. Qualified health care providers should not be required to provide justification for data access in advance of treatment because it would slow down the healthcare delivery. It is enough that they be subject to audit. All access to personal healthcare data must be justified with reference to a specific patient and condition requiring health care provider attention. Access to health care data is often justified by the needs of law enforcement to develop a criminal case against victims of violence, who may not be able or willing to prosecute their attackers. Criminal investigations may also require health care providers to provide records of patient care in the course of developing cases that are not focused on the patient as victim, but as a potential suspect, witness, or other relevant relationship to the crime. Hence, all such records shall be made available to law enforcement with proper oversight and approval.
6.5.2.5	Wireless devices implanted in patients shall require strong authentication in order to operate command and control features.	There are a wide variety of medical devices with electronic circuits that accept commands that change electronic signals and medicine doses. There are not current security standards with which they are controlled.	While there is no know threat to patient health due to wireless cyber security attacks, research into the security of these devices introduces an unnecessary cost. There need to be security standards and equipment certifications for this critical equipment. As these devices allow remote command and control capabilities, any malicious individual who understand how they work may commit murder without any trace of evidence. Until the security options for such devices are well understood, it is not possible to assess the risks to the patient using the devices. At minimum, remote or wireless access should not be allowed unless there is a way to audit who performed what activity performed on devices remotely.
6.5.2.6	Systems such as NHIN shall maintain a Data Use and Reciprocal Support Agreement (DURSA) with companies with whom it shares health information.	Due diligence with respect to data handling by third parties in financial or defense industries requires that those releasing data assure the data protection capability of third parties to whom they release it. The NHIN-like health care networks rely on legal agreements rather than any verification of cyber security features.	Patient data must be immediately available in order to be useful for emergency patient treatment. Any security due diligence requirement for data sharing may restrict a health care provider's ability to save a life. Though ubiquitous information sharing of health care information without pre-vetting of a purpose may not be appropriate for normal operating procedure, all health care information should be shared without question in situations of widespread crisis such as fires and hurricanes. Nationally recognized data sharing with only DURSA-like agreements amount to a handshake and so trusting parties are at the mercy of those who break the rules. As audit-based evidence is not required to join these NHIN-like networks there is no deterrent for anyone within the medical profession to create a market in sensitive health care data.

(Continued)

Table 6.5.2 (*Continued*)

Policy statement	Explanation	Reasons for controversy
6.5.2.7	Access to health care data shall be granted at the institutional level.	This policy accepts the premise that institutional participation in a network such as HSIN should be justification for data download from other institutions, and that access to individual health records need not be justified on a case by case basis.	Where an institution may provide data from multiple sources via a single interface, time is saved in searching for records and decisions based on the data may be made more quickly. Combining database from multiple sources allows this. Access granted at the individual level would preserve accountability for individual possession of information, and provide traceability in the event of data leakage or misuse. The ability to combine health data from multiple sources into a datamart within any HSIN participant will result in complete loss of control over data and synchronization issue with data history. Without a national plan for healthcare data integrity, this is likely to lead to poor decisions due to incomplete data.
6.5.2.8	Software for automated healthcare provider systems such as radiation and medicine delivery shall be designed using safety and security models.	There is a long history of safety and security principles that could be brought to bear on these systems, such as failure in safe mode and allocation of least resources.	Software for specialized equipment should not be burdened with unnecessary subroutines. The best way to control it is to minimize functionality and train operators. Failure to observe known safety and security principles in such potentially dangerous devices amounts to negligence and technology malpractice. The lack of attention to security in the design process of these systems has the effect that they have many of the same security vulnerabilities as industrial control systems.
6.5.2.9	The National Institute of Standards and Technology (NIST) shall maintain standards on the reliability and interoperability of health care provider services equipment.	NIST maintains information security standards for a wide variety of domains, but health care is not one of them.	NIST's expertise in cyber security methodology should be exploited to address cyber security interoperability issues in the healthcare industry. NIST's expertise in security is that of a generalist and health care security issues are better left to specialists. Moreover, there is no evidence that NIST standards are effective in any industry domain.

200

6.5.2.10	Medical standards promoting plug and play interoperability standards shall be enforced.	Current proposals for standards for medical device interoperability emphasize data sharing capability.	The interoperability standard would facilitate security requirements such as not allowing public access to sensitive data, as security protocols are currently criticized as potential hindrances to timely care. The interoperability requirements facilitate economies of scale and minimize data portability problems at health care service providers. Interoperatibilty standards, if not combined with security requirements, may make the problem worse as it would make health care data more widely available. They should not be adopted without companion security models and guidance for appropriate and authorized use of sensitive data. The interoperability requirements are justified by not only by economies of scale and data portability issues, but also by continued development of health care data standards and a significant increase in the technical and material support provided by the federal government for public–private partnerships in this area.
6.5.2.11	Health information shall be required to be digitized so that historical health information can follow the consumer.	This policy requires the health care industry to take advantage of the tools and techniques available in the information age to allow patients to receive the benefit of records from former heath care providers when consulting new ones. It is essential a requirement for service portability.	The availability of digitized health information for every patient will increase the overall accuracy of diagnostics that require knowledge of past history to be accurate, especially in cases where patients are unconscious or otherwise unable to communicate their history in the time of medical crisis. Digitized health information on every patient should be available for analysis to support and improve clinical decision making. Digitized records available in aggregate are appropriate used to improve of healthcare treatment beyond direct patient care to improve population health. In the absence of correct and consistent health care software, which is currently unavailable and for which there are no concrete plans, it does not make sense to require data to be ubiquitous. In fact, requiring the same data to be used across heterogeneous software environments may result in misrepresentation that could result in false diagnosis.

(Continued)

Table **6.5.2** (*Continued*)

Policy statement		Explanation	Reasons for controversy
6.5.2.12	The data collection and integrity protection work done by various uncoordinated government agencies shall be consolidated.	The mission of state emergency operations centers, the Secretary's Operations Center in HHS, the Center for Disease Control Director's Emergency Operations Center and BioPHusion Program, and the Department of Homeland Security's National Biosurveillance Integration Center remain uncoordinated.	Where the government requires health care data collection, it should strive for maximum utility, which can only be achieved via data dissemination to all stakeholders. Currently, there is an overreliance on human factors to connect the dots in correlations between findings across multiple health care data sources. Data collections performed by different agencies have different purposes and requirements for data sharing would impose both distract6.5.3.ion from specific agency purpose and unnecessary expense. Any large repository of health care information will be a target for cyberattack. The current method of multiple data collection and human correlation limits the potential impact of any one data breach.
6.5.2.13	Pharmaceutical manufacturers shall not have access to sales data that identifies the doctors and patients who use their drugs.	Pharmacies share prescription information with drug manufacturers. This policy would limit the type of data about drug purchases made available to pharmaceutical companies.	Pharmaceutical manufacturers have no need to see this level of detail on drug purchases. Kickbacks to doctors by pharmaceutical companies are enabled by the ease with which these companies can verify that doctors are prescribing their drugs. These payments, whether in cash or other benefits, unduly influence the choice of drugs prescribed to patients. Patients have relationships with doctors, not pharmaceutical manufacturers. There have been widely publicized incidents where pharmaceutical companies accidentally release lists of patients email addresses that they hold for use in email advertising, when there was no reason for them to have the list of patients in the first place. Pharmaceutical manufacturers use data on doctors and patients to better understand how their drugs are being used. This information helps them improve customer service and this benefits both doctors and patients.

Table 6.5.3 Cyber Security Policy Issues Concerning Industrial Control Systems

Policy statement		Explanation	Reasons for controversy
6.5.3.1	Systems whose misuse may cause severe damage to persons and property shall require strong authentication to operate.	This policy would require authentication to operate any system where accidents may cause damage, such as boats with wireless autopilots.	There is no reason to believe recreational vehicles will be targeted by cyber threats, and this policy would require significant cost in redesigning electronic components of these systems. Moreover, it is likely to have the unintended consequence that electronic parts from different manufacturers will be difficult to integrate.
			The race to the electronic marketplace has created a dangerous situation wherein many devices are operated with Internet-based and/or wireless commands that can be entered by anyone knowing the manufacturer specifications. It is irresponsible of manufacturers to build capabilities into devices that allow them to be operated by anyone other than the owner.
			There is as much probability to believe that limiting access to control systems will cause accidental damage as there is for them to be controlled by criminals who intend to cause damage.
6.5.3.2	Current cyber security threats and corresponding statutory and legal frameworks that address cyber security for critical industrial control systems shall be reviewed and reported upon annually.	This would require national agencies and other publicly funded organizations that perform cyber security threat intelligence to combine their findings annually into a consolidated report that includes laws related to cyber security.	The findings, conclusions, and recommendations resulting from such a review will be invaluable to inform future legislation.
			Though examination of existing legislation in comparison with a changing environment is a good idea, the way this policy is worded, there is no strategic objective. Such an open-ended review may result in a waste of taxpayer dollars.
			Annual publication of such a report is meaningless, this should not be a report process, but an expectation for government security services that the comparison should be constantly updated and available in order to ensure that controls continuously improve in the face of changing threats.
6.5.3.3	Nations shall mandate the strength of encryption used for identification and authentication credential in critical infrastructure sectors. These extra protections shall also apply to key industrial control systems (ICS) in the critical infrastructure sectors.	Organizations in the critical infrastructure sectors deal with confidential information and the control of industrial systems. This is a requirement for security control commensurate with the amount of potential damage from their abuse.	This policy will match the high criticality of information in these sectors with concomitant protection. These kinds of information should not rely on the insecure systems of the Internet. Encryption and identification credentials are important to help establish higher assurance for these sectors.
			This policy is already in place for many sensitive government systems, and the industrial control systems used to manage critical infrastructure are just, if not more, vulnerable to national security threats.
			This policy will also add cost and complexity to the already difficult to maintain SCADA, PLC, and other ICS component architecture. Additional authentication may not be easy to use, and thus may interfere with operator ability to control these devices. The way to secure these systems is to decrease, not increase complexity.

(Continued)

Table 6.5.3 *(Continued)*

Policy statement	Explanation	Reasons for controversy
6.5.3.4 ICS design criteria shall include requirements for cyber security.	ICS designs are based on performance and safety. This policy would ensure that cyber security requirements are incorporated into designs as well.	The ability to use electronics in unintended ways is commensurate with the functionality and data storage capacity of the circuitry. The ability to use ICS in unexpected ways is at least partially dependent on the capability in these circuits. Awareness that malfunctions or intentional manipulation of the data content of ICS cyber-enabled functionality should inspire overall system designs that protect it from intentional or accident corruption. Awareness that ICS malfunctions or intentional manipulation should motivate cyber malfunction detection measures that are currently missing and need to be developed to identify intentional or unintentional cyber incidents. Electronically controlled physical devices may be controlled physically as well as logically. Malfunction detection measures currently prevalent in ICS should be able to compensate for intentional or unintentional cyber functionality failures.
6.5.3.5 ICS design shall include capability for cyber forensics.	Industrial accidents happen frequently, and investigations inspect cyberspace logs and configurations if they are available. However, many PLCs, DCSs, and SCADA systems often do not identify or store the digital evidence that would be useful in such investigations.	This area is ripe for research and development to determine what specific types of cyber forensics are needed and how they would be utilized in the least noninvasive manner possible. The ICS community has the knowledge-base to understand what physical parameters are required to perform a root-cause analysis of an incident. Consequently, the ICS community has developed the detailed forensics for physical parameters—temperature, pressure, level, flow, motor speed, current, voltage, etc. However, the legacy/field device portions of an ICS have minimal to no cyber forensics. Moreover, it is not clear that adequate cyber forensics exist for even newer ICSs.
6.5.3.6 Research and development shall focus on cyber security technologies specific to industrial control systems (ICS). Interdisciplinary programs on cyber security of industrial control systems should be developed and incorporated into university computer science and engineering programs.	There are currently no universities with interdisciplinary programs on cyber security of industrial control systems. This policy would create a new category with which to track progress in cyber security research specific to ICS	There is little understanding of the actual ICS needs or the ICS technical limitations. ICS cyber security R&D is needed to address appropriate ICS needs. Those working in ICS cyber security are generally either from the IT security community with little knowledge of ICSs or ICS experts knowledgeable in the operation of systems, not security. Little ICS cyber security research is devoted to the non-Windows-based field devices which are not IT-type systems. There is a need to understand the ICS cyber security requirements and develop appropriate ICS cyber security technologies. Separating research into different types of cyber security systems may fragment what little money is available. Rather than create a new field, ICS should be brought into mainstream security curriculum. ICS security, is much less understood, has little expertise, and is often not considered critical. Focused research in this area would be useful in educating both the public and owner/operators on potential risks.

6.5.3.7	Where system functionality affecting performance and safety are controlled by electronics, industrial control systems (ICS) design criteria shall include requirements for cyber security.	The ability to use electronics in unintended ways is commensurate with the functionality and data storage capacity of the circuitry. Awareness that malfunctions or intentional manipulation of the information content of this circuitry should inspire overall system designs that protect it from intentional or accident corruption. Electronically controlled physical devices may be controlled physically as well as logically. Malfunction detection measures currently prevalent in ICS should be able to compensate for electronic failures.
6.5.3.8	The systems that monitor and control public transportation systems should be regulated by the federal government.	Automated surveillance is a deterrent to criminals who may use cyberspace to change public transportation routing if there was no chance of being caught. It also would provide valuable forensic evidence that can be used to remediate and investigate any unauthorized use of these systems. The cost of implementing this policy may not be justified because well-designed manual and mechanical surveillance methods currently in place work well for a wide variety of transportation systems.
6.5.3.9	Public transportation systems that make use of automated switching systems to automatically control traffic shall implement safeguards to ensure that these systems are not tampered with from cyberspace.	Automated surveillance is a deterrent to criminals who may use cyberspace to change public transportation routing if there was no chance of being caught. It would provide valuable forensic evidence that can be used to remediate and investigate any unauthorized use of these systems. Transportation industry operators rely on cyberspace for connectivity to ICS control systems. The ability to allow an authorized person to operate the system inherently introduces the risk of threat due to insider attack. Hence, cyber security tampering opportunities can never be entirely eliminated.
6.5.3.10	The systems that control and monitor water systems shall be designed to automatically alert the public in the event of contamination.	The electronic infrastructure that controls public transportation is currently interconnected to many systems including the Internet. This would establish mandatory national standards for securing the public transportation systems This policy would require that switching systems be placed under automated surveillance and change control and that any detected changes are investigated and correlated with authorized activity. The electronic infrastructure that controls water systems are currently interconnected to many systems and there is no prohibition to connecting to the Internet. This would establish mandatory national standards for securing water systems.

This policy would ensure that cyber security measures are implemented to protect the electronic networks, often including wireless communication, that link monitoring systems and automated analysis that control the treatment and distribution of water.

This policy would result in false alerts to the public every time a system warning signal malfunctioned. It would be sufficient for these systems to alert the operator.

These systems are being automated with remote accessibility to improve monitoring. Retrofitting these systems to improve cyber security would be very expensive and could cause unintended operational consequences. Water monitoring and analysis systems have their genesis in scientific measurement rather than computer operating system technology. To retrofit these systems to operate within cyberspace access control, monitoring, and alert models would be prohibitively expensive. (these systems are being automated with remote accessibility)

(Continued)

Table 6.5.2 (Continued)

Policy statement	Explanation	Reasons for controversy
6.5.3.11	The systems that control and monitor flammable or explosive pipelines shall be designed so that cyber incidents cannot cause pipelines to fail and to safely isolate any anomalies to very small geographic areas.	The electronic infrastructure that controls flammable or explosive pipelines are monitored but not designed to take advantage of many features of automation.	This policy would ensure that cyber security measures are implemented to make use of automated real-time monitoring data at multiple control points to pinpoint the cause of anomalous readings to automatically minimize the impact of both accidental and intentional damage to pipelines and control systems. Today's flammable or explosive pipeline monitoring and control systems are very simple and any change to automate would require comprehensive design changes that present too significant a cost impact to consider implementation.
6.5.3.12	Any system sold to consumers that adjusts energy consumption in their homes shall be solely under their control.	Advances in smart grid technology provide features to monitor home appliance energy and automatically turn them on, off, or adjust their controls.	These features set the stage for network intrusions into the home environment. At best, they may be used by power companies to both spy on and adjust consumer use of electronics. At worst, they may be used by hacker to create local or regional disturbances such as overheated appliances or neighborhood black-outs, respectively. Smart grid features will likely be left to software, which can make better overall decisions for controlling power consumption levels to ensure continuity of service for the community as a whole while minimizing the effect on each homeowner. Energy companies have vested interest in securing this software and associated infrastructure.
6.5.3.13	The critical infrastructure that composes the power plants and electric grid shall be considered a national border.	This policy would establish a national border around the power grid in cyberspace.	The physical and electronic infrastructure that provides power to the nation is currently connected to the Internet. This policy would give the government jurisdiction to protect the power plants and electric grid from cyberattack. Policy does not need to establish a national border in cyberspace in order to give government jurisdiction to protect the power grid. A more reasonable policy would be for the grid to be declared a national asset and set appropriate cyber security standards for the power plants and electric grid. This policy would give the government jurisdiction to monitor and block access to Internet connectivity points adjoining the power grid, and thus interfere with national goals for net neutrality as well as privacy.

6.5.3.14	Energy industry regulatory standards shall be strengthened to address the increasing risk of reliance on cyberspace.	The energy industry used a self-regulatory process to develop a set of cyber secrurity standards—the North American Electric Reliability Corporation (NERC) Critical Information Protection (CIP) cyber security standards.	Current energy industry security standards have been demonstrated to be less than adequate. Applying the NERC CIPs would not have prevented many actual cyber security incidents included several major cyber-related electric outages . NERC CIPs have exclusions such as requiring only routable protocols be addressed that would exclude incidents such as Stuxnet and Aurora from even being considered. It has been observed in other industries that regulatory oversight does not increase security controls. If the industry does not self-identify the controls that are important to their operations, then they will not be adequately addressed.
6.5.3.15	Control system protocols used in automated communication between ICS components shall be reliably secured.	The protocols used to communicate between ICS devices use control system unique protocols such as Modbus, DNP-3, and ICCP. These protocols were developed without security.	There is a move to "wrap" these protocols in TCP/IP to facilitate security and interoperability between IT systems and ICS systems. Wrapping them in TCP/IP can make them even more vulnerable. TCP/IP is not deterministic and consequently, TCP/IP should only be used for nonprocess or nonsafety critical communications. Using similar protocols to IT will allow ICS to benefit from security tools and features available on IT systems that are not currently available for ICS. Increased security for ICS controls may be used to justify increased accessibility for ICS controls, such as Internet connectivity, and the loss of isolation could lead to worse security that currently exists. It will also subject ICS to the same threats that IT systems face.
6.5.3.16	ICS operation shall require clock synchronization wherever time-based electronic processing is done.	Various atomic clocks and satellite services provide robust and reliable time synchronization for electronic systems.	ICSs are deterministic systems and many are programmed to observe real time requirements for sensor activity and /or information flow. Hence, communications must occur within a prescribed period of time prior to automated action changing system state. This policy would minimized the risk of ICS malfunction due to time synchronization issues. Not all ICS systems rely on time-sensitive operation and so this blanket requirement would add unnecessary expense to those environments Reliable and timely communications are critical for maintaining the operations of ICSs. The introduction of some signal validation, minimal authentication, and adequate speed (that is, some latency is acceptable). A major recommendation from the 2003 Northeast Outage was the need for time synchronization. Phasor measurement units for the electric grid will require very precise time measurements.

(Continued)

Table 6.5.2 (Continued)

Policy statement	Explanation	Reasons for controversy
6.3.17	The ICS community shall actively and formally apply software assurance principles to all development of ICS software.	Certain security tests that are widely utilized to test information technology can adversely affect the operation of ICSs or result in operator confusion. Examples include using port scanning tools that result in ICS components freezing-up or worse. Rather than require the same tests, the requirement should be to identify a new set of security tests more suited for ICS software testing.
	Secure software relies on management process designed to maximize adherence to requirements and minimize introduction of accidental or intentional vulnerabilities.	ICS systems should aspire to the same level of security quality as IT systems, and this test policy would drive behavior in the direction of being resilient enough to withstand a wide variety of unexpected input.
	Access controls for ICS focus on physical equipment access rather than logical access. This policy would apply appropriate security access mechanisms to ICS.	Physical intruders in ICS environments may not be challenged to login to computers in order to operate critical infrastructure or machinery. An easy way to quickly add logical to physical access is to provide biometric authentication.
		Password access control systems typically include features that lock the system screen after a specified number of attempted logins have been identified as password failures. If this occurs in an ICS, a time critical control process may not be accessible to the operator that forgot or mistyped the password. This occurrence could have impact on system ability to recover from outages or other off-normal conditions. It would be especially harmful in situations where operators are under great stress.
6.3.18	ICS communication shall be on isolated networks.	Internet connectivity to critical infrastructure should be minimized. Wireless should be configured to restrict access to authorized physical devices, thus eliminating the possibilty of rogue and potentially malicious access.
	This policy would prevent connecting ICS to the Internet and is intended to prevent adversaries from attacking critical infrastructure through publicly available portals.	Not all ICS operate critical infrastructure. Isolated networks are expensive and the decision to incur the cost of network isolation is best left to a risk analysis conducted by a system owner or operator.

6.5.3.19	Cyber Security incidents in ICSs shall be publicly shared.	There have been a few attempts to catalog and share information on ICS cyber security incidents, but this data is not generally publicly available. An Industrial Security Incident Database (ISID) report in 2006 showed that 68% of cyber security related incidents were due to malware, 4% due to deliberate sabotage, and 8% due to hacking activity. Only 12% of the incidents were accidental (Byres and Leversage 2006). This is an outdated and small fragment of the data that should be collected in order to have situational awareness for ICS threats. Data on industrial cyber security incidents is not systematically collected, and only sporadically contributed to member-only forums where the goal is to ensure confidentiality while finding solutions rather than to raise public awareness. Consequently, lessons are not widely shared and common security malfunctions are not systematically addressed. Due to a culture of litigation combined with concern for intellectual property, industrial control operators in the United States do not trust their government to act in their best interests. A nongovernmental ICS CERT is needed to collect and analyze ICS cyber incidents. Industrial control systems security incidents may have devastating consequences, and data on known successful attacks would undoubtedly be used by adversaries to plan the next one.
6.5.3.20	Security certification and testing programs for verifying adequate security in ICS systems shall be established.	The objective of this policy is to develop, implement, and maintain verification strategies to ensure that ICSs address security in their design and implementation as well as to develop new ICS systems that are inherently secure by design. ICSs are systems of systems. It has been demonstrated that ostensibly secure systems can be compromised and it is obvious that insecure systems can be compromised. As security depends on how the systems are installed and maintained, any systems certification is a snapshot in time. When part(s) of the system that can change the cyber environment change (hardware, software, communications, possibly even people), the system needs to be recertified. ICS covers such a wide range of systems an industries, it is not clear how requirements for ICS cyber security testing could be validated and by whom.
6.5.3.21	Security certification and testing programs for ICS security personnel shall be established.	Various ICS operations require certifications for Professional Engineers (PE) but none of the professional engineering disciplines include cyber security competency requirements. Similar to the lack of ICS security curricula, there is a gap in personnel certifications specifically addressing ICS cyber security. Consequently, there is a need for assessing the competency of individuals working in this field that address the union of IT and ICS applications. ICS security is an emerging, highly specialized field of engineering. It combines the disciplines of control system engineering, the specific engineering domain, IT security, industrial networking, risk management, and safety system engineering. It also requires an understanding of commercial platforms (e.g., Windows, UNIX, LINUX, SQL, etc.). IT certifications such as CISSP and CISM are focused on traditional IT and do not address the unique issues of ICS.

exploiting dial-up modems (Meserve 2007). Another major concern is the number of people who have physical access to the controllers that may change the software on the chip sets that issue machine instructions. For example, the Stuxnet "worm" was an attack that was designed to propagate via a universal serial bus (USB) device. It was installed in nuclear facilities in Iran where there was no Internet connectivity (Zetter 2011). Neither exploit required Internet connectivity to initiate.

All policies in Section 6.4 should also be considered for the ICS domain of digital assets. However, existing standards and security features used to secure IT are not as easily transferrable. ICS security is a relatively new field and requires development of ICS-specific security verification procedures to enforce even agreed-upon policies (Stamp, Campbell et al. 2003). Even cyber security management standards are not directly applicable as they specifically address only IT management. Consequently, organizations such as the International Society of Automation (ISA) initiated an effort to develop standards for ICSs-S99-Industrial Automation and Control Systems Security. Some of the other organizations developing standards for ICSs include the Institute of Electrical and Electronic Engineers (IEEE), International ElectroTechnical Commission (IEC), International Council on Large Electric Systems (CIGRE), North American Electric Reliability Corporation (NERC), Nuclear Energy Institute (NEI), and the U.S. Nuclear Regulatory Commission (NRC).

The policy statements in this section are related to protecting private critical infrastructure. Table 6.5.3 includes examples of issues related to specific industries that utilize ICS to operate critical infrastructure and technology control recommendations to minimize the potential for successful execution of cyber sabotage threats at both technology and process levels. The overall set of issues is intended to first impress the reader as to the breadth of the domain, and to use that recognition to facilitate understanding of issue relation to the depth of potential consequences from inattention to ICS cyber security policy (Table 6.5.3).

7

One Government's Approach to Cyber Security Policy

7.1 U.S. Federal Cyber Security Strategy

This chapter examines the cyber security policy that has been adopted by the U.S. federal government from a strategic perspective. Prior to the early 1990s, U.S. cyber security policy was a straightforward response to the proliferation of electronic records, and has been described in Chapter 2. Here, we chronicle more recent history of federal-level cyber security issues that have prompted strategy and associated policy. The chapter explains government action in response to historical events and suggests areas that the government might consider for future action. It begins with a brief historical overview of the most significant events in the past two decades that shape today's policy debates in Washington. While most of the events are clearly cyber-centric, some are not immediately obvious with respect to their contribution to the field of cyber security policy. We start this historical review with terrorist attacks against the United States in the early 1990s, and proceed through actions taken in subsequent administrations. The chapter concludes with general observations of strategy and policy that have been illustrated by the history.

The U.S. Federal Government's policy attitude toward cyber security has ranged from enforcing strong standards developed by the National Institute of Standards and Technology (NIST) and the National Security Agency (NSA) to complete ignorance of the severity of the situation. At any time, several dozen bills related to cyber security are in various states of construction in the U.S. Senate and the U.S. House of Representatives. Many of these bills are rewritten versions of efforts started by a previous Congress, and some of them are brand new efforts. None of the legislation being drafted will alone "fix" the cyber security problems faced by our

Cyber Security Policy Guidebook, First Edition. Jennifer L. Bayuk, Jason Healey, Paul Rohmeyer, Marcus H. Sachs, Jeffrey Schmidt, Joseph Weiss.
© 2012 John Wiley & Sons, Inc. Published 2012 by John Wiley & Sons, Inc.

nation. In fact, it is probably inappropriate for any cyber security policy professional to believe that an Act of Congress will make much difference in securing cyberspace.

There have of course been many attempts to articulate cyber security policy via Congressional action or via actions taken directly by government agencies. There are also many assumptions and misunderstandings about the convergence of policy and strategy. Pure strategy is just a blueprint for how a decision maker would like things to work. To instantiate strategy, policy is combined with process, procedure, standards, and enforcement. Depending on the strategy, this list of things required to instantiate it may be incomplete. Moreover, even well-planned and executed attempts to instantiate a strategy may sometimes fail to achieve strategy goals. This is especially true in environments that evolve as strategy is being executed, such as in the fast-changing world of cyberspace.

For example, in 2006, it became clear that identity theft was an issue that would likely be the subject for public policy. At that time, the major credit card companies likely to be targeted by any potential legislation formed the Payment Card Industry Security Standards Council, which in turn created the Payment Card Industry Data Security Standard. The standards were adopted in order to demonstrate compliance with existing financial privacy protection policy and, the cynical among us would guess, to thwart the perception that there was any need for any further legislation. However, even after the standards were adopted, major payment processors who were compliant with the industry-created standards have been the source of massive data breaches that led directly to identity theft [1]. A similar self-regulating attempt to thwart legislation by voluntary adoption of *do-not-track* consumer privacy standards is under way in the online advertising industry (Wyatt 2012). These examples illustrate the fact that standards and policy are very different things, and standards that are designed to achieve policy compliance do not necessarily do so.

7.2   A Brief History of Cyber Security Public Policy Development in the U.S. Federal Government

7.2.1   The Bombing of New York's World Trade Center on February 26, 1993

The first major terrorist attack on U.S. soil since a 1920 TNT bombing on Wall Street that killed 35 people was meant to topple the city's tallest tower onto its twin, amid a cloud of cyanide gas (Mylroie 1995). Had the attack gone as planned, tens of thousands of Americans would have died. Instead, one tower did not fall on the other, and, rather than vaporizing, the cyanide gas burned up in the heat of the explosion. "Only" six people died and over a thousand were injured. Details of the attack were later found on the terrorist's laptop computer, the first known case of a terrorist using a personal computer to keep track of plans and operational information.

Within a month of the blast, four individuals thought responsible for the attack were apprehended. The suspects went on trial on September 13, 1993. The trial lasted 6 months with the presentation of 204 witnesses and more than 1000 pieces of evidence. A jury convicted the four defendants on March 4, 1994, in federal court on all 38 counts against them. On May 25, 1994, a judge sentenced each of the four defendants to 240 years in prison and a $250,000 fine.

Few Americans are aware of the true scale of the destructive ambition behind the bombing, despite the fact that 2 years later, the key figure responsible for building it—a man who had entered the United States on an Iraqi passport under the name of Ramzi Yousef—was involved in another stupendous bombing conspiracy. In January 1995, Yousef and his associates plotted to blow up 11 U.S. commercial aircraft in one spectacular day of terrorist rage. The bombs were to be made of a liquid explosive designed to pass through airport metal detectors.

But while mixing his chemical brew in a Manila apartment, Yousef started a fire. He was forced to flee, leaving behind a computer that contained the information that led to his arrest on February 7, 1995 in Pakistan. Among the items found in his possession was a letter threatening Filipino interests if a comrade held in custody were not released. It claimed the "ability to make and use chemicals and poisonous gas . . . for use against vital institutions and residential populations and the sources of drinking water." Pakistan subsequently turned him over to U.S. authorities where he was sentenced to 240 years in prison on January 8, 1998.

7.2.2 Cyber Attacks against the United States Air Force, March–May 1994: Targeting the Pentagon

The computer network at Rome Labs, an Air Force facility in New York, came under a cyber attack in spring 1994 (Virus.org 1998). The attack was eventually traced to two young hackers—Kuji and Datastream Cowboy—who originated in the United Kingdom but were using various points of access to hack into other Air Force facilities and the North Atlantic Treaty Organization (NATO).

Datastream Cowboy pled guilty and was fined. Kuji was an Israeli citizen and found not guilty because no Israeli laws applied to this type of incident. This incident cost Rome Labs $500,000 to get their computers online and re-secured; however, this figure did not reflect the cost of the data compromised. One of the hackers admitted that ".mil" sites are typically easier to hack than other sites.

Datastream Cowboy was 16-year-old Richard Pryce, then a pupil at The Purcell School in Harrow, Middlesex (United Kingdom). He was arrested at his home on May 12, 1994 but released on police bail the same evening. Five stolen files, including a battle simulation program, were discovered on the hard disk of his computer. Another stolen file, which dealt with artificial intelligence and the American Air Order of Battle, was too large to fit on his desktop computer. He had placed it in his own storage space at an Internet service provider that he used in New York, accessing it with a personal password. He was located by investigators via an online chat forum where he was bragging about his activities.

Kuji was 21-year-old Mathew Bevan, a soft-spoken computer worker with a fascination for science fiction. His bedroom wall was covered with posters from "The X Files," and one of his consuming interests was the Roswell incident, the alleged crash of a UFO near Roswell, New Mexico, in July 1947. He was arrested on June 21, 1996, at the offices of Admiral Insurance in Cardiff (United Kingdom) where he worked.

How did two rather ordinary young men manage to penetrate the military computer system and spark such a massive security alert? Both were bright and articulate, but there was nothing in their backgrounds to suggest a computer wizardry that would outwit the American military. Their success was based on a mixture of persistence and good luck, which was abetted by crude security mistakes in the Pentagon computer system.

In an interview several years later Pryce said,

> I used to get software off the bulletin boards and from one of them I got a "bluebox," which could recreate the various frequencies to get free phone calls. I would phone South America and this software would make noises which would make the operator think I had hung up. I could then make calls anywhere in the world for free. I would get on to the Internet and there would be hackers' forums where I learnt the techniques and picked up the software I needed. You also get text files explaining what you can do to different types of computer. It was just a game, a challenge. I was amazed at how good I got at it. It escalated very quickly from being able to hack a low-profile computer like a university to being able to hack a military system. The name Datastream Cowboy just came to me in a flash of inspiration.

Pryce easily gained low-level security access to the Rome computer using a default guest password. Once inside the system, he retrieved the password file and downloaded it on to his computer. He then ran a program to bombard the password file with 50,000 words a second. According to Mark Morris, a Scotland Yard investigator on the case, "He managed to crack the file because a lieutenant in the USAF had used the password Carmen. It was the name of his pet ferret. Once Pryce had got that, he was free to roam the system. There was information there that was deemed classified and highly confidential and he was able to see it."

7.2.3 The Citibank Caper, June–October, 1994: How to Catch a Hacker

In mid-1994, an organized Russian crime gang successfully transferred $10 million from Citibank to different bank accounts all over the world. Known as the "Citibank Caper," this incident was partially responsible for prompting the "Security in Cyberspace" hearings in the U.S. Congress chaired by Senator Sam Nunn.

By most measures, those responsible for the Citibank Caper were not world-class hackers—just really poor money launderers. When bank and federal officials began monitoring activities of a hacker moving cash through Citibank's central wire transfer department, they were clueless about where the attack was originating. Monitoring began in July and continued into October, during which there were 40 transactions. Cash was moved from accounts as far away as Argentina and Indonesia to bank accounts in San Francisco, Finland, Russia, Switzerland, Germany, and Israel. In the end, all but $400,000 taken before monitoring began was recovered.

The break came in August 5, when the hacker moved $218,000 from the account of an Indonesian businessman to a BankAmerica account in San Francisco (Mohawk 1997). Federal agents found that account was held by Evgeni and Erina Korolkov of St. Petersburg, Russia. When Erina Korolkov flew to San Francisco to make a withdrawal in late August, she was arrested. By September, recognizing a St. Petersburg link, authorities traveled to Russia. A review of phone records found that Citibank computers were being accessed at AO Saturn, a company specializing in computer software, where Vladimir Levin worked. By late October, confident it had identified the hacker, Citibank changed its codes and passwords, shutting the door to the hacker. In late December, Korolkov began cooperating. Levin and Evgeni Korolkovone were arrested at Stansted Airport, outside London, on a U.S. warrant on March 4, 1995. Unknown is how the hacker obtained passwords and codes assigned to bank employees in Pompano, Florida, and how he learned to maneuver through the system. Citibank says it has found no evidence of insider cooperation with the hacker.

7.2.4 Murrah Federal Building, Oklahoma City—April 19, 1995: Major Terrorism Events and Their U.S. Outcomes

At 9:02 A.M. on April 19, 1995 a truck bomb destroyed the front half of the Alfred P. Murrah Federal Building in Oklahoma City killing 168 citizens, including 19 children, and injuring more than 500. The powerful blast left a 30 ft wide, 8 ft deep crater on the front of the building. Local responders, fire fighters, police force, and urban search and rescue teams rushed to the scene. Within 7 hours, the president ordered deployment of local, state, and federal resources. This was the first time that the President's authority under the Stafford Act (section 501 [b]) was used, granting the Federal Emergency Management Administration (FEMA) primary federal responsibility for responding to a domestic consequence management incident.

The deliberate destruction of the Midwestern office building, located far outside the "nerve centers" of Washington and New York City, had a much larger impact than just the loss of lives and property. Government officials soon discovered that the explosion was felt by other government agencies and private sector businesses across the United States—due to the disruption of functions and data housed in the Murrah building.

The Murrah Federal Building housed several federal offices including the Drug Enforcement Agency, the Bureau of Alcohol Tobacco and Firearms, U.S. Customs Service, U.S. Department of Housing and Urban Development, Veterans Administration, Social Security Administration, and others.

After the attack, government officials realized that the loss of a seemingly insignificant federal building was able to set off a chain reaction that impacted an area of the economy that would not have normally been linked to the functions of that federal building. The idea was that, beyond the loss of human lives and physical infrastructure, a set of processes controlled from that building was lost as well (i.e., a local bureau of the Federal Bureau of Investigation (FBI) and a payroll department), with a hitherto unimaginable impact on other agencies, employees, and/or the private sector down the supply chain and far away from the physical destruction of the building. This made clear that interdependency between infrastructures and their vulnerability were major issues.

One direct outcome of the Oklahoma City bombing was Presidential Decision Directive 39 (PDD 39), which directed the Attorney General to lead a government-wide effort to re-examine the adequacy of the available infrastructure protection. As a result, Attorney General Janet Reno convened a working group to investigate the issue and report back to the cabinet with policy options. The review, which was completed in early February 1996, particularly highlighted the lack of attention that had been given to protecting the cyber infrastructure of critical information systems and computer networks.

Thus, the topic of cyber threats was linked to the topics of critical infrastructure protection and terrorism. Subsequently, President Bill Clinton started to develop a national protection strategy with his Presidential Commission on Critical Infrastructure Protection (PCCIP) in 1996, and the issue has stayed on a high priority ever since.

7.2.5 President's Commission on Critical Infrastructure Protection—1996

Concerns about terrorism have been raised by U.S. officials since the 1970s. However, it was not until after the Vice President's Task Force on Terrorism issued its report in 1985 that U.S. policy was formalized. The following year, the Reagan administration issued National Security Decision Directive 207 (NSDD 207), which focused primarily on law enforcement (crisis) activities resulting from terrorist incidents abroad. It tasked the National Security Council (NSC) with sponsoring an Interagency Working

Group to coordinate the national response and designated lead federal agencies for both foreign and domestic terrorist incidents. The State Department was designated as the lead agency for international terrorism policy, procedures, and programs, and the FBI was designated as the lead agency for dealing with acts of terrorism. No additional major policy changes were implemented in the federal structure until 1995.

Two months after the Oklahoma City bombing in April 1995, President Clinton issued Presidential Decision Directive 39 (PDD 39), which expanded upon NSDD 207. The following year, the PCCIP was formed by an Executive Order (EO). An excerpt from EO 13010 is below, and illustrates the deep understanding that the administration had about the importance of protecting the nation's critical infrastructure.

> Certain national infrastructures are so vital that their incapacity or destruction would have a debilitating impact on the defense or economic security of the United States. These critical infrastructures include telecommunications, electrical power systems, gas and oil storage and transportation, banking and finance, transportation, water supply systems, emergency services (including medical, police, fire, and rescue), and continuity of government. Threats to these critical infrastructures fall into two categories: physical threats to tangible property ("physical threats"), and threats of electronic, radio-frequency, or computer-based attacks on the information or communications components that control critical infrastructures ("cyber threats"). Because many of these critical infrastructures are owned and operated by the private sector, it is essential that the government and private sector work together to develop a strategy for protecting them and assuring their continued operation. (http://frwebgate.access.gpo.gov/cgi-bin/getdoc.cgi?dbname=1996_register&docid=fr17jy96-92.pdf)

The PCCIP was chaired by retired Air Force General Robert (Tom) Marsh and became known as the Marsh Commission. The Commission's final report, *Critical Foundations*, was issued in October 1997, and both formalized the descriptions of the major infrastructures as well as defined threats to them (President's Commission on Critical Infrastructure Protection 1997). It also recommended a series of policies for the federal government, the majority of which became Presidential Decision Directive 63 in May 1998.

As a result of the Commission's findings, the Clinton administration published PDD 63 in 1998, a landmark document outlining in detail a way ahead for protecting the nation's infrastructures from potential attacks. Also in 1998, and also as a result of lessons learned from the Oklahoma City bombing, the Clinton administration published PDD 62 (Combating Terrorism) and PDD 67 (Continuity of Government Operations) which together with PDD 63 form a triad of national policy aimed at addressing weaknesses in various parts of the nation's government and infrastructures. PDD

62 created the position of National Coordinator for Security, Infrastructure Protection and Counterterrorism under the NSC. PDD 63 was the first national policy on critical infrastructure protection creating the framework in which CIP policy would evolve.

7.2.6 Presidential Decision Directive 63—1998

Presidential Decision Directive 63 built on the recommendations of the PCCIP (PDD-63 1998). The Commission's report called for a national effort to assure the security of the United States' increasingly vulnerable and interconnected infrastructures, such as telecommunications, banking and finance, energy, transportation, and essential government services. PDD 63 was the culmination of an intense, interagency effort to evaluate those recommendations and produce a workable and innovative framework for critical infrastructure protection.

PDD-63 created four new organizations:

- The National Infrastructure Protection Center (NIPC) at the FBI fused representatives from FBI, DoD, United States Secret Service (USSS), Energy, Transportation, the Intelligence Community, and the private sector in an attempt at information sharing among agencies in collaboration with the private sector. The NIPC provided the principal means of facilitating and coordinating the Federal Government's response to an incident, mitigating attacks, investigating threats, and monitoring reconstitution efforts. The NIPC was absorbed into Department of Homeland Security (DHS) in 2003.
- Information Sharing and Analysis Centers (ISACs) were encouraged to be set up by the private sector in cooperation with the Federal government and modeled on the Centers for Disease Control and Prevention. Today, there are dozens of ISACs in many sectors of the economy. Several countries have created similar organizations for their industries and economic sectors.
- The National Infrastructure Assurance Council (NIAC) was to be drawn from private sector leaders and state/local officials to provide guidance to the policy formulation of a National Plan. The NIAC was never established. A new "NIAC" (the National Infrastructure Advisory Council) was created by EO 13231 in 2001 and serves to provide the President advice on the security of information systems for critical infrastructure supporting the banking and finance, transportation, energy, manufacturing, and emergency government services sectors of the economy.
- The Critical Infrastructure Assurance Office (CIAO) was created in the Department of Commerce with the responsibility for coordinating the development of critical infrastructure sector plans by the private sector

and their respective federal agency liaisons. Based on the content of the sector plans, CIAO assisted in producing the first National Plan for Information Systems Protection. The office also helped coordinate a national education and awareness program, and legislative and public affairs programs. The CIAO was absorbed into DHS in 2003.

7.2.7 National Infrastructure Protection Center (NIPC) and ISACs—1998

The NIPC had its roots in the Infrastructure Protection Task Force (IPTF), created at the FBI in 1996 in order to increase the "coordination of existing infrastructure protection efforts to better address, and prevent, crises that would have a debilitating regional or national impact." The IPTF was placed at the FBI in order to take advantage of the FBI's newly established Computer Investigations and Infrastructure Threat Assessment Center (CITAC), also created in 1996 to deal with computer crime.

Under PDD 63, the FBI was directed to bring together representatives from U.S. government agencies, state and local governments, and the private sector in a partnership to protect U.S. critical infrastructures. The NIPC was created in 1998 at the FBI to serve as the U.S. government's focal point for threat assessment, warning, investigation, and response for threats or attacks against the critical infrastructures. The NIPC's function was transferred to DHS in 2003.

PDD 63 assigned to industries the task of creating an ISAC, through which companies could share information about attacks, threats, and vulnerabilities. The ISAC was intended to be the NIPC's contact for warning industries about potential threats. Eventually, several ISACs were created for railroad, electric, energy, financial services, and information technology companies. In addition to footing the bill for these councils, companies involved have had to be willing to overcome reticence about their own vulnerabilities in order to share information needed to protect national infrastructure. Several more ISACs were created in the past few years, and unfortunately most are today just a hollow shell of what they were earlier. Information sharing is hard, and depends on building mutual trust between the people (not just the organizations) who participate in them.

7.2.8 Eligible Receiver—1997

In the summer of 1997, the U.S. Joint Chiefs of Staff organized what is known as a "no-notice" exercise that would test the Defense Department's ability to detect and defend against a coordinated cyber attack against various military installations and critical computer networks. It would involve dozens of world-class computer hackers and last for more than a week (Pike 2012a). The Joint Chiefs gave the highly classified exercise the code name "Eligible Receiver 97." The operational details of how the Red Team of pretend-hackers would carry out their attacks were left to senior officials from the NSA.

Prior to launching their attacks on June 9, officials briefed the team of 35 NSA computer hackers on the ground rules. They were told that they were allowed to use only software tools and other hacking utilities that could be downloaded freely from the Internet. The DoD's own arsenal of classified attack tools could not be used. The team was also prohibited from breaking any U.S. laws. The primary target was the U.S. Pacific Command in Hawaii. Other targets included the National Military Command Center in the Pentagon, the U.S. Space Command in Colorado, the U.S. Transportation Command in Ohio, and the Special Operations Command in Florida.

Posing as hackers hired by the North Korean intelligence service, the NSA Red Team dispersed around the country and began digging their way into military networks. The team gained unfettered access to dozens of critical DoD computer systems. They were free to create legitimate user accounts for other hackers, delete valid accounts, reformat hard drives, read email, and scramble data. They did all of this without being traced or identified.

The results of the exercise stunned officials, including the senior members of the NSA responsible for running it. Not only were the attackers potentially able to disrupt and cripple Defense command and control systems, but analysis of their techniques after the exercise ended revealed that much of the private sector infrastructure in the United States, such as the telecommunications networks and power grid, could easily be sent into a tailspin using the same tools and techniques.

7.2.9 Solar Sunrise—1998

In February 1998 several U.S. military system administrators reported a coordinated attack aimed at dozens of unclassified computer systems. The intruders accessed unclassified logistics, administration, and accounting systems that controlled the DoD's ability to manage and deploy military forces (Pike 2012b). Then-U.S. Deputy Secretary of Defense John J. Hamre called it "the most organized and systematic attack to date" on U.S. military computer systems. Although the attacks exploited a well-known vulnerability in the Solaris operating system for which a patch had been available for months, they came at a time of heightened tension in the Persian Gulf. Dr. Hamre and other top officials were convinced that they were witnessing a sophisticated state-sponsored Iraqi effort to disrupt troop deployment in the Middle East.

The U.S. response to this incident required a massive, cooperative effort by the FBI, the Justice Department's Computer Crimes Section, the Air Force Office of Special Investigations, the National Aeronautics and Space

Administration (NASA), the Defense Information Systems Agency (DISA), the NSA, the CIA, and various computer emergency response teams from the military services and government agencies.

In the end, it was found that two young hackers in California had carried out the attacks under the direction of a hacker in Israel, himself a teenager. They gained privileged access to computers using tools available from a university website and installed sniffer programs to collect user passwords. They created a backdoor and then used a patch available from another university website to fix the vulnerability and prevent others from repeating their exploit. Unlike most hackers, they did not explore the contents of the victim computers.

Today, defense officials continue to point to Solar Sunrise as illustrative of the difficulty of separating recreational hacking attacks from the state-sponsored cyber assaults that they are still certain are on the horizon. Law enforcement, meanwhile, holds this investigation up as a textbook example of interagency cyber crime cooperation.

7.2.10 Joint Task Force—Computer Network Defense (JTF-CND)—1998

In response to the findings of the Marsh Commission, the results of Eligible Receiver 1997, and the lessons learned from the Solar Sunrise incident, the DoD began exploring several options for dealing with the clear dangers that were growing from the nation's increased dependency on cyberspace. After months of deliberation and heated discussions, the decision was made to create a JTF that would serve as an operational organization outside of the Intelligence Community (rather than as an arm of the Intelligence Community as many wanted) and would have authority to direct technical changes to DoD computers and networks for cyber defense purposes (Gourley 2010).

Launched in December 1998, the Joint Task Force-Computer Network Defense (JTF-CND) was initially assigned to the Secretary of Defense (SECDEF) then was further assigned to the United States Space Command (USSPACECOM) in October 1999. In 2000, it was redesignated as the Joint Task Force-Computer Network Operations (JTF-CNO), and in October 2002, with the merger of the United States Strategic Command (USSTRATCOM) and USSPACECOM, JTF-CNO became a component of USSTRATCOM.

In June 2004, the SECDEF redesignated the organization as the Joint Task Force-Global Network Operations (JTF-GNO) and appointed the DISA Director to be assigned as its Commander. The JTF-GNO was given authorities and responsibilities for global network operations and defense.

In July 2004, the JTF-GNO formed the Global NetOps Center (GNC) through the functional merger of elements from the JTF-GNO's Operations Directorate, DISA's Global Network Operations and Security Center

(GNOSC), the DoD Computer Emergency Response Team (DoD-CERT), and the Global SATCOM Support Center. As such, the GNC was responsible for guiding, directing, and overseeing daily compliance with NetOps policy, providing common defense of the DoD's Global Information Grid (GIG), and ensuring strategic priorities for information are satisfied.

In November 2008, the JTF-GNO function was assigned to the NSA, and in June 2009 the SECDEF ordered STRATCOM to "disestablish" the JTF-GNO not later than October 2010 as part of the activation of the new Cyber Command. The colors were cased on September 7, 2010, ending its short existence.

7.2.11 Terrorist Attacks against the United States—September 11, 2001 Effects of Catastrophic Events on Transportation System Management and Operations

The terrorist attacks against the United States on September 11th, 2001 exposed not only weaknesses in physical security, airline security, law enforcement investigations, and intelligence analysis, but also demonstrated the close interdependence of the critical infrastructure in lower Manhattan, New York City (DeBlasio, Regan, et al. 2002).

Beneath the streets of New York City, as in most large cities, are miles of tunnels, conduits, pathways, and routes for various infrastructures. When the WTC towers collapsed, hundreds of tons of steel and concrete impacted the surrounding area, severing underground utilities, destroying telecommunications switches, and pulverizing power distribution transformers and backup generators.

The WTC Complex's seven buildings with its 293 floors of office space housed some 1200 companies and organizations. Each floor of the Twin Towers contained over 1 acre of office space. The complex included 239 elevators and 71 escalators. The WTC housed approximately 50,000 office workers and averaged 90,000 visitors each day.

The below-ground Mall was the largest enclosed shopping mall in Lower Manhattan as well as the main interior pedestrian circulation level for the WTC complex.

Approximately 150,000 people a day used the three subway stations located below the towers in the Mall. The below-ground parking garage included space for 2000 vehicles, but only 1000 were used on a daily basis. The number of parking spaces was reduced for safety and security reasons after the 1993 attack.

Because of the terrorist bombing of the WTC in 1993 and subsequent emergencies, such as the 1999 Queens electrical blackout and the 1995 Tokyo Subway gas attack, the New York City region had dramatically increased its planning for major emergencies before September 11, 2001. The New York City Office of Emergency Management (OEM), under the direction of the New York City Mayor's office, significantly upgraded its resources and preparedness, including the completion of a new emergency command center in 1999 at 7 WTC. OEM formed a task force to implement upgrades to the existing emergency response plans for the New York City region. The region used the incident command system (ICS). In addition to following the ICS, individual agencies upgraded their own internal emergency procedures.

The WTC itself was upgraded after the 1993 bombing with over $90 million worth of safety improvements, including a duplicate source of power for safety equipment, such as fire alarms, emergency lighting, and intercoms. Most importantly, building management took evacuation preparedness seriously, conducting evacuation drills every 6 months. Each floor had "fire wardens," sometimes high-ranking executives of a tenant, who were responsible for organizing and managing an evacuation of their floors. In part because of this preparedness, 99% of the occupants of each tower on the floors below the crashes survived.

On the morning of September 11, a Verizon/NYNEX building adjacent to the WTC site did not collapse, but it along with many other buildings bordering the WTC complex suffered significant damage. Not visible in the many photos taken that day is the chaos under the sidewalks and streets. The fiber optic and copper cabling entered the Verizon building from below the streets had been physically damaged by large steel girders that pierced the sidewalks to a depth of several feet. Millions of gallons of water from broken water mains, steam lines, and the Hudson River rushed into the underground conduits that carried not only the telecommunications cables but also pneumatic mailing tubes, electrical cables, and other infrastructure. This damage extended several blocks around the WTC complex. Several large bundles of underground fiber optic cables just outside of the Verizon building were literally sliced in half by the debris, then encased in water, mud, and steam escaping from broken high pressure lines.

The Verizon building at 140 West Street was constructed in 1926 to house the New York Telephone Company. Over the years hundreds of thousands of telephone lines were connected to the building, along with several million data circuits. Next to the Verizon building, in 7 WTC, were two of Con Edison's electric substations that served most of the Lower East Side and virtually every building from Duane Street to Fulton Street to South Ferry. Those substations were instantly destroyed when 7 WTC collapsed late in the day on September 11. Fortunately, all 1737 of the Verizon employees were safely evacuated from the building.

Inside the Verizon building were several floors of switching equipment and communications devices. Many of the components continued to work on backup power in spite of the massive amount of physical damage. One telephone switch was found to be still functioning as it dangled from its rack, held in place only by the strength of the power cable's outer jacket.

This illustrates the remarkable resiliency that many of the electronic components of the nation's communications infrastructure have.

For several weeks after September 11, the sidewalks of the area around the WTC complex were covered with miles of power and communications cables. Because the underground conduits were so badly damaged, Verizon and Con Edison quickly decided to restore operations by using a street-level network.

A similar situation existed in the basement of the Pentagon directly below the impact point of American Flight 77. One of the two major Pentagon Internet gateways was impacted by the crash, but continued to function, thanks to the quick thinking of an employee who was able to crawl into the damaged space with an extension cord to power the routers. The devices were still functioning when the overhead debris was removed several days later.

Many lessons about the communications infrastructure's vulnerabilities to a physical attack were learned following September 11. Unfortunately, it was discovered that the redundancy previously engineered in the networks had been largely reduced due to years of telephone company mergers and acquisitions. For example, the NYSE had designed over a dozen separate communications paths, with roughly half of them terminating at the Verizon building and the remainder traveling over diverse routes to other switching offices further north. On September 11, there were still over a dozen "separate paths," but they were only virtual—all but one physically terminated at the Verizon building.

Many of America's large metropolitan areas have two major central telephone switching centers, a remnant of the days when AT&T dominated the telephone market. It is important for businesses to determine the physical paths that their communications circuits take to their local switching office, and to ensure that they are not paying for what really amounts to "virtual" diversity.

7.2.12   U.S. Government Response to the September 11, 2001 Terrorist Attacks

The United States Commission on National Security in the 21st Century had issued a set of national policy recommendations in February 2001—well before the September terrorist attacks—in a report titled *Seeking a National Strategy* (http://www.au.af.mil/au/awc/awcgate/nssg/phaseII.pdf). Chaired by former Senators Gary Hart (D) and Warren Rudman (R), the so-called Hart-Rudman Commission echoed earlier reports, speaking anxiously of the inevitability of a major terrorist act on U.S. soil and of the nation's weak ability to prevent or respond to such an attack—concerns which were validated just 8 months later on September 11.

Among other things, the Commission called for the creation of a new federal agency, to be named the National Homeland Security Agency (NHSA). The new organization's mission would be "to consolidate and refine the missions of the nearly two dozen disparate departments and agencies that have a role in U.S. homeland security today." Although neither Hart–Rudman nor the earlier Gilmore Commission (1999) focused specifically on critical infrastructure, the reports nonetheless reinforced the basic message of the 1996/97 PCCIP: *the time for action was now, not later.*

While agreeing with Hart–Rudman that a central coordinating point for "homeland security" was called for, President George W. Bush initially chose to establish the function on September 20, 2001 within the White House under the title of Office of Homeland Security (OHS). OHS subsequently became the Homeland Security Council (HSC) the following month. Political pressures ultimately led to the creation of a Cabinet-level organization, the DHS in November 2002. The OHS/HSC director, former Pennsylvania Governor Tom Ridge, was named the nation's first Secretary of Homeland Security in February 2003. The HSC continued as a separately staffed organization through the end of the George W. Bush administration. In 2009, the Barack Obama administration consolidated the staffs of the National Security and Homeland Security councils into a single National Security Staff. The NSC and HSC now exist by statute as separate advisory councils to the President, while supported by a single staff.

Also following the September 11 attacks, President Bush issued EO 13231 (Critical Infrastructure Protection in the Information Age (http://frwebgate.access.gpo.gov/cgi-bin/getdoc.cgi?dbname=2001_register&docid=fr18oc01-139.pdf) making cyber security a priority and accordingly, increasing funds to secure federal networks. EO 13231 created two new White House organizations, the White House Office of Cyberspace Security and the President's Critical Infrastructure Protection Board (PCIPB). While both organizations were officially part of the new HSC, the Cyber Security Office was located in the Eisenhower Executive Office Building (EEOB) and was considered to be part of the NSC staff. The PCIPB offices were located a few blocks from the EEOB, outside of the tight White House security perimeter, thus allowing for easier access to coordinate interagency actions and to involve the private sector in the development of a National Strategy to Secure Cyberspace.

In 2002, the President moved to consolidate and strengthen federal cyber security agencies as part of the proposed DHS. DHS was activated early in 2003, and the National Cyberspace Security Division (NCSD) was created in June 2003. The NCSD and the CERT/CC at Carnegie Mellon University jointly run the United States Computer Emergency Readiness Team (US-CERT) as a single point of contact for addressing emerging national cyberspace security issues.

7.2.13 Homeland Security Presidential Directives

Since its creation in 1947 the NSC has been the principal forum for presidential consideration of foreign policy issues and national security matters. In the process of developing policy recommendations for the President the NSC gathers facts and views of government agencies, and then conducts analyses, determines alternatives, and presents to the President policy choices for his or her decision. The President's decisions are then announced by decision directives. Because the Bush administration had both an NSC and an HSC, there were two sets of decision directives published during his two terms in office—National Security Presidential Directives (NSPDs) and Homeland Security Presidential Directives (HSPDs).

Three HSPDs are worth mentioning here, as they illustrate how different types of cyber security policies needs can ultimately become Presidential decision directives. HSPD 7 replaced PDD 63 (Clinton administration) and increased the number of critical sectors to seventeen. HSPD 12 introduced the requirement for a common identification system for all federal employees and federal contractors. HSPD 23, one of last HSPDs issued by President Bush, was also published as NSPD 54 and outlined a 12-point comprehensive plan for securing the federal government's own networks as well as networks in the private sector that support the critical infrastructure. This plan is commonly known as the Comprehensive National Cybersecurity Initiative (CNCI).

The Bush administration issued HSPD 7 on December 17, 2003, which established a national policy for federal departments and agencies to identify and prioritize U.S. critical infrastructure and key resources and to protect them from terrorist attacks. HSPD 7 tasked the Secretary of Homeland Security with coordinating the overall national effort to enhance the protection of the critical infrastructure and designated other departments and agencies with sector-specific responsibilities.

HSPD 7 replaced PDD 63 and raised the total number of critical infrastructure sectors to 17. (An eighteenth sector—critical manufacturing—was added in 2009.) The following paragraphs from HSPD 7 show how the sectors were realigned after the creation of DHS:

> (15) The Secretary [of Homeland Security] shall coordinate protection activities for each of the following critical infrastructure sectors: information technology; telecommunications; chemical; transportation systems, including mass transit, aviation, maritime, ground/surface, and rail and pipeline systems; emergency services; and postal and shipping. The Department [of Homeland Security] shall coordinate with appropriate departments and agencies to ensure the protection of other key resources including dams, government facilities, and commercial facilities. In addition, in its role as overall cross-sector coordinator, the Department shall also evaluate the need for and coordinate the coverage of additional

critical infrastructure and key resources categories over time, as appropriate.

(18) Recognizing that each infrastructure sector possesses its own unique characteristics and operating models, there are designated Sector-Specific Agencies, including:

(a) Department of Agriculture–agriculture, food (meat, poultry, egg products);

(b) Health and Human Services–public health, healthcare, and food (other than meat, poultry, egg products);

(c) Environmental Protection Agency–drinking water and water treatment systems;

(d) Department of Energy–energy, including the production refining, storage, and distribution of oil and gas, and electric power except for commercial nuclear power facilities;

(e) Department of the Treasury–banking and finance;

(f) Department of the Interior–national monuments and icons; and

(g) Department of Defense–defense industrial base.

(19) In accordance with guidance provided by the Secretary [of Homeland Security], Sector-Specific Agencies shall:

(a) collaborate with all relevant Federal departments and agencies, State and local governments, and the private sector, including with key persons and entities in their infrastructure sector;

(b) conduct or facilitate vulnerability assessments of the sector; and

(c) encourage risk management strategies to protect against and mitigate the effects of attacks against critical infrastructure and key resources.

Sector Specific Agencies, in conjunction with their Sector Coordinating Councils (industry) and Government Coordinating Councils (government), work together via a framework of risk analysis and information sharing that is specified in the National Infrastructure Protection Plan (NIPP). Development of the NIPP was called for in HSPD 7 (see paragraph 27) and is maintained by DHS. The first interim NIPP was published in 2004, and the latest version was published in 2009.

7.2.14 National Strategies

While publishing national strategies is a routine function of the federal government, a handful of national strategies written in the wake of the 2001 terrorist attacks are worth mentioning in the context of homeland and cyber security. These publications are the ultimate in presidential strategic policymaking, and set for visionary statements and concepts that are then used by the various departments and agencies to develop their own strategic and operational policies.

The *National Strategy for Homeland Security* (2002) defined "homeland security" and identified a strategic framework based on three national objectives:

- Preventing terrorist attacks within the United States
- Reducing America's vulnerability to terrorism
- Minimizing the damage and recovering from attacks that do occur.

Improved "information sharing" has always been an objective of the government, and the Homeland Security Strategy recognized both the power of using information systems to improve information sharing, as well as the many gaps that remained to be filled. From the *Strategy's* executive summary:

> Information systems contribute to every aspect of homeland security. Although American information technology is the most advanced in the world, our country's information systems have not adequately supported the homeland security mission. Databases used for federal law enforcement, immigration, intelligence, public health surveillance, and emergency management have not been connected in ways that allow us to comprehend where information gaps or redundancies exist. In addition, there are deficiencies in the communications systems used by states and municipalities throughout the country; most state and local first responders do not use compatible communications equipment. To secure the homeland better, we must link the vast amounts of knowledge residing within each government agency while ensuring adequate privacy.

The *National Strategy for Homeland Security* identifies five major initiatives in this area:

- Integrate information sharing across the federal government;
- Integrate information sharing across state and local governments, private industry, and citizens;
- Adopt common "meta-data" standards for electronic information relevant to homeland security;
- Improve public safety emergency communications; and
- Ensure reliable public health information.

An updated *National Strategy for Homeland Security* was published in October 2007 that set forth four new goals:

- Prevent and disrupt terrorist attacks;
- Protect the American people, our critical infrastructure, and key resources;
- Respond to and recover from incidents that do occur; and
- Continue to strengthen the foundation to ensure our long-term success.

The 2007 *Strategy* expanded the scope beyond terrorism to include man-made and natural disasters. The first three goals listed above focused on organizing national efforts. The last goal was designed to create and transform homeland security principles, systems, structures, and institutions. This included a comprehensive approach to risk management, building a culture of preparedness, developing a comprehensive Homeland Security Management System, improving incident management, better utilizing science and technology, and leveraging all instruments of national power and influence.

The *National Strategy to Secure Cyberspace* (2003) outlined an initial framework for both organizing and prioritizing efforts. It provided direction to the federal government departments and agencies that have roles in cyberspace security. It also identified steps that state and local governments, private companies and organizations, and individual Americans could take to improve the nation's collective cyber security. The *Strategy* highlighted the role of public/private engagement and provided a framework for the contributions that can be made to secure all parts of cyberspace. Because the dynamics of cyberspace would require adjustments and amendments to the *Strategy* over time, the original concept was to update the strategy annually. However, no changes have been made to it since being published in February 2003.

The *National Strategy for the Physical Protection of Critical Infrastructures and Key Assets* (2003) identified a clear set of national goals and objectives and outlined the guiding principles that underpin our efforts to secure the infrastructures and assets vital to our national security, governance, public health and safety, economy, and public confidence. The *Strategy* also provided a unifying organization and identified specific initiatives to drive our near-term national protection priorities and inform the resource allocation process. Most importantly, it established a foundation for building and fostering the cooperative environment in which government, industry, and private citizens could carry out their respective protection responsibilities more effectively and efficiently. Like the *National Strategy to Secure Cyberspace*, it has not been updated since its publication in February 2003. However, two recent cyber strategies were published by the Obama administration, one on trusted cyberspace identities and the other addressing international cyberspace practices.

The National Strategy for Trusted Identities in Cyberspace (NSTIC) is a White House initiative to work collaboratively with the private sector, advocacy groups, public sector agencies, and other organizations to improve the privacy, security, and convenience of sensitive online transactions (http://www.nist.gov/nstic/about-nstic.html). The Strategy calls for the development of interoperable technology standards and policies—an "Identity Ecosystem"—where individuals, organizations, and underlying infrastructure—such as routers and servers—can be authoritatively authenticated. The goals of the Strategy are to protect individuals, businesses, and public agencies from the high costs of cyber crimes like identity theft and fraud, while simultaneously helping to ensure that the Internet continues to support innovation and a thriving marketplace of products and ideas.

In 2011, President Obama issued an *International Strategy for Cyberspace* to pursue a policy that would empower innovation as well as the ability to seek, receive, and impart information and ideas through any medium and regardless of frontiers, protected from fraud, theft, and threats to personal safety. As a goal, it was stated that, "The United States will work internationally to promote an open, interoperable, secure, and reliable information and communications infrastructure that supports international trade and commerce, strengthens international security, and fosters free expression and innovation." The goal was followed by several specific policy statements that reflect our national values:

- States must respect fundamental freedoms of expression and association, online as well as off.
- States should in their undertakings and through domestic laws respect intellectual property rights, including patents, trade secrets, trademarks, and copyrights.
- Individuals should be protected from arbitrary or unlawful state interference with their privacy when they use the Internet.
- States must identify and prosecute cybercriminals, to ensure laws and practices deny criminals safe havens, and cooperate with international criminal investigations in a timely manner.
- Consistent with the United Nations Charter, states have an inherent right to self-defense that may be triggered by certain aggressive acts in cyberspace.

7.3   The Rise of Cyber Crime

In any culture there will be criminals who take advantage of the less fortunate, the gullible, and those who do not pay attention to their own personal security. The Internet culture is no different, with the exception that many criminals can ply their trade nearly anonymously and away from the reach of most law enforcement activities. Typically, Internet crime centers on credit card theft, fraud, online gambling, and pornography, and attempts to swindle users through the use of fake email and fake web sites. Other crimes include theft of intellectual property, including peer-to-peer file swapping and the sale or distribution of cracked or copied software.

In the 1990s, many security professionals believed that we were on a collision course with some major type of Internet disruption—a "cyber Pearl Harbor" as it was frequently called. However, beginning around the end of 2003 and early 2004, another threat emerged and has dominated the scene since then. Organized crime has discovered that there is just too much value online to ignore it. That makes all online users the new victims of crime, and often they have no idea that they have been robbed or swindled.

To make matters worse, the explosion of "Web 2.0" technologies (wikis, peer-to-peer, social networking, and other forms of self-expression) have made it even easier for the criminals to take advantage of unsuspecting victims. In industrial plants it is even worse—many of these new technologies are replacing older systems as they are upgraded. By bringing in Web 2.0 technologies to monitor and run ICS/SCADA systems, we are potentially opening our internal control networks to the outside criminal community. There is an enormous amount of value in a critical infrastructure control system, and criminal groups around the world are only milliseconds away from exploiting any small mistake you might make.

Each year since 2008, Verizon has published a report called the *Data Breach Investigation Report* (DBIR), an analysis of investigations into the sequence of events that lead to breaches into large databases of information. Year after year the Verizon team has claimed the vast majority of all large data breaches are driven by criminal intentions. The latest statistics, based on nearly 800 breaches that were investigated in 2010 (number in parenthesis is the percentage change from 2009) and published in 2011, show that (Baker, Hutton et al. 2011):

- 92% stemmed from external agents (+22%)
- 17% implicated insiders (−31%)
- 9% involved multiple parties (−18%)
- 50% utilized some form of hacking (+10%)
- 49% incorporated malware (+11%)
- 29% involved physical attacks (+14%)
- 17% resulted from privilege misuse (−31%)
- 11% employed social tactics (−17%)
- 83% of victims were targets of opportunity (<>)
- 92% of attacks were not highly difficult (+7%)
- 76% of all data was compromised from servers (−22%)
- 86% were discovered by a third party (+25%)
- 96% of breaches were avoidable through simple or intermediate controls (<>)
- 89% of victims subject to PCI-DSS had not achieved compliance (+10%).

Crime fighters are quickly learning how to detect and chase criminals in cyberspace, but this is not an easy fight to win. The clear advantage goes to the criminals today. Hopefully, the advantage will shift to the good guys in a few years but for now the Internet is just like the Wild West of 150 years ago.

A more sinister criminal technique has come to light in the past few years—counterfeit computer and networking equipment manufactured in Southeast Asia that is bound for the American markets. Investigations by the FBI and other law enforcement agencies have found that an estimated 10% of all electronics coming into the United States is counterfeit, or contains a significant amount of counterfeit parts. Even worse, there is growing evidence supporting a theory that foreign governments are deliberately installing backdoors and other hidden access capabilities into products made in their country that are sold on the open world market. The Defense Department, Homeland Security, and others are gravely concerned about what this could mean for critical infrastructure systems and networks in the long term.

7.4   Espionage and Nation-State Actions

During the Cold War and in the centuries prior to it, nations took great risks to recruit and train spies to operate on foreign soil. Today, the Internet has made spying as easy as opening up a web browser then querying a search engine, and has reduced the risk of loss of human life to nearly zero. Of course, that theory is only good for spying on countries that are well connected.

Beyond governments, many companies engage in an activity known as "competitive intelligence," a euphemism for corporate espionage. It has become so popular that there is even a well-recognized professional association for all of the corporate spies to belong to—the Strategic and Competitive Intelligence Professionals, or SCIP (formally known as the Society of Competitive Intelligence Professionals, they changed their name in May 2010; http://www.scip.org.)

In the late 1990s, several U.S. government systems were found to have hidden accounts and large amounts of unauthorized activity. As the investigation developed, more computers and systems outside of the federal government were found to have unauthorized accounts. "Data exfiltration" became the new buzzword, rather than "intrusion" or "unauthorized access." The targets seemed to be large databases that contained atmospheric data, bathymetric data, and other information that took decades to accumulate. The source of the attacks was not clear—the intruders used complex methods to route attacks through multiple compromised computers and used "drop sites" as collection points for the data being stolen. In no cases were any signs of disruption present. It all appeared to be electronic espionage, a classic case of theft of intellectual property, only via the Internet rather than using microfilm and a spy camera as James Bond would have done.

During the Cold War, the spy community was clearly focused on the United States versus the USSR espionage. But in recent years, the focus has moved from former Soviet countries to China. The culture in China supports academic and scholarly achievement. Many students and professors treat the Internet as an experiment, and routinely gain access to remote systems or locate bugs in vulnerable software purely for academic purposes. Their findings are published in academic papers, and the researchers move along to the next project. Some, however, have found that there is incredible value in this research and have begun to make a business out of it, selling their findings to governments, criminal groups, and perhaps even terrorists.

In 2003, a series of cyber attacks that were believed to be of Chinese origin were found to be targeting American computer systems. Dubbed "Titan Rain" by the Defense Department, the investigation of the intrusion remained classified until the story was leaked to the press. Following the press leak, it was revealed that the attackers had gained access to many computer networks, including those at Lockheed Martin, Sandia National Laboratories, Redstone Arsenal, and NASA. While the names of the investigations have changed over the years, the espionage continues to the present day.

Chinese cyber-spying came into the public realm in the spring of 2006 when a private sector system administrator noticed that many of his users were receiving emails with Microsoft Word attachments containing Chinese. When opened, Word would crash and the dialog box asking the user if they wanted to share the data with Microsoft appeared. The sysadmin contacted the SANS Internet Storm Center, which in turn published a diary about the problem. In a few days, the issue was traced to a zero-day vulnerability in Word. The intruders had found a way to modify Word documents, using the vulnerability to write information into a specific memory location using Object Link Extensions (OLE) in Microsoft's Office products. This technique gave the intruders a path to install malicious code of their choosing, which could range from simple key-logging software to complete "rootkit" packages that give full control of the hijacked computer to the intruder.

But China is not the only suspect in terms information technology products modified for espionage or cyber warfare purposes. Perhaps the best (and scariest) example of this trend was the discovery of the Stuxnet worm in the middle of 2010. Thought to be written by one or more Western nations, the software was designed to physically damage specific components of nuclear fuel refinement installed in Iran. Rather than spreading over a network like the Internet, Stuxnet was designed to jump across network "air gaps" by infecting common universal serial bus (USB) memory sticks. The origins of Stuxnet remain a mystery, but the source code is available for anybody to modify and redeploy against new targets.

7.5 Policy Response to Growing Espionage Threats: U.S. Cyber Command

In 2009, the Defense Department's Cyber Command (USCYBERCOM) assumed the duties of the JTF-GNO, a "temporary" organization launched in 1998 to counter the growing threat of cyber intrusions coming from foreign countries. The highly complex attacks of the late 2000s led the White House to rethink how best to counter the growing threat and to permanently institutionalize cyber security into military plans and operations. Today, USCYBERCOM directs the operations and defense of most DoD networks, and when directed by the President can also conduct "full spectrum" military cyberspace operations. However, USCYBERCOM has no authority over the operation of private sector networks like the Internet or the public telephone system.

According to the Defense Department,

> USCYBERCOM will fuse the Department's full spectrum of cyberspace operations and will plan, coordinate, integrate, synchronize, and conduct activities to: lead day-to-day defense and protection of DoD information networks; coordinate DoD operations providing support to military missions; direct the operations and defense of specified DoD information networks and; prepare to, and when directed, conduct full spectrum military cyberspace operations. The command is charged with pulling together existing cyberspace resources, creating synergy that does not currently exist and synchronizing war-fighting effects to defend the information security environment.

> USCYBERCOM will centralize command of cyberspace operations, strengthen DoD cyberspace capabilities, and integrate and bolster DoD's cyber expertise. Consequently, USCYBERCOM will improve DoD's capabilities to ensure resilient, reliable information and communication networks, counter cyberspace threats, and assure access to cyberspace. USCYBERCOM's efforts will also support the Armed Services' ability to confidently conduct high-tempo, effective operations as well as protect command and control systems and the cyberspace infrastructure supporting weapons system platforms from disruptions, intrusions and attacks.

> USCYBERCOM is a sub-unified command subordinate to U. S. Strategic Command (USSTRATCOM). Service Elements include Army Forces Cyber Command (ARFORCYBER); 24th USAF; Fleet Cyber Command (FLTCYBERCOM); and Marine Forces Cyber Command (MARFORCYBER).

It remains to be seen how effective the USCYBERCOM will be with respect to increasing the security of the nation's most sensitive networks. One of the most significant challenges will be the long-standing "stove pipe" mentality of military organizations—that what is mine is mine and no other group or command should have any authority over what is on my plate. Because of the millisecond nature of cyberspace and the realization that risks created by one group can quickly affect other groups, this attitude will have to change in order for the USCYBERCOM to be successful.

Unfortunately for organizations that refuse to collaborate or interlock their defenses, they are more exposed to adversarial groups which have learned to exploit weaknesses along these boundaries.

7.6 Congressional Action

As this book is being written, several bills are in various states of construction in the U.S. Senate and the U.S. House of Representatives. Many of these bills are rewritten versions of efforts started by the previous Congress, and some of them are brand new efforts. None of the legislation being drafted will alone "fix" the cyber security problems faced by our nation. In fact, it is probably inappropriate for any cyber security policy professional to believe that an Act of Congress will make much difference in securing cyberspace.

The 111th Congress (2009–2010) produced over 50 separate "cyber bills" that attempted to fix cyber security problems with legislation. In the Senate, two bills dominated most of the discussion—the Lieberman/Snowe (Homeland Security Committee) bill and the Rockefeller/Collins (Commerce Committee) bill. The former bill introduced a "kill switch" concept that was widely ridiculed in the media and around Washington. It was ultimately removed from the bill's language, but the concept has remained as a reminder of how far the Congress had planned to go with respect to their legislative agenda. There was a strong desire to pass comprehensive cyber security legislation before the 2010 mid-term elections in order to show bipartisan support for addressing a growing national threat, but neither the Senate nor the House was able to produce a bill that reached their respective floors for a vote.

The 112th Congress (2011–2012) at the time of this writing has at least a dozen cyber security bills introduced in both the Senate and the House. Most of these bills are rewrites of bills introduced in the 111th Congress, although some are a fresh start. However, as the focus of the Congress is on budgets and economic issues, it is unlikely that a comprehensive cyber security bill will get enacted into law very soon. More likely is the approach advocated by the House majority to draft and pass smaller pieces of legislation that address specific problems.

Some cyber security related bills have already been discarded. For example, the Stop Online Piracy Act (SOPA, H.R. 3261) and the Preventing Real Online Threats to Economic Creativity and Theft of Intellectual Property Act (PROTECT IP Act, or PIPA, S.968) were congressional bills intended to expand the ability of U.S. law enforcement to fight online trafficking in copyrighted intellectual property and counterfeit goods. Both of these bills were widely criticized in the technical community and were eventually rejected by Congress after influential Internet sites such as Wikipedia shut down for a day in protest.

Two House bills, H.R. 3523 ("Cyber Intelligence Sharing and Protection Act of 2011," introduced by Congressman Mike Rogers and Congressman Dutch Ruppersberger) and H.R. 3647 ("'Promoting and Enhancing Cyber-security and Information Sharing Effectiveness Act of 2011," introduced by Congressman Daniel Lungren) seem to have less controversy. The former bill addresses specific legal restrictions that prevent the private sector and the government from sharing critical and time-sensitive cyber security data. The latter bill is much more comprehensive and includes provisions for a new information sharing organization, designates a lead cyber security official at DHS, promotes research at DHS to find new solutions to technical cyber security issues, and directs DHS to develop a national cyber security incident response plan in conjunction with private sector critical infrastructure asset owners.

A major consideration in both the House and Senate cyber security legislation is the concept of "covered critical infrastructure"—or what parts of the private sector the legislation applies to. In one House bill, the definition includes those facilities or functions that, if disrupted or destroyed by way of cyber vulnerabilities, could result in significant loss of life, a major economic disruption, mass evacuations of major population centers, or severe degradation of national security capabilities. Several industry sectors are seeking specific "carve-outs," or exceptions to this definition, so that they remain outside any new government oversight or regulation. Their argument is that their sectors are subject to external forces beyond their control and that any restrictive legislation would either hamper technical growth or limit asset owners from being able to profitably operate their infrastructure systems.

According to several Senators, the prime motivator for action is the fear that an attack on the United States' critical infrastructure via the Internet is not only possible but is highly likely in the near future. The Congress does not want to be left holding the bag, they would rather be in a position to show that they had taken action ahead of the crisis, and could not be accused of inattention to the issue. The private sector, on the other hand, would rather that the government fixes its own house first before imposing any regulatory or punitive framework onto businesses. Industry would rather that government provide incentives to be more secure, along the lines of reduced regulatory burden, lower business taxes, and perhaps credits or grants to offset costs. However, in the budget-conscience world of today, it is very unlikely that the Congress will enact any cyber security legislation that costs taxpayers money. Cost-neutral incentives are what industry needs to identify, and then perhaps a middle ground can be found.

7.7 Summary

The U.S. federal government's policy attitude toward cyber security has ranged from enforcing strong standards developed by NIST and the NSA to complete ignorance of the severity of the situation. This chapter has attempted to show how federal government policy has changed over the past two decades in response to changing threats and growing dependence on cyberspace. As the Internet and cyberspace have evolved over the past 20 years, so have government's cyber security policy efforts. Unfortunately, the threats and vulnerabilities of cyberspace are evolving faster than public policy can keep up (Brenner 2011). The best efforts may only have slowed attacks or restricted the amount of damage that can be done.

Cyber security policy is not static and must be just as flexible as the cyberspace it is designed to protect and manage. Often, governments cannot adapt to rapid change and quickly fall behind with respect to public policies while attack strategies, systems, and human education and awareness continue to evolve. It is possible that the federal government's own organization, being very hierarchical and linear, is its own worst enemy when it comes to securing computers and computer networks. By contrast, adversary networks may be expected to be operated by very loosely linked administrative leadership and sparse operational structures that are nevertheless capable of strategic coordinated attacks (Robb 2007). Cyberspace is complex and interconnected with no single point of authority or control. Defending networks may also require a decentralized and nonhierarchical approach to organizational management (Brafman and Beckstrom 2006). Some private sector companies have moved to a flat, decentralized organizational construct, and have thereby become more successfully resilient to outside forces. It may also be time to rethink governmental organization models to make them look more like cyberspace.

8

Conclusion

Each chapter in this book introduces a different perspective on cyber security. Though each may stand on its own as an essay, together they illustrate that cyber security policy is a multidimensional topic. Chapter 1 framed cyber security policy in the context of its current state of professional practice. Chapter 2 presented the field of cyber security as a rapidly expanding arms race for technology control. Chapter 3 reflected on the goals of cyber security policy, and described attempts to both verify and validate that goals are achieved. Chapter 4 emphasized that decision makers need to carefully evaluate the impact of cyber security policy alternatives in the context of strategic enterprise goals. Chapter 5 explained the catalog approach to cyber security policy. Chapter 6 provided a plethora of examples of policy issues. Chapter 7 described how cyber security policy is addressed by government.

Each chapter introduced a different layer of detail with which to frame the overall cyber security decision-making process. However, these layers are not cumulative levels of abstraction, but entirely different perspectives on the same basic ground truth: the evolving complexity of security issues presented by cyberspace. Combined, the chapters illustrate the complexity of cyber security policy, and the corresponding difficulties faced by cyber security policymakers. Even cyber security policymakers who have clear goals and organizations firmly grounded in principles are hesitant to state mandates, and are constantly monitoring cyberspace to ensure that policy does not result in unintended consequences. We conclude that, as cyberspace and corresponding cyber security measures evolve, so will any taxonomy of cyber security policy issues.

Cyber Security Policy Guidebook, First Edition. Jennifer L. Bayuk, Jason Healey, Paul Rohmeyer, Marcus H. Sachs, Jeffrey Schmidt, Joseph Weiss.
© 2012 John Wiley & Sons, Inc. Published 2012 by John Wiley & Sons, Inc.

Hence, a great deal of the effort in creating this book has been to summarize enough background information to ensure that the reader is prepared to face, understand, and reason analytically about any cyber security policy issue, whether legacy or new. To that end, it has been necessary to encourage a thorough understanding of the past, in order for our readers not to repeat it. Nevertheless, the pace of change in cyberspace is accelerating so much that those immersed in cyber security policy issues may find omissions in the range of possibilities for topics that might potentially have been included. To those whose favorite issue has been unintentionally omitted, we leave it for you to publicize, and just hope that this book will bring more informed participants to your cyber security policy debates.

We hope that at least one message is clear: that there is no blueprint available to produce cyber security, no standards provide a magic bullet, no course of action is clear of potential obstruction. It should also be crystal clear that the choices made by cyberspace strategists and entrepreneurs to date have not been based on cyber security concerns, nor are they likely to be in the future. Every stakeholder, whether an individual Internet user, a small business, a global conglomerate, or a nation-state, must decide its own strategy for maintaining security in cyberspace, and this strategy should be utterly dependent on their own mission and purpose in cyberspace occupation. Whatever cyber policies are adopted should be critically scrutinized by all for compatibility with one's own strategy.

It is indeed a situation in which every person must decide their own best interests. There is no Magna Carta of cyberspace, and no constitution. Like colonists in the New World, what governance exists is remote and has little power without the consent of the governed. Like the wild west, lawlessness and vigilantism operate in parallel while helpless victims and bystanders frequently succumb to attacks. What laws exist are antiquated for the purpose of prosecuting cyber criminals and some parts of society sometimes appear to celebrate Billy the Kid over the banks and the railroads.

This book does not champion control over cyberspace by any one or more entities. The solution most likely lies in the balance between control over cyberspace operations and maintaining the flexibility that is required for innovation. However, today's choices between control and flexibility are usually not made conscientiously by those who feel the impact of the consequences of such choices. In general, cyberspace stakeholders are naively unaware of the circumstances that lead to their inability to protect themselves against cyber attack. We hope this book will reduce the level of such naiveté.

Even if it did, mere recognition of the factors that led to today's cyber insecurity is not a sufficient condition for successful achievement of cyber security. Even the most enlightened and benevolent governance structure would have its hands full trying to address the myriad of cyber user policy issues and at the same time keeping a lid on cyber conflict. This strange new world requires new paradigms in cyber security policy beyond the current nation-state and diplomatic structures that exist today. For example, it is necessary for private sector global conglomerates to set internal cyber security policy that is consistent across such boundaries and still maintains harmony with all of them.

Cyber security policy development is not an easy task, and it is not confined to the boundaries of law, or management, or technology. It requires a blended way of thinking that crosses professional boundaries and highlights requirements for innovation. As in the dawn of the industrial revolution, new ways of thinking about the world must prevail. This is not to say that cyber security policy decisions should be the sole province of the digital generation. It is rather to say that, unless this generation comes to terms with the potential for catastrophe that is consequent in not dealing with this problem, the society who built the Internet will undoubtedly continue to lose ground to well-organized, well-equipped, determined threats who know how to define, articulate, and achieve cyber security goals which are adversarial to our own.

To assist with this coming-to-terms, we have established a reference framework for cyber security policy issues and a taxonomy within which they may be interpreted. It is hoped that this reference will contribute to the layman's ability to properly interpret cyber security directives and to assist today's cyber security policymakers in creating these directives. With this groundwork, future editions of this guidebook, or others like it, can use the foundation herein as a launch point to describe the ever-altering cyber security landscape of the future.

Glossary

Though there may be more technical definitions for the list of words, terms, and phrases that we have included in this book on cyber security policy, these definitions are purposely worded in layman's terms. Readers who seek further clarity may achieve it by consulting more technical publications.

Access control lists (ACLs, pronounced ak-els): Permissions with respect to files and programs allocated to computer users, for example, read, write execute; may be listed for individual users or groups of users, where groups are designated by membership lists or attributes of a user record designated as a role.

Account hijacking: Using credentials for a computer that belongs to someone else without their knowledge.

Advanced persistent threat (APT): An adversary who is continually actively engaged in reconnaissance to collect information for purposes of cyber espionage and/or cyber attack.

Anti-malware: Software designed to detect and minimize the damaging impact of malicious software.

Antivirus: Software designed to detect and minimize the damaging impact of malicious self-replicating software.

Availability: A system security attribute that refers to the delivery of functional capability when required.

Badness-ometer: A scale on which every reading indicates security is bad.

Bandwidth: A measure of the amount of data that can simultaneously traverse through a telecommunications line.

Cyber Security Policy Guidebook, First Edition. Jennifer L. Bayuk, Jason Healey, Paul Rohmeyer, Marcus H. Sachs, Jeffrey Schmidt, Joseph Weiss.
© 2012 John Wiley & Sons, Inc. Published 2012 by John Wiley & Sons, Inc.

Bit: An electronic representation of a 1 or a 0, typically combined with other bits to represent information in binary message formats.

Black hats: Cyber criminals. The origin of the term is old Western movies where the bad guy typically wore black while the good guy wore white.

Blacklist: In the context of the Internet, a list of sites to avoid due to evidence of malice by site operators (e.g., the sites deliver malware) or due to organization determination of inappropriate use of organizational computing resources (e.g., gambling sites).

Bluetooth: A network protocol for close range wireless communication.

Bogon: Short for bogus networks, this term refers to packet on the Internet that identifies its source as unallocated address space.

Border Gateway Protocol (BGP): A network communications protocol used to send data between Internet sites.

Bot: Short for robot, it refers to software.

Botnet: Multiple bots controlled by the same operator.

Bug: a coding error in software.

Business logic: In the context of security, rules for handling information that are programmed in software.

Byte: An ordered set of 8 bits; may represent a single character.

Carrier: A telecommunications company that transports data between physical locations, may be satellite, cellular, and/or land-based.

Certificates: Cryptographic keys which may be verified to be associated with organizations or individuals.

Certified Information Security Auditor (CISA): A technology audit certification offered by the Information Audit and Control Association (formerly the EDP Audit Association). Certification requires a test in information systems audit tools and techniques as well as independent attestation of education and experience. See www.isaca.org.

Certified Information Security Manager (CISM): An information systems security management certification offered by the Information Audit and Control Association. Certification requires a test of an enterprise security body of knowledge as well as independent attestation of education and experience. See www.isaca.org.

Certified Information Systems Security Professional (CISSP): A security certification offered by the International Information Systems Security Certification Consortium, Inc. Certification requires a test in tools and techniques for information security as well as endorsement by an existing CISSP. See www.isc2.org.

Chief Information Security Officer (CISO): A title associated with the highest ranking individual whose sole function within an organization is to manage an organization-wide security program.

Click fraud: The act of charging an Internet site for a user selecting a link to it, when no real person clicked on the link, often accomplished with automated software.

Compensating control: A security measure that mitigates the security risk of a vulnerability for which a primary control is ineffective. Typically a detection and response capability, the measure would compensate for the lack of system features that would prevent the vulnerability from exploit.

Computer Emergency Response Team (CERT): An organization whose mission is to receive reports of cyber incidents and gather a team qualified and motivated to resolve them.

Confidentiality: A system security attribute that refers to its ability to restrict access to information to an identified set of system users.

Content: In the context of cyberspace, refers to information represented by data.

Content filters: Strings of text that may be compared to data to determine whether it contains specific information, for example, NNN-NN-NNNN where N translated to any number is often used as a content filter for a U.S. social security number.

Control activity: Any combination of people, process, and technology whose purpose is to achieve a control objective.

Control objectives: Statement of management intention on security posture.

Credentials: information used to identify a user and authenticate that user to a computer; also referred to as *login credentials*.

Crime as a service (CAAS): Cyber attacks for hire, such as denial of service attacks.

Crimeware: Software created for the purpose of executing CAAS.

Cryptography: A method of hiding data in bit format by using complex methods of diffusion and confusion in combination with large sequences of other bits (keys). In this context, diffusion means disseminating the message into a statistically longer and more obscure format, and confusion means to make the relationship between the message and the key very long and involved.

Cyber security: Security modified with an adjective referring to the cyberspace properties of the thing to be secured. In general, cyber security refers to methods of using people, process, and technology to prevent, detect, and recover from damage to confidentiality, integrity, and availability of information in cyberspace.

Cyberspace: The global collection of electronic circuits that allow people to share information without physical connectivity.

Defense Industrial Base (DIB): Companies whose primary customer is the U.S. government.

Denial of control: Deprivation of the ability to enter system commands.

Denial of service (DOS): An intentional shutdown of system communications.

Denial of view: Deprivation of the ability to view systems status, or otherwise corrupt the data normally viewed by a system operator.

Dial-back: A mechanism that records a phone number calling, disconnects the incoming call, and initiates an outbound call to the same number only if it has been previously authorized to connect to that number.

Discretionary access control (DAC): Computer access control mechanisms that allow a user who can access data to grant that access to another user without administration collusion.

Distributed control systems (DCSs): Systems that allow multiple avenues of administration.

Distributed denial of service (DDOS): An intentional shutdown of system communications caused by multiple, independently operating computers whose activities are purposefully coordinated.

Distributed Network Protocol (DNP3): A set of industrial control system communications protocols that segment messages into three components (physical, data, and application).

Domain Keys Identified Mail (DKIM): A cryptographic protocol that allows users to verify the integrity of email and its provenance.

Domain Name Services (DNSs): A way to identify at which Internet address the computer corresponds to an Internet Universal Resource Locator.

Domain squatting: Using a company or individual trademark, copyright, or an identifier similar to register a domain name on the Internet that appears with probability to belong to that company or individual.

Doxing: Disclosing embarrassing or otherwise damaging personal information about someone on the Internet.

e-Commerce: "e" is short for electronic, and e-commerce refers to business conducted over the Internet.

Email: Originally, email as in e-commerce, where "e" stood for "electronic," now in mainstream vocabulary as email, or messages sent or received using Internet mail protocols.

Encryption: The process of using cryptography to hide data content.

End user: a person who uses a computer or mobile device, typically used to refer to those without the advantage of administrative privileges.

End User License Agreements (EULAs): Software industry standard verbiage created to form a legal compact between software buyers and sellers.

Federal Emergency Management Administration (FEMA): The U.S. federal government agency with primary responsibility for responding to a domestic consequence management incident.

Field instrumentation: Physical sensors and mechanism with electronic circuits that integrate with industrial control systems (ICSs).

Firewall: An electronic device deployed to intercept all traffic sent and received between two networks for the purpose of restricting the type of data protocols allowed between them.

Flaw: In the context of software, a flaw is a design that is unable to meet all requirements for the intended functionality simultaneously. "Flaw" may also refer specifically refer to the portion of software code that, if and when replaced, would allow for a design that met specifications.

Freeware: Software that anyone may use, though authorized use may require acceptance of a license agreement. Often confused with Open Source, but different because freeware source code is not always available.

FUD Factor: Fear, uncertainty, and doubt in the context of a discussion about security, usually introduced in order to influence a spending decision.

Global Positioning System (GPS): A system that allows software on an electronic device to communicate with multiple satellites in order to determine its location on earth.

Graphical user interface (GUI): Software representation of information used to view information on and/or operate computers.

Hactivism: Political protest conducted in cyberspace. Typically accomplished by sabotaging one or more government or enterprise websites that are associated with the political protest target.

Host intrusion detection system (HIDS): A file integrity detection and alerting system, such as tripwire.

Identity theft: Impersonation of an individual using data that are associated with computerized records that identify the individual.

Impersonation: A method by which a user may manipulate data within an authentication session or order to appear to the authenticating system as a different individual, who is also an authorized system user.

Improvised explosive device (IED): An explosive configured with trigger mechanisms customized to explode when approached by a specific target.

Industrial control system (ICS): A system that monitors and controls physical processes.

Information Systems Audit and Control Association (ISACA): An international association of cyber security and audit professionals who certify members for the professional practice of Information Systems Audit, Security, Governance, and Risk Management.

Information technology (IT): Refers in general to the computer systems and associated management processes designed to achieve organizational goals for information processing.

Integrity: An information attribute that refers to its authenticity, accuracy, and provenance. When applied to a system, integrity refers to its ability to maintain the authenticity, accuracy, and provenance of recorded and reported information.

Intelligent electronic device (IED): Component that provides software configuration, monitoring, and communications functions within a SCADA or other control component of an ICS.

Inter-Control Center Communications Protocol (ICCP or IEC 60870-6/TASE.2): An international protocol for industrial control system communcation that conforms to the sever-layer OSI model.

Internet Assigned Numbers Authority (IANA) or a delegated Regional Internet Registry (RIR): Organizations that facilitate the assignment of Internet addresses.

Internet Corporation for Assigned Names and Numbers (ICANN): The organization that sets the rules for determining how Internet users may claim ownership to address space and name space.

Internet Engineering Task Force (IETF): An organization that allows technologists to propose and collaborate on Internet standards.

Internet-facing: An adjective to describe a system that may be accessed via the public Internet.

Internet protocol (IP): A method of electronic communication used to convey information on the Internet.

Internet Registrar: A service business that provides registration of Internet domain names within top-level domains (TLDs) such as ".com."

Internet service provider (ISP): A business that sells connections to the Internet.

Intrusion detection system (IDS): With respect to *physical security* implies monitoring algorithms using images from cameras and personnel badge or physical access card readers, while in *cyber security*, the term IDS refers to host or network monitoring for malware and/or damaging impact to cyberspace resources.

Intrusion prevention system (IPS): A cyber security term to describe software that terminates the network connection of any user identified to be sending malware or commands known to be part of a cyber attack.

Job control technician: A professional who manage large quantities of computer processes, ensuring that the required dependencies of each are available at the time they are executed, and the output of each is available when required.

Joyride: To use computers in an unauthorized fashion to play online games or for other peaceful purposes.

Key management: People, process, and technology coordinated to keep track of encryption keys to ensure availability of encrypted data.

Login: Information use to identify a user and authenticate that user to a computer, also referred to in shortened form as *credentials*.

Malvertising: Advertisements that contain links to websites that download malware onto end-computers without raising suspicions of the computer users.

Malware: Software designed with malicious intent, to spy on user activities, steal data, or damage the integrity of targeted computers.

Mandatory access control (MAC): A method of maintaining permission to access system information or execute system functions that must be performed by a system administrator or operator, and cannot be changed by users of system information.

Man-in-the-middle: A type of cyber attack wherein the attacker intercepts communication from a user destined for a server and communicates with the server instead, pretending to be the user. The server responds to the attacker, and the attacker responds to the user, in effect, impersonating both the user and the server simultaneously.

Mash-up: A website that incorporates links from many other websites in order to maintain its full set of features, such as linking to calendar applications and shopping cart applications running on a different web service provider, and displaying status from those applications continually throughout the user experience on its primary site.

Mean-time-to-repair (MTTR): The amount of time it is expected to take to recover from a specific type of system failure, based on historical data of actual recovery times recorded.

Messaging: a generic term to refer to any process by which messages are sent electronically, via server protocols such as email, chat, or peer-to-peer protocols.

Modbus: A messaging structure used to communicate commands within industrial control systems.

Multifactor authentication: Authentication factors are what you have, what you know, and what you are. Any authentication process that uses more than one of these techniques to authenticate a user is multifactor authentication.

Mutual identification: Any process by which two devices connected over a network can identify the other simultaneously prior to creating a communications channel between them.

Name space: In the context of the Internet, the convention of names that ends in global top-level domains such as ".com."

National Infrastructure Advisory Council (NIAC): Created by Executive Order 13231 in 2001, the NIAC advises the U.S. President on the security of information systems for critical infrastructure.

National Infrastructure Protection Plan (NIPP): A U.S. Department of Homeland Security publication that specifies the working relationship between public and private sector organizations that is expected to be used to respond to unforeseen emergencies that negatively impact national infrastructure.

National Security Telecommunications Advisory Committee (NSTAC): A committee of telecommunications industry stakeholders whose goal is to develop recommendations for the President of the United States to assure vital telecommunications links through any event or crisis, created under Executive Order 12382.

Net neutrality: A cyber security policy position that endorses unrestricted ability of content to move freely over the Internet, and opposes attempts to regulate Internet information flow or to allow Internet Service Providers to have control over routing of information as opposed to electronic transmission.

Network Address Translation (NAT): A communications protocol that allows a network routing device to label the same computer with different network addresses depending on which network interface is communicating with the computer.

Network listening: Copying network traffic to a device for which it was not addressed, for the purpose of eavesdropping on network communications.

Network zone: A set of network addresses for which communications security is managed by surrounding them with common traffic choke-points with similar traffic filters.

Node: A network-connected electronic device which has communication capabilities.

North Atlantic Treaty Organization (NATO): An alliance of countries from North America and Europe committed to fulfilling the goals of the North Atlantic Treaty signed on April 4, 1949.

Online behavioral advertising: Gathering information about an individual's behavior on the Internet in order to provide customized advertising to be displayed to that individual.

Open source: Software whose source code is freely available on the Internet and whose owners encourage others to add features; participation in such software projects may require the participant to observe license agreements.

Operating system: A computer program that allows hardware to be controlled using a standard set of utilities that are the same no matter what hardware is being accessed.

Operations: A generic term for a department whose mission is to ensure that systems function as expected.

Packet: In the context of the Internet communications protocols such as the Transmission Control Protocol, a packet is a string of bytes representing data fields that are read by Internet routers in sequential order in order to extract the IP address and other fields required to send the information in the packet to the destination identified by its sender.

Patch: A portion of software code contrived to replace portions of code that are operating incorrectly without replacing the entire code base for the affected application or product.

Penetration test: A software security quality assurance technique that checks for known vulnerabilities, a form of badness-ometer.

Personally identifiable information (PII): Information that can be used to create consumer relationships of financial liability.

Pharming: Changing the method that a user resolves domain names services to send them to malicious websites, either on their local machine or on a domain name server.

Phishing: Sending an unsolicited email or other message that appears to be from a friendly source, but instead lures a user into accepting malware onto their computer.

Phone home: A software or malware feature that initiates communication back to the software vendor who supports it or the crimeware operator who operates it, respectively.

Policy servers: Computers that store variable configurations for security technologies, not to be confused with management policy.

Port: An addressable place in memory on a computer that sends and receives network communications.

Programmable logic controller (PLC): A digital computer used for automation of electromechanical processes. PLCs are used in many industries and machines. A PLC is designed for multiple input and output arrangements.

Proxy servers: A computer that is designed to intercept network communications bounds for a given destination, such as the Internet, and check it against a set of rules for acceptable use prior to allowing it to continue to its destination.

Public key cryptography: A cryptographic algorithm that uses split keys to allow a user to keep the private component while allowing others to identify the user using a public component.

Reference monitor: Software that allows an operating system to allocate its resources to only authorized users by interrupting all resource requests and comparing them to access control lists before allowing them to be answered.

Remote access: The ability to use the resources of a computer without being collocated with it, usually via a phone line or Internet connection, but may be wireless or satellite enabled.

Remote access tool (RAT): Malware that enables remote access.

Remote terminal unit (RTU): Any device that allows manual command entry in a SCADA system.

Repudiate: To deny.

Request for comment (RFC): The standard name for a proposed Internet technology standard, indexed by number, title, author, and keywords.

Reverse engineer: A process of examining systems and/or software to determine how it works.

Secure Socket Layer (SSL): A generic term to refer to all secure communications protocols that allow traffic between end users and web servers to be encrypted.

Security information management (SIM): An industry-specific term in computer security referring to the collection of data (typically log files, e.g,. event logs) into a central repository for trend analysis.

Sender authentication: Sender ID Framework (SIDF) or Sender Policy Framework (SPF).

Security operations center (SOC): A department within an enterprise whose mission is to detect and respond to security incidents.

Smart grid: A digitally enabled electrical grid that gathers, distributes, and acts on information about the behavior of all participants to improve the efficiency, reliability, and sustainability of electricity services. It utilizes two-way communications making it cyber vulnerable.

Smart meters: Devices that measure electricity and alter power distribution based on the measured value.

Social engineering: Using friendly persuasion to gain information that may be used to commit account hijacking, identity theft, and theft of intellectual property, including espionage.

Social networking: Using collaboration software to share content with friends and colleagues on the Internet or privately operated networks used by persons of similar goals and/or interests.

Spam: This term originated as a canned meat product, but now refers to undesirable messages, most frequently email.

Spoof: A method by which one system may manipulate data within a communication protocol in order to display the technical attributes of another system through a network interface, spoofing is the system equivalent of impersonation.

Spyware: Malware designed to capture user keystrokes and other activities in order to complete profile information on them, to sell to advertisers or crimeware operators, or to conduct espionage or APT activities.

Supervisory Control and Data Acquisition (SCADA): A subset of industrial control systems generally used in large, geographically dispersed applications such as electric, gas, and water transmission and distribution systems.

System of systems: A system that has a specific mission or purpose only in combination with other independently operating systems that have mission or purposes separate from their use in combination.

Technology malpractice: Negligence in management techniques to meet information security requirements.

TNT: Trinitrotoluene, a type of explosive.

Top-level domain (TLD): A string of letters that corresponds to a set of Internet names that end in that string. For example, "com," "org," and "net." A gTLD is a generic top-level domain, and a ccTLD is a country code top-level domain. TLD is the general term that encompasses both.

Traffic filters: Specification of the network traffic protocols to be allowed into a network zone, may also include the source or destination Internet address of the machines within the zone. Traffic filters are typically the basis for firewall rules.

Transmission Control Protocol (TCP): A specification for data sent between network devices, specifies, among other things, how may bits are reserved in what order for the network address to which the data should be sent, the protocol under which it should be interpreted, and the application which should be used to process the date upon receipt.

Transport Layer Security (TLS): A more recent specification and update to SSL.

Tripwire: Software that monitors file attributes to detect and alert when files are modified or deleted.

Unallocated address space: Internet addresses that are purposely not assigned to any entity in order for all entities to use them internally, as defined in Internet Engineering Task Force (IETF) Requests for Comment (RFC) 1918.

Universal serial bus: Protocol for data communications between an operating system and peripherals.

Virtual private network (VPN): A cryptography-enabled method of confidential communication between multiple computers over a public network.

White hat: A cyber security professional who emulates cyber criminal behavior in order to test systems security. The origin of the term is old Western movies where the bad guy typically wore black while the good guy wore white.

White list: A list of email domains which should not be blocked by spam filters, or a list of software programs that should not be quarantined by antivirus, or any other list of exceptions to security filters.

Zero-Day: When used as a modifier for the word threat, attack, or vulnerability, zero-day means that the vulnerability used by the threat agent is not publicly known.

Zone: An network configuration that requires traffic filters to specify all authorized access to systems within the zone.

References

Abend, V., et al. (2008). Cybersecurity for the banking and finance sector. In *Wiley Handbook of Science and Technology for Homeland Security*, ed. J. G. Voeller. Hoboken, NJ: John Wiley & Sons, Inc.

Acohido, B. and J. Swartz (2008). *Zero Day Threat*. New York: Sterling Publishing Co., Inc.

Adair, S., R. Deibert, et al. (2010). Shadows in the cloud: Investigating Cyber Espionage 2.0. A joint report of the Information Warfare Monitor and Shadowserver Foundation.

Alexander, K. (2011). Congressional testimony. House Armed Services Committee. Washington, DC.

Alperovitch, D. (2011). Revealed: Operation shady RAT, McAfee.

Amoroso, E. (1999). *Intrusion Detection*. Sparta, NJ: Intrusion.Net Books.

Amoroso, E. (2006). *Cyber Security*. Summit, NJ: Silicon Press.

Amoroso, E. (2010). *Cyber Attacks*. Burlington, MA: Butterworth-Heinemann.

ANSI and ISA (2010). The financial management of cyber risk. An Implementation Framework for CFOs, American National Standards Institute (ANSI) and the Internet Security Alliance (ISA).

Assante, M. (2009). Critical cyber asset identification letter. Chief Information Security Officer, North American Electric Reliability Corporation (NERC).

ASTM (2009). ASTM Standard F2761 Integrated Clinical Environment, or ICE. From http://www.astm.org, ASTM International, West Conshohocken, PA.

Baker, W., A. Hutton, et al. (2011). Data breach investigations report. From http://www.verizonbusiness.com/go/2011dbir, Verizon Business.

Cyber Security Policy Guidebook, First Edition. Jennifer L. Bayuk, Jason Healey, Paul Rohmeyer, Marcus H. Sachs, Jeffrey Schmidt, Joseph Weiss.
© 2012 John Wiley & Sons, Inc. Published 2012 by John Wiley & Sons, Inc.

Barrera, D. and P. Van Oorschot (2011). Secure software installation on smartphones. *IEEE Security & Privacy*, 42–51.

Bayuk, J. (2000). Information security metrics: An audit-based approach. Computer Systems Security and Privacy Advisory Board (CSSPAB) Security Metrics Workshop (Sponsored by NIST).

Bayuk, J. (2005). *Stepping through the IS Audit, A Guide for Information Systems Managers*, 2nd Edition. Rolling Meadows, IL: Information Systems Audit and Control Association.

Bayuk, J. (2007). *Stepping through the InfoSec Program*. Rolling Meadows, IL: Information Systems Audit and Control Association.

Bayuk, J. (2010). *Enterprise Security for the Executive: Setting the Tone at the Top*. Santa Barbara, CA: Praeger.

Bayuk, J., D. Barnabe, et al. (2010). Systems security engineering, a research roadmap, final technical report, Systems Engineering Research Center. From http://www.sercuarc.org.

Bilgerm, M., L. O'Connor, et al. (2006). Data-centric Security, IBM.

Bishop, B. (2010). China's internet: The invisible birdcage. *China Economic Quarterly* September. Available at http://www.theceq.info/.

BITS (2007). BITS email security toolkit. From http://www.bitsinfo.org, The Financial Services Roundtable.

BITS (2011). Malware risks and mitigation. From http://www.bitsinfo.org, The Financial Services Roundtable.

Boardman, J. and B. Sauser (2008). *Systems Thinking: Coping with 21st Century Problems*. Boca Raton, FL: Taylor & Francis.

Botha, R. A., S. M. Furnell, et al. (2009). From desktop to mobile: Examining the security experience. *Computers & Security* 28(3–4): 130–137.

Boyd, J. (1987). A discourse on winning and losing. Briefing slides. Maxwell Air Force Base, AL, Air University Library Document No. M-U 43947.

Brafman, O. and R. A. Beckstrom (2006). The starfish and the spider: The unstoppable power of leaderless organizations portfolio hardcover.

Brenner, J. (2011). *America the Vulnerable*. New York: Penguin Press.

Byres, E., J. Karsch, et al. (2005). Good practice guide on firewall deployment for SCADA and process control networks. UK National Infrastructure Security Coordination Centre (NISCC).

Byres, E. and D. Leversage (2006). The industrial security incident database. Metricon 1.0, From http://www.securitymetrics.org.

Carlson, J. (2009). Financial services. In *Enterprise Information Security and Privacy*, ed. C. W. Axelrod, J. Bayuk, and D. Schutzer. Norwood, MA: Artech House.

Ceruzzi, P. E. (2003). *A History of Modern Computing*, 2nd Edition. Cambridge, MA: MIT Press.

CETS (2004). Convention on cybercrime. CETS No.: 185. From http://conventions.coe.int.

Charette, R. (2009). Now is the time to define software never-events. *IEEE Spectrum*.

Chatzinotas, S., J. Karlsson, et al. (2008). Evaluation of security architectures for mobile broadband access. In *Handbook of Research on Wireless Security*, ed. Y. Zhang, J. Zheng, and M. Miao. Hershey, PA: IGI Global.

Cheswick, W. R. and S. M. Bellovin (1994). *Firewalls and Internet Security*. Reading, MA: Addison-Wesley.

Chew, E., M. Swanson, et al. (2008). *Performance Measurement Guide for Information Security*. (Rev 1, first version 2003). Washington, DC: National Institute of Standards and Technology.

CISWG (2005). Report of the best practices and metrics teams. Corporate Information Security Working Group, US House of Representatives, Subcommittee on Technology, Information Policy, Intergovernmental Relations and the Census, Government Reform Committee.

Clarke, R. A. and R. K. Knake (2010). *Cyberwar*. New York: HarperCollins.

Cleland, S. and I. Brodsky (2011). *Search and Destroy: Why You Can't Trust Google Inc*. St. Louis, MO: Telescope Books.

Cloppert, M. (2010). Evolution of APT state of the ART and intelligence-driven response. US Digital Forensic and Incident Response Summit. From http://computer-forensics.sans.org, SANS.

COSO (2009). Guidance on monitoring internal control systems. Internal Control—Integrated Framework Introduction, Committee of Sponsoring Organizations of the Treadway Commission, Members include: American Accounting Association, American Institute of Certified Public Accountants, Financial Executive Institute, Institute of Internal Auditors, Institute of Management Accountants. From http://www.coso.org.

CSIS (2008). *Securing Cyberspace for the 44th Presidency*. Washington, DC: Center for Strategic and International Studies.

DeBlasio, A., T. Regan, et al. (2002). Effects of Catastrophic Events on Transportation System Management and Operations, New York City—September 11, U.S. Department of Transportation, ITS Joint Program Office, April 21, 2002. From ntl.bts.gov/lib/jpodocs/repts_te/14129_files/14129.pdf.

Denmark, A. M. and J. Mulvenon, Eds. (2010). *Contested Commons: The Future of American Power in a Multipolar World*. Washington, DC: Center for a New American Society (CNAS).

Denning, D. (1982). *Cryptography and Computer Security*. Reading, MA: Addison-Wesley.

DHS (2009). National infrastructure protection plan (NIPP). U.S. Department of Homeland Security. Available at http://www.dhs.gov/xlibrary/assets/NIPP_Plan.pdf.

DoD (1985). *The Orange Book, Trusted Computer System Evaluation Criteria*. Washington, DC: Department of Defense. (supercedes first version of 1983).

DoD (2005). Information assurance workforce improvement program. US Department of Defense, DoD 8570.01-M.

Drew, C. (2011). Stolen data is tracked to hacking at lockheed. *The New York Times*, June 3.

Drucker, P. (2001). *The Essential Drucker*. New York: HarperCollins.

DSB (1970). Security controls for computer systems. Defense Science Board.

DSB (1996). Information warfare—Defense. Defense Science Board.

DSB (2005). High performance microchip supply. Defense Science Board.

FBIIC and FSSCC (2007). Banking and finance, critical infrastructure and key resources, sector-specific plan as input to the national infrastructure protection plan. Financial and Banking Infrastructure Information Committee and Financial Services Sector Coordinating Council.

FDIC (2004). Putting an end to account-hijacking identity theft. Federal Deposit Insurance Corporation Division of Supervision and Consumer Protection Technology Supervision Branch.

Fernandez, E. B. and N. Delessy (2006). Using patterns to understand and compare web services security products and standards. Proceedings of the Advanced International Conference on Telecommunications and International Conference on Internet and Web Applications and Services (AICT/ICIW 2006), IEEE.

FFIEC (2006). *IT Examination Handbook—Information Security Booklet*. Washington, DC: Federal Financial Institutions Examination Council, www.ffiec.gov.

FS-ISAC (2011). Threat viewpoint, advanced persistent threat. Financial Services Information Sharing and Analysis Center, www.fsisac.com.

FSSCC (2008). Research and development agenda. Financial Services Sector Coordinating Council for Critical Infrastructure Protection and Homeland Security, Financial Services Sector Coordinating Council, www.fsscc.org.

FTC (2011). *Consumer Sentinel Network Data Book*. Washington, DC: U.S. Federal Trade Commission. From http://www.ftc.gov/sentinel/reports/sentinel-annual-reports/sentinel-cy2010.pdf.

Furr, J. (1990). Wikepedia entry attributes spam usage to him.

Gallaher, M. P., A. N. Link, et al. (2008). *Cyber Security, Economic Strategies and Public Policy Alternatives*. Cheltenham, UK: Edward Elgar.

Garcia, M. L. (2008). *The Design and Analysis of Physical Protection Systems*. Burlington, MA: Butterworth-Heinemann.

Gilliland, A. and R. Gula (2009). SCAP panel discussion. Financial Services Information Security Caucus. New York.

Gilmore Commission (1999). First annual report to the President and the Congress of the Advisory Panel to Assess Domestic Response Capabilities for Terrorism Involving Weapons of Mass Destruction. Available at www.rand.org.

Gordon, L. A. and M. P. Loeb (2005). *Managing Cybersecurity Resources*. New York: McGraw-Hill.

Gorman, S. (2012). Chinese hackers suspected in long-term Nortel breach. *The Wall Street Journal, February 14.*

Gourley, B. (2010). JTF-CND to JTF-CNO to JTF-GNO to Cybercom, ctovision.com, September 8, 2010. Available at http://ctovision.com/2010/09/jtf-cnd-to-jtf-cno-to-jtf-gno-to-cybercom/.

Grampp, F. T. and M. D. McIlroy (1989), Why we moved crypt to /usr/games, and other fatherly advice. AT&T Bell Laboratories Technical Memorandum nos. TM 11275-890302-03TMS and TM 11270-890301-06TMS.

Guinnane, T. W. (2005). Trust: A concept too many. Economic Growth Center, Yale University, www.econ.yale.edu/~egcenter/research.htm.

Hathaway, M., et al. (2009). Cyberspace policy review, assuring a trusted and resilient information, and communications infrastructure. United States Executive Branch.

Hayden, L. (2010). IT security metrics: A practical framework for measuring security & protecting data: McGraw-Hill Osborne media.

Herley, C. (2009). So long, and no thanks for the externalities: The rational rejection of security advice by users. New security paradigms workshop. Oxford, United Kingdom, ACM.

Herrmann, D. (2007). *The Complete Guide to Security and Privacy Metrics.* Boca Raton, FL: Auerbach Publications.

HHS (2010). Nationwide Health Information Network (NHIN) exchange architecture overview. DRAFT v.0.9, US Department of Health and Human Services.

HIPAA (2003). Health Insurance Portability and Accountability Act of 1996 (HIPAA) security rule. US Department of Health and Human Services. Federal Register Vol. 68, No. 34.

Hoglund, G. and G. McGraw (2008). *Exploiting Online Games.* Boston, MA: Pearson Education.

Hubbard, D. W. (2007). *How to Measure Anything.* Hoboken, NJ: John Wiley & Sons, Inc.

Hubbard, D. W. (2009). *The Failure of Risk Management.* Hoboken, NJ: John Wiley & Sons, Inc., p. 6.

IETF (ongoing). Request for Comments (RFC). Internet Engineering Task Force Archives. Available at http://www.ietf.org/rfc.html.

Igure, V. M., S. A. Laughter, et al. (2006). Security issues in SCADA networks. *Computers & Security* 25(7): 498–506.

INCOSE (2011). INCOSE systems engineering handbook, version 3.2.1.

ISA. International Society of Automation S99—Industrial Automation and Control Systems Security.

ISACA (2007). Control Objectives for Information Technology (COBIT). Rolling Meadows, IL, Information Systems Audit and Control Association, IT Governance Institute.

ISF (2007). The standard of good practice for information security. Information Security Forum, http://www.isfsecuritystandard.com.

ISO/IEC (2002). Information technology—Systems Security Engineering—Capability Maturity Model (SSE-CMM, ISO/IEC 28127). International Organization for Standardization (ISO) and International Electrotechnical Commission (IEC).

ISO/IEC (2005a). Information technology—Security techniques—Information security management systems—Requirements (ISO/IEC 27001). From http://www.iso.org.

ISO/IEC (2005b). Information technology—Security techniques—Code of practice for information security management (ISO/IEC 27002). International Organization for Standardization (ISO) and International Electrotechnical Commission (IEC).

ISO/IEC (2007). Systems and software engineering—Measurement process (ISO/IEC 15939). International Organization for Standardization (ISO) and International Electrotechnical Commission (IEC).

ISO/IEC (2009a). Information technology—Security techniques—Evaluation criteria for IT security—Part 1: Introduction and general model (ISO/IEC 15408). International Organization for Standardization (ISO) and International Electrotechnical Commission (IEC).

ISO/IEC (2009b). Information technology—Security techniques—Information security management—Measurement (ISO/IEC 27004). International Organization for Standardization (ISO) and International Electrotechnical Commission (IEC).

ISO/IEC (2009c). Systems and software engineering—Systems and Software Assurance—Part 2: Assurance case (ISO/IEC 15026). International Organization for Standardization (ISO) and International Electrotechnical Commission (IEC).

Jacobs, A. and M. Helft (2010). Google, citing attack, threatens to exit China. *The New York Times*, January 12.

Jakobsson, M. (2009). Academia. In *Enterprise Information Security and Privacy*, ed. C. W. Axelrod, J. Bayuk, and D. Schutzer. Norwood, MA: Artech House, 191–198.

Jansen, W. (2009). Directions in security metrics research. National Institute of Standards and Technology Interagency Report. NISTIR 7564, www.nist.gov.

Jaquith, A. (2007). *Security Metrics*. Upper Saddle River, NJ: Pearson Education.

Jaquith, A. and D. Geer (2005). Security Metrics, a community website for security practitioners. From http://www.securitymetrics.org.

Khusial, D. and R. McKegney (2005). e-Commerce security: Attacks and preventive strategies. From http://www.ibm.com/developerworks/websphere/library/techarticles/0504_mckegney/0504_mckegney.html#N10078.

Kim, G., P. Love, et al. (2008). *Visible Ops Security*. Eugene, OR: Information Technology Process Institute.

Kim, G. and E. H. Spafford (1994). *The Design and Implementation of Tripwire: A File System Integrity Checker.* Proceedings of the 2nd ACM conference on computer and communications security. Fairfax, VA: ACM Press.

King, S. (2010). *Science of Cyber Security,* JST-10-102. McLean, VA: MITRE.

Kocieniewski, D. (2006). Six animal rights advocates are convicted of terrorism. *The New York Times,* March 3.

Kuehl, D. T. (2009). From cyberspace to cyberpower: Defining the problem. In *Cyberpower and National Security,* ed. F. D. Kramer, S. H. Starr, and L. Wentz. Dulles, VA: Potomac Books, Inc.

Landwehr, C. E. (2009). A national goal for cyberspace: Create an open, accountable internet. *IEEE Security & Privacy,* 7(3): 3–4.

Littman, J. (1990). Shockwave rider. *PC Computing,* June.

Loveland, G. and M. Lobel (2011). Global state of information security survey. Price Waterhouse Coopers, CIO Magazine, and CSO Magazine.

Lynn, W. (2010). Defending a new domain. *Foreign Affairs* 89(5): 97–108.

Markoff, J. (2012). Researchers find a flaw in a widely used online encryption method. *The New York Times,* February 15.

Maughan, D. (2009). A roadmap for cybersecurity research. US Department of Homeland Security.

McGraw, G. (2006). *Software Security.* Boston: Pearson Education.

McHugh, J. (2000). Testing intrusion detection systems. *ACM Transactions on Information and System Security,* 3(4).

McMillan, R. (2010). More than 100 companies targeted by Google hackers. *Computerworld,* February 27. Available at www.computerworld.com.

McNeil, J. (1978). The Consultant, Coward, McCann, and Geoghegan, Inc., also a BBC television series.

MD FIRE (ongoing). Medical device free interoperability requirements for the enterprise. From http://www.mdpnp.org.

Menn, J. (2010). *Fatal System Error.* New York: Perseus Books Group.

Meserve, J. (2007). Staged cyber attack reveals vulnerability in power grid. *CNN News.* From http://www.youtube.com/watch?v=C2qd6xXbySk.

Miniwatts (ongoing). Internet World Stats, Miniwatts Marketing Group. http://www.internetworldstats.com/stats.htm.

MITRE (ongoing). Common Vulnerabilities and Exposures, dictionary of common names for publicly known information security vulnerabilities. http://cve.mitre.org.

MITRE (2009). Common Weakness Enumeration (CWE/SANS) top 25 most dangerous programming errors. From http://cwe.mitre.org/. S. Christey.

Mohawk (1997). Putting the terror in terrorism, busted in 97. December 26. Available at http://web.textfiles.com/ezines/OCPP/ocpp05.txt.

Monty Python (1970). Monty Python's flying circus spam sketch. From http://www.youtube.com/watch?v=anwy2MPT5RE.

Mylroie, L. (1995). The World Trade Center bomb: Who is Ramzi Yousef? And why it matters. *The National Interest*, December 1. Available at http://nationalinterest.org/article/the-world-trade-center-bomb-who-is-ramzi-yousef-and-why-it-matters-1035.

National vulnerability database. http://nvd.nist.gov/.

NCPI (2001). *Understanding Crime Prevention*, 2nd Edition. National Crime Prevention Institute. Woburn, MA: Butterworth-Heinemann.

Nelson, A. J., G. W. Dinolt, et al. (2011). A security and usability perspective of cloud file systems. SoSE 2011 6th International Conference on System of Systems Engineering, Albuquerque NM.

NERC (2010). High-impact, low-frequency event risk report. From http://www.nerc.com/files/HILF.pdf, North American Electric Reliability Corporation, June 2010.

Neumann, P. G. (2004). Principled assuredly trustworthy composable architectures. SRI International. Available at http://www.csl.sri.com/~neumann/chats4.pdf.

NIST (2011). Managing information security risk. National Institute of Standards and Technology, Joint Task Force Transformation Initiative Interagency Working Group.

NRC (1996). *Cryptography's Role in Securing the Information Society*. National Research Council. Washington, DC: National Academy Press.

NSPD-54/HSPD-23 (2008). The Comprehensive National Cybersecurity Initiative, National Security Presidential Directive 54/Homeland Security Presidential Directive 23.

NTIA (1998). Improvement of technical management of internet names and addresses. National Telecommunications and Information Administration (Editor), *Federal Register*, Vol. 63, No. 34, FR Doc. 98-4200.

NTSB (2010). San Bruno pipeline incident, preliminary report. Accident No.: DCA10MP008. From http://www.ntsb.gov/Surface/pipeline/Preliminary-Reports/San-Bruno-CA.html, National Transportation Safety Board.

OCC (2008). Bulletin OCC 2008-16. Subject: Information Security Description: Application Security, US Office of the Comptroller of the Currency.

Pande, P., R. Neuman, et al. (2001). *The Six Sigma Way*. New York: McGraw-Hill.

Pariser, E. (2011). *The Filter Bubble*. London: Penguin Group.

PCI (2008). Payment Card Industry (PCI) Data Security Standard, Version 1.2. Payment Card Industry (PCI) Security Standards Council, https://www.pcisecuritystandards.org.

PDD-63 (1998). U.S. Presidential Decision Directive 63. Available at http://www.fas.org/irp/offdocs/pdd/pdd-63.htm.

Peltier, T. R. (2001). *Information Security Policies, Procedures, and Standards*. Boca Raton, FL: CRC Press.

Pike, J. (2012a). Eligible receiver. Available at http://www.globalsecurity.org/military/ops/eligible-receiver.htm.

Pike, J. (2012b). Solar sunrise. Available at http://www.globalsecurity.org/military/ops/solar-sunrise.htm.

PMI (2008). *A Guide to the Project Management Body of Knowledge (PMBOK® Guide)*, 4th Edition. Newton Square, PA: Project Management Institute.

Ponemon Institute (2009). Electronic health information at risk. Available at www.ponemon.org.

Powell, C. (2009). Security leadership. Fortify Executive Summit & ISE Mid-Atlantic Awards Washington, DC, Executive Alliance, Inc.

Preckshot, G. G. (1994). Method for performing diversity and Defense-in-Depth analyses of reactor protection systems. UCRL-ID-119239. US Nuclear Regulatory Commission Lawrence Livermore National Laboratory, Fission Energy and Systems Safety Program.

President's Commission on Critical Infrastructure Protection (1997). Critical foundations: Protecting America's infrastructures, http://www.fas.org/sgp/library/pccip.pdf.

Proctor, P. (2001). *The Practical Intrusion Detection Handbook*. Upper Saddle River, NJ: Prentice Hall.

Ramachandran, J. (2002). *Designing Security Architecture Solutions*. Hoboken, NJ: John Wiley & Sons, Inc.

Rattray, G. (2001). *Strategic Warfare in Cyberspace*. Cambridge MA: The MIT Press.

Rekhter, Y., R. G. Moskowitz, et al. (1996). Address allocation for private internets. Request for Comments: 1918 Internet Engineering Task Force, Network Working Group.

Rescorla, E. and T. Dierks (1999). The Transport Layer Security (TLS) protocol, version 1.2. Request for Comments: 5246, Internet Engineering Task Force, Network Working Group.

Rice, D. (2008). *Geekonomics*. Boston: Pearson Education.

Robb, J. (2007). *Brave New War, The Next Stage of Terrorism and the End of Globalization*. Hoboken, NJ: John Wiley & Sons, Inc.

Rohmeyer, P. (2010). Technology malpractice. In *Cyberforensics: Understanding Information Security Investigations*, ed. J. Bayuk. New York: Springer.

Ross, R., S. Katzke, et al. (2007). Recommended security controls for federal information systems, SP 800-53 Rev 2. National Institute of Standards and Technology.

Rost, J. and R. L. Glass (2011). *The Dark Side of Software Engineering*. Hoboken, NJ: Wiley.

RSTA (ongoing). Root Server Technical Operations Association, www.root-servers.org.

Ruitenbeek, E. V. and K. Scarfone (2009). The Common Misuse Scoring System (CMSS): Metrics for software feature misuse—DRAFT NISTIR 7517. National Institute of Standards and Technology.

Safire, W. (1994). On language—Cyberlingo. *The New York Times Magazine*, December 11, 1994.

Sarno, D. (2012). Phone apps dial up privacy worries. *Los Angeles Times*, February 18.

Savola, R. M. (2007). Towards a taxonomy for information security metrics. International Conference on Software Engineering Advances (ICSEA). Cap Esterel, France, ACM.

Schacht, J. M. (1975). *Jobstream Separator System Design*. NIST History of Computer Security. McLean, VA: MITRE.

Schewe, P. F. (2007). *The Grid*. Washington, DC: Joseph Henry Press.

Schmidt, H. (2006). *Patrolling Cyberspace*. N. Potomac, MD: Larstan Publishing.

Schneider, F. B., Ed. (1999). *Trust in Cyberspace*. National Research Council. Washington, DC: National Academy Press.

Schneier, B. (2003). *Beyond Fear*. New York: Copernicus.

Schwartz, N. D. and C. Drew (2011). RSA faces angry users after breach. *The New York Times*, June 7.

Schweitzer, J. A. (1982). *Managing Information Security, A Program for the Electronic Age*. Woburn, MA: Butterworth Publishers Inc.

Schweitzer, J. A. (1983). *Protecting Information in the Electronic Workplace*. Reston, VA: Reston Publishing.

Shannon, C. E. (1949). Communication theory of secrecy systems. *Bell Labs Technical Journal*, 28(4).

Siegel, M. (2005). *False Alarm, the Truth about the Epidemic of Fear*. Hoboken, NJ: John Wiley and Sons, Inc.

Singleton, F. (1994). The evolution of EDP auditing in North America. *IS Audit and Control Journal* IV: 38–48.

SIT (2010). *Global Cybersecurity Policy Conference*. Washington, DC: Stevens Institute of Technology.

Skoudis, E. and L. Zeltser (2004). *Malware: Fighting Malicious Code*. Upper Saddle River, NJ: Prentice Hall.

Slater, R. (1987). *Portraits in Silicon*. Cambridge, MA: MIT Press.

Smedinghoff, T. J. (2009). Legal and regulatory obligations. In *Enterprise Information Security and Privacy*, ed. C. W. Axelrod, J. Bayuk, and D. Schutzer. Norwood, MA: Artech House.

Spamhaus (ongoing). The Spamhaus Project. From http://www.spamhaus.org.

SSE-CMM® (2003). Systems Security Engineering Capability Maturity Model®. Model Description Document, Version 3.0.

Stamp, J., P. Campbell, et al. (2003). Sustainable Security for Infrastruture SCADA, Sandia National Laboratories. SABD2003-4670.

State (2010). International traffic in arms regulations. http://www.pmddtc. state.gov/regulations_laws/itar_official.html, US Department of State.

Sterling, B. (1992). *Hacker Crackdown*. New York: Bantam Doubleday Dell Publishing Group.

Stoll, C. (1989). *The Cuckoo's Egg*. New York: Doubleday.

Stouffer, K., J. Falco, et al. (2009). Guide to Industrial Control Systems Security, SP 800-82. National Institute of Standards and Technology.

Thompson, H. H. (2003). Why security testing is hard. *IEEE Security & Privacy*, 1(4).

Thompson, H. H. and S. G. Chase (2005). *The Software Vulnerability Guide*. Hingham, MA: Charles River Media.

Toner, E. S. (2009). Creating situational awareness: A systems approach. Workshop on Medical Surge Capacity, Institute of Medicine Forum on Medical and Public Health Preparedness for Catastrophic Events.

UCF (ongoing). Unified Compliance Framework™, http://www. unifiedcompliance.com/.

US-CERT (ongoing). The original CERT was privately operated, and has since been supplemented with one run by the US Department of Homeland Security, From http://www.cert.org/ and http://www.us-cert.gov/.

Vijayan, J. (2008). McColo takedown: Internet vigilantism or online neighborhood watch? *Computerworld*, November 17. Available at www. computerworld.com.

Virus.org (1998). Targeting the Pentagon, Rome labs attack story. *InfoSec News*, March 31. Available at http://lists.virus.org/isn-9803/msg00123. html.

Ware, W. (1970). Security controls for computer systems. From http://seclab.cs.ucdavis.edu/projects/history/papers/ware70.pdf, Report of Defense Science Board Task Force on Computer Security.

Weiss, J. (2010). *Protecting Industrial Control Systems from Electronic Threats*. New York: Momentum Press.

Wolf, C. (2008). *Proskauer on Privacy: A Guide to Privacy and Data Security Law in the Information Age*. New York: Practising Law Institute.

Wyatt, E. (2012). White House, consumers in mind, offers online privacy guidelines. *The New York Times*, February 23.

Zetter, K. (2011). How digital detectives deciphered Stuxnet, the most menacing malware in history. *Wired*. Available at http://www.wired. com/threatlevel/2011/07/how-digital-detectives-deciphered-stuxnet/ all/1.

Zimmer, B. (2009). On language. *The New York Times Magazine*, October 5.

Index

Cyber Security Policy Guidebook, First Edition. Jennifer L. Bayuk, Jason Healey, Paul Rohmeyer, Marcus H. Sachs, Jeffrey Schmidt, Joseph Weiss.
© 2012 John Wiley & Sons, Inc. Published 2012 by John Wiley & Sons, Inc.

CPSIA information can be obtained
at www.ICGtesting.com
Printed in the USA
BVHW01*0617290618
520264BV00003B/3/P

9 781118 027806